T0312591

LIVES OF GREAT RELIGIOUS BOOKS

The Life of Saint Teresa of Avila

LIVES OF GREAT RELIGIOUS BOOKS

FORTHCOMING

FRONTISPIECE. Portrait of Saint Teresa by Fray Juan de la Miseria, 1576. *Santa Teresa de Jesús*, Convento de Santa Teresa de Jesus, Ávila, Spain. Album / Alamy Stock Photo.

The Life of Saint Teresa of Avila

A BIOGRAPHY

Carlos Eire

PRINCETON UNIVERSITY PRESS

Princeton and Oxford

Published by Princeton University Press
41 William Street, Princeton, New Jersey 08540
6 Oxford Street, Woodstock, Oxfordshire OX20 1TR

press.princeton.edu

Library of Congress Control Number: 2019936638
ISBN 978-0-691-16493-9

British Library Cataloging-in-Publication Data is available

Editorial: Fred Appel and Thalia Leaf
Production Editorial: Karen Carter
Jacket and Text Design: Lorraine Doneker
Jacket Credit: Josefa de Óbidos, The Transverberation of
Saint Teresa of Avila, 1672
Production: Erin Suydam
Publicity: Tayler Lord and Kathryn Stevens
Copyeditor: Cathryn Slovensky

This book has been composed in Garamond Premier Pro

Printed on acid-free paper. ∞

Printed in the United States of America

10 9 8 7 6 5 4 3 2 1

CONTENTS

THE CHARACTER OF THE *VIDA*

Written five centuries ago under vexing circumstances by a nun who claimed to commune with God, *The Life of Teresa de Jesús* is much more than an autobiography. The text has multiple levels of meaning and serves many functions simultaneously, spiritual as well as mundane. At its deepest spiritual level, it is all about the intermingling of heaven and earth, and about the highest levels of divinization attainable by humans. At its most mundane, it is a remarkable woman's account of her life in golden age Spain.

Kept under lock and key by the Spanish Inquisition for two decades, this book could have been swept into oblivion as mere ashes, since some of its early readers itched to burn it. Alonso de la Fuente (1533–92), a Dominican friar, had this to say about the *Vida* when he denounced it to the Inquisition: "This book . . . has the venom of heresy within it, so secretly expressed, so well disguised, so smoothly varnished, that those who are ignorant as well as those who are the subtlest of theologians in the world can use it as a sealed and closed manual or as scripture read in the dark of night, unnoticed by Catholic ears." The only inspiration Teresa could have received, charged Fray Alonso, was from "an evil angel, the same one who fooled Mohammed and Luther and all other heresiarchs." And the most convincing proof of its demonic derivation, he added, was the fact that Teresa dealt with subjects that "exceeded the capacity of any woman."[1]

Fortunately, other early readers were awed by its unique contents, reckoned its rare worth, and kept the flames at bay, circulating some clandestine copies, waiting impatiently for the right moment to share the text with the world. When that moment finally came, not long after the author's death, this book—which she was ordered to write so theological experts and ecclesiastical elites could discern whether or not she was genuinely holy—quickly became one of the most significant in the Catholic tradition. Then, over the next few centuries, as quarreling cooled among Christians, it gradually gained recognition outside Catholic circles, even in the secular world, as one of the most extraordinary autobiographies ever penned, and as one of the world's greatest religious books.

Fittingly, as this text prevailed over all who sought to suppress it in its own day, so does it continue to prevail over all reductionist attempts to circumscribe its essence or to wedge its significance into any tidy pigeonhole, spiritual or secular. And so does it also continue to attract disparate readers and interpreters of all sorts, many of whom would loathe to share space with one another on a bus seat or a footnote.

Many twenty-first-century readers—perhaps most—will find this book to be weird or outrageous, and some will dismiss it as delusional. Much of this text is about prayer and the humdrum details of convent life, and other such issues of slight concern to a secularized world. Much of it is also about otherworldly trysts that defy reason and test the limits of language. When all is said and done, the book is as much about God and about human potential as about the author herself, though the narrative is squarely focused on her own experiences. In page after page its author struggles to give voice to the ineffable, aching constantly for a dimension other than the one in which she is trapped—one she knows to be far higher and better, into which she ventures repeatedly—expressing her longing for it, as well as for her disdain of whatever stands in her way, including her own five senses and her beating heart. Near the end of the *Vida* she says: "Everything I see with my bodily eyes is like a dream that mocks me; and what I have seen with the eyes of the soul is what she [my soul] desires; and seeing she is so far away from it, she longs to die."[2]

The *Life*, or *Vida*, as it is known in Spanish, is not really an autobiography, strictly speaking, and its title of *Vida* is somewhat misleading, for it was not chosen by the author but rather by its earliest editor, Luis de León, when it was first published in 1588. Before that, during the twenty-five years when it circulated surreptitiously in manuscript form among a very small number of readers, it was simply known as "the book" (*el libro*).[3] Its immediate intended audience was tiny and exclusive, and as it was being written, no one involved in the project—including the author—could imagine what would eventually become of it. Those first few male clerics who read it were unnerved by it, even those who found much to like in it. The author, a sickly nun who suffered seizures and fell into trances, and was suspected by some of being a heretic or of being under demonic influence, wrote under extreme duress, knowing that what she was writing would be minutely examined by readers who had the power to condemn her, and that every word could be negatively construed.

Yet, despite the dire circumstances under which she wrote, and the steep slippery slopes down which every word of hers could tumble, it has always been obvious to anyone who knows how to spot talented writing that this nun had a unique poetic gift for expressing the ineffable while avoiding censure, and that—contrary to all her carping about being forced to write about herself, unwillingly—she really loved writing, and excelled at it.

Teresa de Jesús, the author, was a sixteenth-century Carmelite nun who lived in the walled city of Ávila. Before becoming a nun and taking on a religious name, she was known as Teresa de Ahumada y Cepeda. In the English-speaking world she is more commonly known as Teresa of Avila, without the accent on the capital "A." In the last three decades of her life Teresa wrote a great deal, despite her constant engagement in practical affairs as the leader of a new religious order—four books, some two dozen poems, hundreds of letters, and various other texts—but it is her *Vida*, or *Life*, that has had the greatest impact of all, not just because it tells the remarkable story of her evolution into a mystic and monastic reformer from her own perspective but also because of the details she provides about her many otherworldly encounters. Few other books in the Christian tradition contain as rich a description of supernatural visions and ecstasies, or as gripping a narrative of one soul's search for intimacy with God.

Teresa's *Vida* is a mystical text, above all, or, more precisely, an autobiographical exposition of mystical theology. "Mysticism" is a troublesome term, loaded with various meanings, some of which are pejorative. Take, for instance, one of its definitions in the *Oxford English Dictionary*: "mysticism is religious belief that is characterized by vague, obscure, or confused spirituality; a belief system based on the assumption of occult forces, mysterious supernatural agencies, etc." Teresa's mysticism was anything but "vague" or "confused," and the forces she assumed were anything but "occult." Such a definition of "mysticism" is inappropriate for Teresa. A more accurate definition that applies to Teresa and her *Vida* can be found in the same dictionary: "mysticism is belief in the possibility of union with or absorption into God by means of contemplation and self-surrender; belief in or devotion to the spiritual apprehension of truths inaccessible to the intellect."[4] In other words, a "mystical experience" is an encounter with divine or heavenly realities, and a "mystic" is someone who claims to have such encounters. This is precisely the definition that will be assumed in this book when the terms "mystic," "mystical," "mystical experience," or "mystical theology" are used.

Encounters with divine or otherworldly realities are the very stuff of religion, and claims about such encounters can be found in most cultures around the world. But there are as many different kinds of mysticism as there are religious traditions. Christian mysticism is theocentric, that is, focused on encounters between humans and the God of the Bible, the God who revealed himself to the ancient Jews and then became incarnate in Jesus Christ. The fact that the Christian God is triune—Father, Son, and Holy Spirit—and that this Trinity is an unfathomable mystery, makes all encounters with the divine in the Christian tradition quite different from those in the two other monotheistic Abrahamic religions, Judaism and Islam. The additional fact that the Son,

the second person of the Christian Trinity, is simultaneously divine and human, and that his humanity does not
cancel out his divinity—or vice versa—makes Christian
mysticism have even less affinity with Judaism and Islam.
The differences between Christian mysticism and that of
polytheistic or nontheistic religions are even greater.

Teresa's *Vida* is more than a narrative of her encounters
with the Christian triune God. It is also an analysis of those
rare supernatural encounters, and of the ways in which such
mystical states can be attained. In some ways, the *Vida* is also a
manual, or instruction book, for by outlining the precise ways
in which she came to have these encounters, and by analyzing
different methods of prayer, Teresa provides instruction for
anyone who desires to follow the same path. Although providing such instruction was not the sole motivation for writing the book, that instructive function became one of its most
distinctive traits for centuries, down to our own day. When
Pope Paul VI raised Teresa to the exalted rank of "doctor of
the church" in 1970—one of the first two women ever to be
so honored—it was due as much to the practical usefulness of
the *Vida* as to the way in which she drew theological lessons
from her encounters with the divine.[5]

When all is said and done, however, it is not just the
Vida's how-to approach to prayer and to developing a life of
the spirit, or its engrossing narrative, or its feminine perspective that have made it one of the world's great religious
books. It could be argued that above all, it is really its audacious, unrestrained optimism about the human potential for
love and divinization, and its affirmation of the ultimate tri-
umph of good over evil, that have earned it a special place
among the other texts in this series.

LIVES OF GREAT RELIGIOUS BOOKS

The Life of Saint Teresa of Avila

Teresa's Life Story

The city of Ávila squats defiantly on a semiarid plateau in the old Spanish kingdom of Castile, as if unnaturally sprung from the earth, a boxy rectangular outcrop teeming with stone buildings and tiled rooftops, ringed by massive walls thirty-six feet high and nine feet thick. Eighty-eight curved towers extend outward from the crenellated ramparts at regular intervals, like mute giant sentries, making the whole city seem ever ready for a siege. Ávila's fortifications were built in the twelfth century, when war was constant and such bulwarks were needed, not just to keep enemies at bay but also to make them think one's city was an impregnable fortress, as invincible as its own arrogance.

Symmetrical Ávila mocks the landscape that surrounds it, so given to extremes of stifling heat and bitter cold, so implacably parched and vast and empty, so devoid of visible boundaries, so sorely bereft of the straight lines, obtuse angles, deltoid curves, and all the precise order that humans can impose on the world with the aid of Euclidian geometry.

On 28 March 1515, long after those battlements had last seen any action, and shortly before the start of the Protestant Reformation in faraway Saxony, Teresa de Ahumada y Cepeda was born in this utterly medieval city. She was the fifth oldest of twelve children in her household. The two oldest ones in this brood were from her father's first marriage, a boy and a girl whose mother, Catalina del Peso, had died in 1507. The other children were eight boys and two girls from her father's second wife, Beatriz Dávila y Ahumada, who had married him when she was fifteen years old. Beatriz had given birth to Teresa when she was twenty, and would die at the age of thirty-three, shortly after the birth of Teresa's youngest sister. Nearly all of Teresa's nine brothers followed military careers and sought their fortunes far beyond Ávila's old walls, in the so-called New World that Christopher Columbus had stumbled upon in 1492, and that Spain claimed for itself.

Her father, Alonso Sánchez de Cepeda, was a hidalgo, a member of the lower nobility. Her mother, Beatriz, belonged to two of the leading families of the city. A well-disguised blemish lurked in the family tree, however: a secret so shameful and so potentially injurious—and so well hidden—that it would remain unknown for four more centuries, until the 1940s, when someone stumbled upon it accidentally, in an unlikely place. Tucked away in lawsuit records from Ciudad Real, two hundred kilometers south of Ávila, the secret had never surfaced in any official documents connected to Teresa herself, including those from her encounters with the Inquisition or those pertaining to her beatification and canonization inquests. Whether or not Teresa was in on the secret remains a matter of dispute, but many experts suspect that she was aware of it, indeed, and that this awareness shaped her life and her work.

This skeleton in the closet was as frightful as they came in sixteenth-century Spain, where one's social status depended so much on lineage: Teresa had Jewish ancestors. Worse yet, her father's father had been punished by the Inquisition in 1485 for the sin of Judaizing, that is, for secretly observing Jewish rituals and customs. Authorities in church and state looked upon Judaizing as an amalgam of heresy, apostasy, and hypocritical deception, and as an especially heinous offense.[1]

Teresa's grandfather Juan Sánchez de Toledo was the son of a Jewish convert to Catholicism who chose baptism for himself and his family in the mid-fifteenth century. Like many other such conversos, that is, Jewish converts and descendants of Jewish converts in Spain, Teresa's grandfather had either found it impossible to discard his ancestral religion completely or to convince his neighbors that he had indeed done so. Tens of thousands of Jews had been coerced into converting, especially after widespread massacres in 1391, and throughout the fifteenth century, thousands more converted in fear of popular violence and a rash of new laws that placed many segregationist restrictions on them. Preaching campaigns launched at Spain's remaining Jews only served to incite anti-Jewish sentiment and to produce waves of questionable conversions after 1391, creating a new social class with an ambivalent identity. Conversos were fully Christian, legally, and were not subjected to the same restrictions as Jews who refused baptism, but they and their progeny were tagged as "*new* Christians," to distinguish them from the "*old* Christians" who had no Jewish ancestry.

Questions hovered over all conversos, no matter how devoutly Catholic any of them might have been or might have seemed. Suspicions surrounding converso backsliding—or Judaizing—increased rather than decreased throughout the fifteenth century, so much so that the monarchs Ferdinand and Isabella petitioned Rome in 1478 for the right to create and run an independent tribunal of their own in Spain that would identify and punish all Judaizers. Pope Sixtus IV granted this request, and so it came to be that Ferdinand and Isabella established the Tribunal of the Holy Office of the Inquisition and that the hunt for Judaizers began in 1480.

When this relatively new Inquisition tribunal came to Toledo in 1485 to ferret out Judaizers, Teresa's converso grandfather Juan was a well-to-do cloth merchant who had successfully blended in with Toledan society by marrying a woman from a distinguished old Christian family. Fearing the wrath of the Inquisition, or sensing inevitable persecution regardless of innocence or guilt—or perhaps feeling remorse about secretly observing some Jewish traditions—Juan willingly confessed that he was a Judaizer. The fact that he had freely revealed his sin, expressed contrition, and begged for forgiveness earned him a full pardon and moderate punishment. But the price he had to pay for his offenses was steep.

Every Friday for seven weeks in a row, Juan, his children, and other *reconciliados* who had been forgiven had to walk from church to church through the streets of Toledo, garbed in a yellow penitential tunic known as a *sanbenito*. Undergoing this status-crushing shaming ritual was not the end of Juan's debasement, however, but only its starting point, for every penitent's yellow *sanbenito* would be hung permanently in his or her parish church, with the offender's name and sins clearly displayed for all to see.

In a culture that placed an extremely high value on honor and reputation, such as that of late medieval Spain, such humiliation could be devastating, not only to the penitent but to all of his relatives, for generations to come. In essence, that *sanbenito* was an edict of permanent marginalization that sent a clear message as long as it hung in public, year after year: Juan Sánchez de Toledo and his kin were untrustworthy.

Juan responded to this situation by moving his family from Toledo to Ávila, where he had business contacts. In addition to transplanting his family, and to substituting his own surname and that of his children, Sánchez, with that of his old Christian wife, Cepeda, Juan was also clever enough to affirm his family's hidalgo status in a court of law in Ciudad Real, where he owned some property. Although his Jewish ancestry was mentioned in some of those court documents, that fact remained buried in those papers, far from Ávila.[2] What mattered most to Juan, and what allowed him to establish a new identity successfully, was obtaining the court document that affirmed his nobility, which allowed him and his progeny to pass themselves off as old Christians.

The basic assumption of his claim was simple enough: anyone who lives as a hidalgo and is recognized by his neighbors as a hidalgo must be a hidalgo, and, of course, also an old Christian. A witness from Ávila who testified in court on behalf of Juan had this to say about him and his family: "Those Toledans are considered hidalgos and also gentlemen and they mingle with the children of great hidalgos and with relatives of the leading gentlemen of Ávila . . . they have very fine horses and are very well attired, and are treated as top-notch people."[3]

Teresa's grandfather timed his move to Ávila most adroitly, for anti-Jewish and anti-converso sentiment continued to increase after his public shaming. In 1492 Ferdinand and Isabella responded to this crisis by issuing a harsh ultimatum to Spain's Jews: convert or leave. Although tens of thousands of Jews fled from Spain in response, tens of thousands also chose to stay and convert. This sudden increase in the number of new Christians created by the 1492 Edict of Expulsion only served to worsen suspicions about insincere conversions among all conversos, and helped unleash a new wave of repressive and discriminatory measures against new Christians.

Eventually, by the time Teresa reached adulthood, the persecution of Judaizers by the Inquisition had begun to diminish, due largely to the fact that it ran out of new Christians to haul in, and turned its attention instead to all sorts of heretics and deviants. But discrimination against new Christians continued to increase. "Purity of blood" statutes that barred new Christians from holding government or church posts and from testifying in courts of law were enacted throughout Spain in the mid-sixteenth century. By the time of Teresa's death in 1582, discrimination had become the law of the land, and proving that one had *limpieza de sangre* or purity of blood had become a prerequisite for social advancement and membership in many religious orders. The ultimate irony of this turn of events is that according to the letter of these blood purity laws, Teresa would have been unable to join the Carmelite order, much less reform it, and—to top it off—she would also have been ineligible for canonization as a saint.

We know relatively little about Teresa's childhood, and the details we do have, mostly from her *Vida*, hide almost as much as they reveal. The *Vida* portrays her parents as very "virtuous and fearful of God," and credits them with instilling in her a reverence for things divine at an early age. "My father liked to read good books," she said, "and had some in Spanish so that his children could read them too. And my mother always took great care to make sure we said our prayers, and to instill in us devotion to Our Lady and to some saints." Such efforts paid off, she claimed, for she "began to awaken" to piety "around the age of five or six" (1:1.34).

From the very first page of her *Vida*, Teresa dwells on the effect that books had on her, as well as on others, and this theme is carried through the entire narrative. In various ways, "the book of her life" (*el libro de su vida*) is a book about books and about how the right combination of reading and prayer, and the right kind of spiritual direction from the right kind of person, can lead one to God. This linkage of reading, praying, and following directions is essential in Teresa's mind, for reading on one's own without the other two components can lead one astray. Teresa stresses this point in the first few pages of her *Vida*, mostly through story-telling and carefully chosen examples from her childhood.

For instance, Teresa gives no details about her education but instead simply relates how she and one of her brothers took to reading the lives of the saints on their own, and how reading about martyrs inspired her and that brother to leave home in search of martyrdom. "We agreed to run away to the land of the Moors," she says, "so that they might behead us there." Although their parents stopped them before they could get very far, Teresa and her brother continued to be inspired by the lives of the saints in other ways. "When I saw that it was impossible to go anywhere where we'd be killed for God's sake, we decided to become hermits, and we would build hermitages out of rocks, as best we could, in an orchard we had at home." Similarly, Teresa says that when she played with other girls, she loved "building convents and pretending to be nuns" (1:6.35).

Teresa also highlights the undesirable effects that the wrong kind of books had on her as a child. Much like the fictional character of Don Quixote (and also much like her flesh-and-blood contemporary Saint Ignatius Loyola), Teresa became addicted to reading chivalric romances, "so excessively," she says, "that I could never be happy unless I had a new book." These romances, as she later saw it, made her focus on frivolous, worldly things such as her clothes, hairbrushes, cosmetics and perfume, and harmful "childish" trifles rather than on things divine. They also inclined her to strike up a close friendship with some cousins, who were equally addicted to worldly frivolities, and with some other unnamed relative from whom she learned "all kinds of evil" (2:3.37). Teresa's dalliance with bad books and bad company, which was compounded by the absence of good advice, led to a love of sin so profound that she "lost nearly all" of her soul's "natural inclination to virtue." Teresa provides no details about these sins of hers, or about her "depraved" behavior, but she does say that it was due to her "wickedness" that in 1531, at the age of fifteen, she was sent to live at the Augustinian Convent of Our Lady of Grace, where other girls of her social status—but "less depraved" than her—were educated (2:1–6.36–38).

Teresa's confinement in a convent outside the walls of Ávila might have had less to do with her behavior, however, than with circumstances at home. Teresa's mother had died three years earlier, in 1528, when Teresa was only thirteen years old, and the mother's role had been assumed by Teresa's older half sister María. When María married in 1531 and moved to her husband's household in a nearby village, Teresa's widowed father faced a daunting challenge. Preserving a teenage daughter's honor was a high priority for any hidalgo father, but to do that properly his household needed an older female presence. As Teresa put it, "now that my sister had married, being alone in the house without a mother was not a good thing" (2:6.38).

Teresa had no burning desire to become a nun when she was sent to Our Lady of Grace, but she enjoyed her life at the convent, and it was there that she got her first taste of monastic life and began to develop the habit of praying regularly. After only a year and a half, unfortunately, as she was beginning to contemplate a life as a nun, illness suddenly forced her to return to her father's house. According to Teresa, the illness was "serious," and she recovered very slowly. Fevers and fainting spells plagued her, and she needed constant care. After some months with her father, she was sent to María's house, and it was on her way there, while she stopped for a brief stay with one of her father's brothers, a widower who liked to read devotional texts, that she was introduced to the genre of literature that would shape her personality most intensely.

Later on in life, as she was writing her *Vida*, she would look back on the few days she spent at her uncle Pedro's house as a significant turning point. It was there, while reading devotional texts to her uncle and discussing them with him that she "began to understand the truth . . . that all things are as nothing, and that the world is vanity and quickly passes away." Fearing that she would soon die from her illness and go directly to hell, and "inspired by servile fear more than by love," she decided to become a nun. It seemed like a safe bet for her. Although life as a nun might be a lot like purgatory, she thought, spending a few years suffering an earthly purgation might give her the chance to gain eternal life in heaven (3:5–6.40).

When Teresa finally regained her health, in November 1535, at the age of twenty, she entered the Carmelite Convent of the Incarnation in Ávila, against her father's wishes. This convent was a relatively lax monastic community, in which the rule of the Carmelite order was not strictly interpreted. All of its nuns hailed from the top tier of society, the same class as Teresa, and to enter the convent, every nun had to bring a dowry, just as if she were getting married. This was the way this convent and most others had been funded since medieval times, and exceptions to this requirement were very rare. Teresa's father did what was required, providing a generous yearly income from one of his properties and paying for all of his daughter's clothing and furnishings.

These privileged nuns at the Incarnation convent were not truly cloistered, that is, forced to remain behind the convent walls; nor were they required to cut off their connections to the outside world. Far from it: these nuns could come and go, with permission from their superiors, and they could also spend time visiting relatives and friends, or conversing with them at the convent, in the *locutorio*, a room set aside for such gatherings. Nuns like Teresa, who had the means to afford it, could live in a two-room suite, while others of lesser means had no more than a bed in a large common dormitory. Consequently, the nuns at the Incarnation had plenty of interaction with the world from which they were ostensibly fleeing, and the convent was a busy socially stratified space, always full of visitors. It was also common for some of the nuns to be sent to live with patrons who requested the presence of a nun in their household during a time of grief, or for a nun to be given permission to take care of an ailing relative out in "the world." Similarly, some nuns who had room to spare, like Teresa, could take in a boarder for a spell, when circumstances seemed to demand it. Teresa, for instance, took in a younger sister in 1543 after their father died.

All of this so-called laxity was relative in comparison to convents that observed strict enclosure—and Teresa would later decry her own lassitude—but, in fact, when all is said and done, Teresa's convent was no haven for slackers. The daily routine for nuns at the Convent of the Incarnation was a tough grind, to say the least, and self-denial was expected of all of its nuns. Prayer times were strictly observed from the predawn hours to late into the night and consisted of eight daily prayer events that no one was supposed to skip: lauds, prime, terce, sext, none, vespers, compline, and the night office, also known as vigils, during which the nuns would recite or sing set prayers in unison. In addition, from early autumn until Easter season in springtime the nuns ate meat only three times a week, and on the other four days of those six months of abstinence they would eat only one meal a day. Teresa and her sisters also kept strict fasts during the penitential seasons of Lent in late winter/early spring and Advent in December, a sum total of roughly seventy days of fasting per year. Constant introspection was required too, for every nun was supposed to confess her sins to a priest once a week.

In addition, Teresa and her sisters at the convent observed a rule of silence in their dining hall and in the common dormitories of the relatively less privileged nuns. This means that no one spoke a word at mealtime, as one of their sisters read to them from some devotional text, and that after the relatively less privileged nuns had gone to bed in their dormitories, none of them could utter a word. Regardless of their family's rank or of the size of their dowry, every nun was also required to perform mundane tasks throughout the convent day after day, such as cooking or cleaning, hard work that was deemed undignified—or even downright dishonorable—for upper-class women such as Teresa and her fellow sisters. Needless to say, these menial tasks were lessons in humility for Teresa and others of her social class, as well as bitter pills to swallow.[4]

Teresa seems to have chosen a nun's life at the Convent of the Incarnation because she had friends there, especially one named Juana Suárez, who would become her constant companion for many years. At first, it was difficult for Teresa to come to terms with her choice. "Leaving my father's house hurt so much," she says in her *Vida*, "that I do not think that death will be any less painful. All my bones felt as if they were being wrenched asunder" (4:1.41).

Teresa adjusted to convent life quickly, however, and found great joy in her new life. She would have to serve one year as a postulant before being formally admitted to the Carmelite order and the Convent of the Incarnation, and then another year as a novice. Everything in her routine as a postulant—even sweeping the floor—made her very happy. A year after entering the convent, in November 1536, Teresa became a novice and donned the habit of the Carmelite order. As that year passed, Teresa continued to adjust to the rhythms and rigors of monastic life. In November 1537, before professing her final vows, she made a general confession, as required, making an account to a priest of all the sins she had committed up to that point in her life. Shortly thereafter, at a solemn ceremony, Teresa left behind her status as a novice and became a full-fledged member of her monastic community.

All was not well, however. Once again, her health began to decline. Teresa provides few details about the frequent fainting fits, irregular heartbeats, and other ailments she began to endure, other than to say that she often lost consciousness and that all medical treatments failed to cure her. Years later, some of her fellow nuns would recall that she grew pale and thin during this time, and that she would weep often and suffer convulsions. By the autumn of 1538 her symptoms had worsened so much that her doctors gave up hope of finding a cure. Sheer desperation drove Teresa's father to remove her from the convent and to take her to a *curandera* (folk healer) who lived at some distance from Ávila. In Teresa's day and age, healers of this sort who relied on herbs and other natural remedies had not yet been stigmatized as witches, and it was not at all uncommon for elites as well as peasants to seek their help. The timing of her exit could not have been worse for Teresa, however, because the healer in question could not offer any treatments in the autumn and winter, when there were no fresh herbs to be found.

Unfortunately, Teresa's father did not realize this until Teresa was already on her way to the healer. This meant that Teresa would continue to deteriorate for several months outside of her convent, under her family's worried and helpless gaze, waiting for spring to arrive, or praying for a miraculous cure.

As had happened in 1533, during her previous illness, Teresa's father took her to María's house. On the way there, as before, they stopped for a brief stay at Uncle Pedro's house, and that visit would have significant consequences for Teresa, even though she could not be aware of it at that time. Uncle Pedro, who had earlier introduced Teresa to devotional texts, now gave her a gift that would have an immense impact on her: a copy of *The Third Spiritual Alphabet*, a newly published book by the Franciscan friar Francisco de Osuna.[5]

Teresa began to read his book as soon as she reached her sister's house, and eventually—by her own admission—it would shape her spiritual life more intensely than any other text. Osuna's *Alphabet* was a distillation of late medieval mysticism, especially of the kind that flourished in Germany, the Netherlands, and England in the fourteenth century. Its basic premise is that God dwells at the core of every human being and that loving intimacy with the divine can be achieved in one's earthly life through a process of self-denial coupled with inner or silent prayer. An emphasis on silent prayer is essential to this tradition, as is the process of delving inwardly, to find the divine within the human and to rise above one's heart in perfect stillness. Osuna's book was one of several such texts circulating in Spain at that time. Spanish translations of various texts in this tradition had been commissioned in the early sixteenth century by the reforming cardinal Francisco Jiménez de Cisneros, and these texts quickly found favor with many Spanish readers.[6] Osuna's *Alphabet* was a how-to book, a primer for anyone who wanted to delve into this particular type of mysticism. The practice of silent prayer advocated by Osuna, and especially the "prayer of quiet," which would give rise to much controversy, involved reaching states of *recogimiento* (recollection, or inner stillness) and *dejamiento* (self-abandonment), and, ultimately, states of ecstatic prayer and of union with the divine.[7]

Teresa spent the rest of that winter with María, languishing in the same sad state in which she had arrived, hovering too uncomfortably close to death but still able to read, pray, and achieve a fleeting foretaste of Osuna's prayer of quiet. Once spring arrived and she began to be treated by the healer, her condition worsened quickly. Teresa's *curandera*, who specialized in digestive disorders, gave her potent laxatives and emetics made from herbs and some ingredients straight out of the witches' brew in Shakespeare's *Macbeth*, including frog's toes, snake excrement, and pulverized wings from flies. Contrary to her father's expectations, the cure proved worse than the disease, and after enduring three months of "the greatest tortures" at the hands of the folk healer, Teresa grew increasingly sicker. Constantly feverish, frighteningly weak, and wracked by "intolerable pain," she could no longer stand, sit up, or eat solid food. Disconsolate, her father had no choice but to take her home to Ávila in July 1539, and to await her death.

A few weeks later, on 15 August 1539, Teresa died. Or so it seemed.

Shortly after receiving the last rites due to the alarming speed of her decline, she suddenly lost consciousness and stopped breathing. No one could detect any sign of life, and when a mirror was pressed to her nostrils to determine whether or not she was still breathing, the absence of any moisture on the mirror made it seem clear that she was dead indeed. Preparations began for burial, and—as was customary—hot wax was poured over her eyes to seal them.

At the convent, the nuns prepared for her entombment. Teresa's grieving father could not reconcile himself to the circumstances and insisted, against custom, that her burial be delayed for a day or two. Family members kept vigil next to her corpse constantly, taking turns around the clock. Late on the third night of this vigil, shortly before she was about to be buried, her brother Alonso accidentally knocked over a candle, setting a curtain on fire. During the ensuing commotion, much to everyone's surprise and delight, Teresa gasped for air and sprang back to life. As the flames were extinguished, all rejoiced.

But this joy was muted. Teresa might have come back from the dead, but she was still in dreadful shape, totally paralyzed, seemingly incurable. Gradually, Teresa regained some strength and the ability to eat solids. In 1540, a few months after her close brush with death, Teresa asked to be moved back to the Convent of the Incarnation. Her recovery there was painfully slow but steady. Though she arrived as a bedridden paralytic who needed constant care, she gradually gained strength and climbed out of bed. At first she could only crawl on her hands and knees, but bit by wondrous bit, her health returned as mysteriously as she had lost it. Teresa would eventually recoup the ability to walk and to care for herself, but it was not until 1542—four years after she fell seriously ill and left the convent—that she was finally able to resume a normal schedule with all her fellow nuns. And even then, her recovery was incomplete. For the remainder of her life, bouts of paralysis in her left arm would be a recurring problem, compounded by many other ailments, such as migraine headaches, fevers, frequent colds, fatigue, and an odd assortment of pains in major organs of her body, including her heart. By all external physical signs, it would seem that Teresa was doomed to live out the rest of her days at the Convent of the Incarnation as a cripple, perhaps even as a burden to her community. But Teresa would end up surprising everyone, including herself.

During her long illness, Teresa lost some of her spiritual fervor, and—in her own words—"began to indulge in one pastime after another, in one vanity after another." Worse yet, her soul was "so led astray by all these vanities" that she became ashamed of "turning toward God and finding him in the intimate friendship of prayer" (7:1.52). Teresa joined her community every day and night during the scheduled times for vocal prayer, as she was required to do, but she abandoned mental (silent) prayer. The other nuns at her convent apparently saw nothing wrong in Teresa's behavior, although she thought of herself as "wicked" and estranged from God. The problem—as Teresa saw it—was that as she gained more and more strength, she began to spend more of her time meeting with visitors. This behavior, which she viewed as a distraction that pulled her ever farther away from God, was not viewed negatively by the other sisters. Teresa confessed that she wanted nothing more than to be thought well of, or admired, and her constant conversations with those from the outside world were a perfect way of making herself seem more worthy of esteem, especially since many of the patrons of the convent came to visit the nuns for advice or for comfort in times of distress. Teresa's convent was very keen on cultivating close relations with patrons, and would frequently send some of its nuns to live in their homes during times of need, especially when patrons or someone in their family fell ill or died. Teresa herself would be sent on these errands of mercy a number of times, including one to her own father, who became gravely ill in 1543 and was attended by her. Alonso Cepeda would die at home that year, with Teresa by his side.

Teresa spent the next twelve years observing a perfunctory routine of vocal prayer at set times each day, weekly confession, menial duties, and the "pestilential pastime" of conversing with visitors. This "stormy sea"—those many "grievous" years of glum, passionless, humdrum existence during which she could "find no joy in God and no pleasure in the world" (8:2.60)—came to an abrupt end for Teresa in 1555, on a special feast day when a new image of Christ was brought into the convent for veneration. The figure in this image was the suffering Christ of the passion, wounded and bleeding, and seeing it affected her so much that she fell to the ground, and in a fit of weeping repented for having abandoned mental prayer for so many years, begging for Christ's help, asking him to "strengthen her once and for all" so she could devote herself wholly to a life of prayer (9:1.63). Teresa considered this her "conversion," for from that pivotal moment forward her life changed completely. Gone was the sickly, lukewarm nun who prayed and fulfilled her duties perfunctorily, frittering away too many hours with visitors, chatting about insignificant issues instead of praying or seeking intimacy with the divine. Teresa was a new woman. Now she would become an exceptional nun, bold and gifted and highly energetic, wholly engaged in silent prayer, a mystic who routinely crossed the boundaries established for religious women by society and the Catholic Church, as well as the dimensional boundaries between heaven and earth.

Teresa the avid reader would compare her conversion to that of the great saint Augustine (354–430), whose autobiographical *Confessions* she devoured and used as a model for her own *Vida*. The comparison is most apt and an acknowledgment of her indebtedness to Saint Augustine, for just before her conversion she had been given a newly published Spanish translation of the *Confessions* as a gift. The link between this gift and her conversion was clear to her: the fact that she had not asked for it or ever seen it meant that "the Lord had ordained it." Teresa projected herself into the text, and Augustine's description of his own tearful conversion, especially, made her weep and shook her soul out of its long, indolent slumber. Dissolving in a weeping fit at the feet of the wounded Christ's image, just as Augustine had done under a fig tree, confirmed the mimetic dimension of this pivotal moment for Teresa. Once again, as she had done with her books of chivalry, Teresa sought to transform herself through imitation. Moreover, this was no self-transformation, as Teresa saw it. This was a divine irruption, an act of God. As God had transformed Augustine in his moment of repentance and tear-soaked self-abandonment (dejamiento), so would God transform Teresa in hers (9:7–9.65).

Filled with enthusiasm, the new Teresa returned to spiritual reading and mental prayer, and the recogimiento and dejamiento recommended in Osuna's *Third Spiritual Alphabet*. Soon thereafter, Teresa began to experience "consolations" in return, that is, trances and visions, raptures, divine locutions, intense experiences of God's presence, and supernatural physical phenomena such as levitations. These intimate encounters with the divine, which she would later identify and classify as nine distinct states of prayer, became ever more frequent between 1555 and 1560.

Never trained in scholastic theology, and unfamiliar with all of its carefully drawn terminology and precise distinctions, Teresa would struggle to explain these ineffable experiences. Her *Vida* is in large measure an attempt to come to grips with these experiences and place them in some intelligible theological context.

One passage from the *Vida* that focuses on some of her experiences shortly after 1555 reveals the dexterity with which Teresa intertwined description and analysis in an effort to make sense of something that was beyond sensory experience or rational thought. "A feeling of the presence of God used to come over me, unexpectedly, which made it impossible to doubt that He was within me and I was wholly engulfed in Him. This was not like a vision: I believe it is called 'mystical theology.' The soul is then suspended as if it were completely outside itself" (10:1.66). In another sentence densely packed with terms drawn from devotional texts and monastic culture, Teresa would express befuddlement and, at the very same time, claim some expertise on the subject of her mystical encounters with the divine, saying, "I would like, with the help of God, to be able to describe the difference between union (*unión*) and rapture (*arrobamiento*), or elevation (*elevamiento*), or what they call flight of the spirit (*vuelo de espíritu*), or transport (*arrebatamiento*)—which are all one. I say these are all different names for the same thing, which is also called ecstasy (*éstasi*)" (20:1.108).

Teresa evolved into a mystic very quickly, in leaps rather than mere steps, so it did not take long for her to run into resistance from male confessors who disapproved of her visions and raptures, interpreting them as delusions. One of her confessors, Father Gaspar Daza, a *letrado* (learned priest well versed in theology), scolded her, saying that no one with a life as imperfect as hers could receive divine favors of the sort she described. Much to Teresa's relief, she found a new confessor, Baltasar Álvarez, who validated her experiences. Álvarez was a priest from the Society of Jesus (the Jesuits), a religious order with a strong tradition of recogimiento, and he would serve as her confessor from 1559 to 1564, as she began to emerge as a mystic and reformer. He assured Teresa that her encounters with the divine were indeed genuine, and also arranged for some well-respected religious figures to meet with Teresa and pass a very positive and affirming judgment on her experiences.

One of these luminaries brought in by Álvarez was none other than one of the most powerful men in Spain, Francis Borgia, former duke of Gandia and viceroy of Catalonia, who had given up his titles and his vast fortune to join the Society of Jesus. Francis Borgia would eventually become the third general of the Jesuit order, but when he met Teresa he was simply serving as the inspector of the new Jesuit school in Ávila. Teresa received approval and encouragement from Francis Borgia, who advised her not to resist her divine trances, visions, and ecstasies. "He consoled me greatly," Teresa would later say (24:3.132).

The other great figure Teresa met during this difficult time was Pedro de Alcántara, leader of a reform movement in the Franciscan order and author of a very influential devotional text, *Treatise on Prayer and Meditation*. A mystic well known for his ecstasies and levitations, Alcántara was revered as a living saint and had even been offered the post of spiritual advisor to the king of Spain.[8] A severe ascetic who fasted constantly and slept no more than two hours a day, Pedro was described by Teresa as "emaciated to such an extreme that he seemed to be made of nothing but tree roots." The fact that this holy man was impressed by Teresa did much to enhance her own reputation in ecclesiastical circles. As far as Teresa was concerned, meeting this kindred spirit and earning his praise was a great gift from God. "He was very holy and also very amiable," she said, adding, "he was a man of few words—except when answering questions—and his responses were exquisite because his mind was so sublime" (27:18.148).

Around this time, as she was receiving encouragement from Borgia and Alcántara, Teresa's otherworldly experiences intensified. Visions of Christ became frequent, in which he revealed his full humanity and divinity simultaneously, dazzling and enrapturing Teresa. These visions had a profound effect on her. "A great love of God grew within and I did not know who had put it there, because it was very supernatural, and I had not sought it out. I found myself wanting to die from the desire to see God, and I knew no other way of seeking that other life except through death" (29:8.156).

It was also during this period that Teresa first experienced the transverberation—arguably the best known of all of her ecstasies—during which an angel pierced her heart with a flaming lance.[9] Her own description of this ecstasy suggests that she did not see angels in corporeal form very often, but that the Lord sometimes (*algunas veces*) granted her "this vision" (*esta visión*) of an angel poised beside her, to her left, "in bodily form," and that the angel she saw must have been one of the cherubim, because he was so handsome (*hermoso*) and his face was so resplendent. Whether "this vision" (*esta visión*) refers to one specific experience or to a recurring experience is unclear, but tradition has interpreted the vision known as the transverberation as a singular event. According to Teresa, this ecstasy was a paradoxical wounding that caused her to experience ultimate bliss and ultimate pain simultaneously:

> I saw in the angel's hand a long dart of gold, and at the iron's point there seemed to be a little fire. He appeared to me to be thrusting it at times into my heart, and to pierce my very inner depths; when he drew it out, he seemed to draw them out also, and to leave me all aflame with a great love of God. The pain was so great, that it made me moan; and yet so surpassing was the sweetness of this excessive pain, that I could not wish to be rid of it, and the soul could not be satisfied with nothing less than God. The pain is not bodily, but spiritual; though the body has its share in it. (29:13.158)

After 1558, due to her otherworldly raptures, Teresa the frail nun was transformed into a dynamic figure and a force to be reckoned with, assuming greater authority through three closely intertwined roles: that of a mystic, that of a writer, and that of a religious reformer. This new triple identity and the authority that came with it were not easily attained, but Teresa prevailed, overcoming many obstacles and sustaining a constant pace of feverish activity up until her death. Tracing the arc of her ascendancy to fame requires dealing not just with her dynamism, then, but also with the three closely intertwined roles that she played.

Of all her three roles, Teresa the writer is undoubtedly the best known. This aspect of her life and work provided

Teresa with a wide audience, not only during the early modern age but down to the present as well. Teresa's two other roles, those of mystic and reformer, were the subjects she wrote about. Writing about herself, her life of prayer, and her efforts to reform the Carmelite order gave Teresa the unique chance to shape and control her legacy to a considerable extent. Although hundreds of texts have been written *about* Teresa ever since her death, it is in the texts written *by* Teresa that subsequent generations have found—and continue to find—the key reference point for all narratives and analyses, and this is especially true of her *Vida*, for it is in that unique text that Teresa expresses her own understanding of her life and work.

When it comes to her two other roles, Teresa the mystic is perhaps better known nowadays than Teresa the reformer for one reason, above all: while her mysticism transcends its very Catholic essence and its historical setting by dealing with issues that are still of great concern beyond Catholic culture—such as the meaning and purpose of human existence and the nature of reality itself—her reforming work, which was limited to one order of cloistered nuns, does not easily transcend its very specific sixteenth-century monastic milieu. Moreover, for readers of the *Vida*, the Teresa they come in contact with is not the reformer but the mystic, for the narrative of that text is focused on her mysticism, not on her efforts to reform the Carmelite order, which actually began in earnest after she was done writing the *Vida*. Nonetheless, isolating the mystic from the reformer is not only impossible but wrongheaded, for contemplation and action were always linked for Teresa, and the fact that her reform of the Carmelite order is directly related to some of her most dramatic mystical experiences—such as her vision of hell—is something Teresa makes very clear.

Teresa the Reformer

Displeased with the relative laxity with which the Carmelite rule was observed at the Convent of the Incarnation, and convinced that God had chosen her to return her order to its original strictness, Teresa formulated plans to establish a new Carmelite convent in Ávila. Her goal was to emulate the reform of the Franciscan order carried out by Pedro de Alcántara, the venerable mystic who had assured her in 1557 of the divine origin of her ecstasies and visions. This reform entailed a return to strict enclosure and to absolute poverty, and a commitment to silent prayer. The nuns were to be *descalzas* (discalced), that is, they were to wear sandals rather than shoes as a visible sign of their commitment to absolute poverty; and the new convent was to support itself by its own labors, such as sewing, and by securing alms from benefactors and patrons rather than by owning land and collecting rents, as was common for most monastic institutions. In addition, the reformed order would open its doors to any woman who proved herself spiritually and temperamentally worthy of joining, regardless of her class or status, or the ability to come up with a dowry, as was customary at most nunneries. Dowries—while welcome—were not to be required of anyone.[10]

Since Ávila already had five religious houses for women and six for men, opposition to the establishment of yet another convent was intense, especially to one that would compete with the others for alms to ensure its survival, but Teresa prevailed. In August 1562 she established the Convent of Saint Joseph in Ávila, where she and three nuns from the Convent of the Incarnation began a reform of their Carmelite order. Teresa would spend the rest of her life crisscrossing Spain tirelessly, seeking patrons, establishing fourteen new Discalced Carmelite convents, and fomenting a parallel reform among the male Carmelites through John of the Cross, a younger mystic deeply influenced by her.

Since most of Teresa's work as a reformer took place after 1562, it is an aspect of her life that is explicitly excluded from her *Vida* and therefore also from our purview in this study, which focuses only on that text. Yet, that reforming work is invisibly woven into the fabric of the *Vida*, for Teresa deemed it an essential component of her conversion and of the increasingly intense spiritual life that flowed from it, described by her in chapters 32 to 36. That spiritual growth and all its intense transports and visions had a purpose beyond personal illumination, as she saw it, so writing the *Vida* was much more than an attempt to understand and explain the "favors" God showered on her. For Teresa, the project was also an attempt to discover the outcome of all those favors. It could be argued, in fact, that this link between action and contemplation is so significant to Teresa that the climax of the *Vida* is reached in those chapters that link her visions to the founding of the Convent of Saint Joseph and of the Discalced Carmelite reform.

Teresa the writer and reformer kept very busy after finishing the *Vida*. During the last two decades of her life, between 1562 and 1582, Teresa penned three other major books: *The Interior Castle*, an intensely poetic yet analytical summary of her mystical experiences that relies heavily on metaphors; *The Way of Perfection*, a how-to guide for the nuns under her direction, which she called a "living book," for achieving the ultimate goals of the Carmelite spiritual life; and *The Book of Foundations*, a history of her reforming efforts and of the establishment of the Discalced Carmelite order in Spain. A master at multitasking, Teresa also wrote poems, meditations, instructions, and more than five hundred letters during this stretch of time, while continuing to experience many of her transports, raptures, and ecstasies. And, as if all this were not enough, Teresa also traversed Castile and Andalusia ceaselessly, always uncomfortably, often in searing heat or freezing cold, in beggarly carts and carriages, establishing seventeen Discalced Carmelite convents hither and yon against constant local opposition, launching a similar enterprise among male Carmelites— against even stronger opposition—and handling the innumerable practical details and unpleasant disputes that were part and parcel of such activism.

Teresa died at the age of sixty-seven on 4 October 1582 at the Discalced Carmelite convent she had founded in Alba de Tormes at the estate of the duke of Alba. She arrived there exhausted, having just handled unpleasant business at her convents in Burgos, Palencia, and Valladolid. Her constant companion, Ana de San Bartolomé, would later say that she couldn't look at Teresa during that trip without crying because Teresa's face looked "half dead." Ana would also say: "This final journey ... was a prolonged martyrdom ... It is only fair to report what I heard [from Teresa herself], which given her great strength and courage, must have been most difficult for her to say: that in spite of all the many travails she had endured through her life, she had never been as distressed and afflicted as she was at that moment."[11]

Teresa died from a hemorrhage that began shortly after her arrival at Alba and lasted several days. Those who thronged around her deathbed, however, had a different interpretation. According to their eyewitness accounts, Teresa died in the midst of a mystical trance, and it was the intensity of that rapture, which wrenched her soul from her body too violently, that had caused the profuse bleeding. In other words, they believed that Teresa's death was caused by the ultimate mystical ecstasy, and that her final moments were utterly blissful. One of her early biographers said:

> She remained wholly absorbed in God, with the greatest serenity and stillness, totally enraptured with the novelty of what she was beginning to discover, rejoicing and enjoying her nearness to that which she had so keenly desired . . . Who would doubt that the King of Glory attended on her there, revealing a thousand new joyful things, and calling her to Himself with those sweet words: "Come, my beloved, my dove, hurry, my friend, for the winter of this life is now over, and the beautiful flowers of my eternity and my glory are starting to bloom."[12]

In death, as in life, Teresa exerted a forceful presence. Suddenly, all of the objects that had come in contact with her body and the body itself acquired the wondrous qualities possessed by relics of the saints. In addition, many of those who were close to Teresa claimed she had visited them from the afterlife. Her corpse became the greatest wonder of all, and the source of much contention.

Fearful that a relic as potentially wondrous as Teresa's corpse would be taken to Ávila, the nuns at Alba buried her quickly in their chapel and filled the grave with heavy stones to ensure she could not be easily dug up. Meanwhile, the nuns at Saint Joseph's convent in Ávila claimed legitimate ownership of the corpse and demanded it be turned over to them. As an unseemly dispute dragged on between the two convents, Teresa's corpse was exhumed and moved twice. In October 1585, Teresa's body was taken to Ávila. To console the nuns at Alba for this loss, her left arm was cut off and left there. Less than a year later, however, the duke of Alba—one of the most powerful men in Spain—obtained orders from Pope Sixtus V to have the corpse returned to Alba. So, once again, in August 1586, Teresa's remains were disinterred and returned to their original burial spot, despite howls of protest from Ávila. Appeals were made to Rome by the Ávila nuns, but to no avail. In 1589 Pope Sixtus V reaffirmed his decision that Alba should be Teresa's final resting place.

A miracle intensified all of this wrangling, for the exhumations had revealed that Teresa's corpse refused to decompose. This was not totally unexpected, for incorruptibility was a trait associated with saints' corpses, along with other miraculous phenomena, such as the so-called odor of sanctity, and the oozing of miraculous oil. But the fact that incorruptibility was not granted by God to every saint—even great ones—made Teresa's miracle all the more wondrous.

Teresa's corpse manifested all of these miraculous attributes, and others as well. The fragrance emitted by the corpse was not only immensely pleasing but also capable of overwhelming anyone who came near it, and causing headaches. According to many who handled Teresa's remains, her flesh remained supple for decades, and capable of bleeding when cut. Miraculous oil also began to flow after some years, and the cures ascribed to this oil and to other bits and pieces of Teresa were more numerous than the bits and pieces themselves.

Why speak of bits and pieces? Because, paradoxically, the incorruptibility of Teresa's corpse ensured its disintegration. Gradually, as news of the marvel of her corpse spread, so did the desire to gain access to it, and the only way to fulfill that desire was to carve it up and disperse fragments of it, large and small. This process of *découpage millimetrique*, or of cutting up the relics of saints into minute fragments, was an old Christian tradition, based on the belief that the presence of the saints is manifested equally in every bit of their remains, no matter how small, and that this presence is a link between heaven and earth.

Teresa's corpse remained at Alba, where a proper shrine was eventually built for it, but by the 1590s it was already grossly mutilated. The heart had been removed and enshrined in a reliquary, and the arm that had been severed to placate the nuns at Alba when the corpse was moved to Ávila in 1585 was displayed in another reliquary. One hand ended up in Lisbon. One foot went to Rome, along with other fragments, including her lower jaw. One finger from the left hand was clipped by Jerónimo Gracián, a confessor deeply devoted to her, and he wore it around his neck for the remainder of his life. Other fingers ended up in various locations, and other relics—slivers of flesh, some teeth and bones, and one eye—eventually made their way to other places in Europe, or overseas to far-off Mexico and the Philippines. Someone who saw the corpse at Alba in 1594 lamented that "there was a great deal of flesh missing from the back, and almost half the belly was gone." And one of Teresa's nieces was shocked to learn that "the body is all cut up and that they parcel out pieces of flesh to those who ask for them out of devotion."[13]

While all of this carving was going on, Teresa quickly became an iconic representative of the Catholic Reformation. Since the Council of Trent had established new rules in 1563 for the beatification and canonization of saints, Teresa became one of the first to undergo this new process, which involved interviewing hundreds of people who had known her and examining her writings closely. The beatification inquest proceeded very smoothly, and Teresa was beatified in 1614 by Pope Pius V. Soon thereafter, a canonization inquest began, and a mere eight years later, in 1622, Teresa was officially declared a saint by Pope Gregory XV, along with Ignatius Loyola, Francis Xavier, and Philip Neri, great figures of the Catholic Reformation. Teresa's canonization expanded the appeal and reach of her writings, which could ask for no grander seal of approval than to be declared the work of a saint.

In addition to becoming an authority on spiritual matters and an intercessor venerated throughout the Catholic world, Teresa also became an iconic national figure in Spain. The Spanish royal family had a role to play in this development, for King Philip II had greatly admired Saint Teresa and gathered her manuscripts at his library in the palace of the Escorial. One of the most avid relic collectors of his day,

Philip had brought more than seven thousand relics to that palace. He may not have acquired any of Teresa's corporeal relics, but he did manage to gather some of the most valuable contact relics of all: the books she had written with her own right hand. Philip guarded those manuscripts as closely as any of his other precious relics.

Devotion to Saint Teresa remained strong in the royal family after Philip II's death in 1598. In 1627, his grandson, King Philip IV, expressed his own devotion to Teresa by elevating her to the role of patroness of Spain, alongside the apostle Saint James, who had been the sole patron since the early Middle Ages. One of the sermons preached in Madrid during the celebration of Teresa's new role as patroness summed up the sentiments that informed the king's decree: "Everything about this saint is Spanish: her life, her death, her holiness, her religious order, her miracles, her teachings, and the fame she has earned throughout the world, all of these are Spanish."[14] Although some Spaniards did not approve of making Saint James share his role with a woman, and eventually convinced Pope Urban VIII to proclaim Saint James the sole patron of Spain, very few of these naysayers dared to question Teresa's *españolidad* (Spanishness) or the reverence due to her.

All of her Spanishness did not hem in Teresa, however, or prevent her from becoming one of the best known and most universally revered saints in the Catholic world beyond Spain. Ultimately, much of what Catholics came to know about Teresa was derived from her *Vida*, a text that became inseparable from her role as an exemplary Catholic. Teresa the saint and Teresa the author of the *Vida* could not be unyoked. In the iconography that developed after her elevation to sainthood, Teresa would often be depicted with a quill pen in her hand, or in the act of writing. In her own day and age, and for several generations, as Catholics and Protestants continually battled each other, Teresa came to represent some of the core beliefs about divine-human relations most beloved by Catholics and most loathed by Protestants. As one of her early biographers put it: Teresa was the antidote to Luther's poison.

> This, too, was planned by God, that at almost the same time that the wicked Luther began to plot his lies and deceptions, and to concoct the poison with which he would later kill so many, He should be forming this sainted woman so she could serve as an antidote to his poison, so that whatever was withdrawn from God on one side by Luther should be gathered and collected on another side by her.[15]

One of these relics, her right hand, would play a very peculiar role in the history of Spain four centuries later. This was the hand with which Teresa did all of her writing, always very rapidly. We will return to this relic in chapter 6.

How, When, and Why
the Book Was Written

CHAPTER 2

Forced Confession

Teresa did not write the *Vida* because she itched to tell her life story to the world or longed to be admired for her extraordinary experiences. She wrote it because she was commanded to do so by the clerics who served as her confessors and spiritual advisors, and she did it as an act of obedience and as an exercise that classifies as a "judicial confession."[1] In other words, Teresa was forced to write the *Vida* because various authorities in her order and in the Catholic Church wanted to examine her prayer life and her mystical claims in detail.

But how was it that a cloistered nun's prayer life could attract the kind of attention that Teresa received? In Teresa's case, as in many others like hers, it was the fact that her raptures, transports, and ecstasies occurred at unpredictable times and always had some observable trancelike aspect to them. Since many of these trances produced physical changes in her appearance while she was in the company of other nuns, or even of visitors, the trances could not be ignored, and reports of her extraordinary altered states began to circulate rapidly in monastic, clerical, and lay circles throughout Spain and beyond. Nonetheless, gaining a reputation as a mystic or a saint—especially one who falls into trancelike states, or floats in the air miraculously, or claims to commune with God—was somewhat perilous in mid-sixteenth-century Spain, where suspicions of heresy, fraud, or demonic activity ran high.

Certain questions had to be asked by ecclesiastical authorities of anyone who claimed to have experiences such as Teresa's, and these questions were deemed especially necessary in the case of women, for it was widely believed that females were less intelligent and less stable than males, and much less trustworthy when it came to any claim of supernatural encounters. Was Teresa genuinely engaging with the divine, or was she a fraud? Was she "inventing the sacred," a charge that the Inquisition made in cases of fraudulent claims to mystical experience?[2] Was it possible that her experiences involved the devil rather than God? Did her behavior in any way contradict or challenge authority? Was her behavior appropriately holy? What kinds of revelations was she claiming? Were her messages orthodox or heretical? Was she in any way linked to any heresy?

Teresa's *Vida* attempts to answer all of these questions as clearly as possible. Of course, the *Vida* is a multilayered text that transcends these questions, but to fully understand its contents one must first acknowledge that its very essence is apologetic, and that it was written under orders, as an act of obedience, with a very specific purpose in mind, as well as a very select audience. That purpose was to provide the correct answers to all of the questions above; the audience consisted of her superiors, the inquisitors, and fellow nuns. Addressing a lay audience was the last thing Teresa had in mind. In other words, the text is not so much an autobiography as it is a lengthy apologia, or defense, of Teresa's orthodoxy and of the genuine divine origin of her mystical experiences.[3]

The timing of the *Vida*'s writing—roughly 1560 to 1565— has much to do with a growing climate of suspicion and anxiety in Spain. Around 1558 and 1559, just as Teresa was beginning to acquire a reputation as a holy woman and a mystic, networks of Protestants were discovered in Spain, principally in Seville and Valladolid. The Inquisition swooped down on these Protestants quickly and ferociously. Between 1559 and 1562, around one hundred Protestants were executed by the Inquisition. All in all, this was a relatively small number, given the intensity of the search for "Lutherans," but the mere fact that Protestantism had sunk roots in Spain alarmed the authorities of church and state and gave rise to a climate of suspicion and hypervigilance in which the slightest perceived deviation from Catholic orthodoxy could earn one a place in the Inquisition's prisons. No one felt safe. Even Bartolomé Carranza, archbishop of Toledo, ended up being accused of heresy in 1558. Despite his position as the highest of all clerics in Spain, and despite the fact that he had served as confessor to Queen Mary of England and shared responsibility with "Bloody Mary" for the execution of hundreds of Protestants, Carranza was helpless. He would remain in the hands of the Inquisition for seventeen years—seven of those in Spain and ten in Rome—before being cleared of the most serious charges against him. Commanded to renounce sixteen questionable statements, Carranza died seven days after abjuring these niggling errors.[4]

In the wake of Carranza's arrest, which had sent a chilling message to everyone, mysticism became more suspect than ever before. In that fateful year of 1559, the Grand Inquisitor Fernando de Valdés issued an index of forbidden books that included many of the vernacular devotional texts that had inspired Teresa and some authors she revered, such as Pedro de Alcántara, Luis de Granada, and Francis Borgia. Although the orthodoxy of these authors was beyond dispute, hypersensitivity to Protestantism had reached such intensity among guardians of orthodoxy in Spain that some of their texts—previously hailed and enthusiastically embraced—were now deemed potentially dangerous and capable of leading the faithful astray.[5] Teresa obediently discarded these newly forbidden books with sadness. "When they took away many books written in the vernacular, so that they would not be read," she said, "I was very troubled, because some of them delighted me, and I could not read them in Latin. But the Lord said to me, 'Don't be sad, I will give you living books.'" That "living book" was nothing other than her encounters with the divine. "The Lord showed me so much love and taught me by so many methods," she claimed, "that I have had very little or hardly any need for books. His Majesty Himself has been the true book where I have found all that is true" (26:6.142). This statement speaks volumes about Teresa's daring (no pun intended), for to claim direct contact with the Lord in the early 1560s was to set oneself up for close scrutiny.

The first of the questions asked of Teresa—whether or not she was a fraud—was a pressing concern. False mystics of all sorts, male and female, could be found in sixteenth-century

Spain. Faking an ecstasy and making it seem genuine is not too difficult, it seems, for the Inquisition found plenty of monks and nuns guilty of "inventing the sacred" during Teresa's lifetime. False mystics could also be found outside convent walls, particularly among women known as *beatas* who took no vows and lived on their own, praying constantly, frequenting churches, and acquiring a reputation for holiness among the laity.

The issue of deception had to be addressed in order to safeguard belief in genuine mystical experiences. This belief was an integral part of the theology and piety of the Catholic Church, as well as of its identity vis-à-vis Protestants who denied the validity of all mystical claims. Every fraud was a challenge to the truth as well as to the authority of the church, especially frauds who fooled prominent people.

A contemporary of Teresa unmasked as a fraud was Maria de la Visitación, a nun in Lisbon who was acclaimed as a divinely inspired saint and prophet by many elites of church and state, including King Philip II and the Dominican theologian and spiritual writer Luis de Granada. In 1588—six years after Teresa's death—Sister Maria was tried by the Inquisition and found guilty of faking her ecstasies and her much-revered stigmata. Luis de Granada, who had written a glowing account of her holiness, would lament how easy it had been for him to be fooled by Maria.[6]

Another issue that needed addressing was that of demonic influence, for it was unquestioningly assumed that women were more susceptible to the devil's tricks than men. One of the most shocking cases of a feigned sanctity in the sixteenth century was that of the Franciscan nun and abbess Magdalena de la Cruz (1487–1560), which blurred the lines between fakery and demonic activity, two issues based as much on traditional beliefs concerning the devil's power to deceive as on assumptions regarded as "common sense." Like Teresa, Sister Magdalena had gone into trances frequently and claimed to be in constant communication with God. She had also supposedly survived by eating nothing but the consecrated host, levitated during some ecstasies, and received the gift of the stigmata. Magdalena had gained the approval of many elites, including the royal family, the general of the Franciscan order, and the venerable Francisco de Osuna, author of *The Third Spiritual Alphabet*, the book that changed Teresa's prayer life. In 1543, during a serious illness that brought her close to death, Sister Magdalena confessed that she had faked her mystical ecstasies, as well as her stigmata and other miracles attributed to her, and that all her deceptions could be blamed on demonic possession. In 1546, after publicly unmasking her as a fraud and a demoniac at an auto-da-fé in Córdoba, the Inquisition sentenced her to perpetual imprisonment in a Franciscan convent.[7]

Belief in the devil's ability to pass himself off as an "angel of light" or even as Jesus Christ himself was an ancient Christian belief, deeply embedded in monastic culture.[8] This was an unquestioned assumption, linked to another: a belief that a devil always assailed those who aimed for holiness and closeness to God. In Teresa's case, as soon as she began to have visions and other mystical transports, her confessors suspected the worst, and warned her that her experiences were demonic in origin. As Teresa dutifully confessed that Christ kept appearing to her, the confessors grew increasingly alarmed, and ordered her to greet her visions of Christ with an obscene hand gesture known as "giving the fig," an equivalent of today's "giving the finger." Dealing with the devil on his own level with obscenities and insults was fairly common advice in monastic culture, as common as the belief that the devil could easily deceive anyone. Teresa dutifully obeyed, despite the pain it caused her to greet Christ in such an offensive way (29:5–6.155–56). Years later, in 1622, in his bull of canonization for Teresa, Pope Gregory XV would emphasize the value placed on such obedience: "She was wont to say that she might be deceived in discerning visions and revelations, but could not be in obeying superiors."[9]

Another set of questions asked of Teresa also gave shape to her narrative in the *Vida*. Had she challenged authority in any way? Was she genuinely holy? Questions about a mystic's behavior and relations with superiors were asked because it was commonly assumed that genuinely divine experiences led to exemplary behavior, such as an aversion to sin and pride, a dedication to one's vows of poverty, chastity, and obedience, delight in self-denial, a humble attitude, total deference to superiors, and unquestioning submission to church authority. Teresa's *Vida* very carefully and constantly highlights all of these qualities, with additional heavy doses of deference and self-abasement. This constant appeal to her own humility and unworthiness, and to all of the shortcomings of being a woman rather than a man—her "rhetoric of femininity"—is essential to the narrative of the *Vida* and gives it structure.[10] Being too sure of herself could easily brand her as overly proud and contumacious. Nonetheless, Teresa needed to strike a careful balance between self-deprecation and self-assertion, for admitting that she was clueless or confused could lead the Inquisition to find fault in her. Genuine mystics who communed with God were supposed to correctly discern what they were experiencing. In other words, Teresa the writer had a very difficult and delicate balancing act to perform in defending her role as a genuine mystic.

No other account in the *Vida* displays Teresa's dexterity with this balancing act more clearly—or more dramatically— than that of her obedience to those confessors who ordered her to greet all visions of Christ with obscene gestures. On the one hand, Teresa says in no uncertain terms that she knew she was right and her confessors were wrong. This was a potentially dangerous assertion, a likely sign of pride and therefore also of error. On the other hand, however, Teresa stresses her obedience to her confessors, even adding for good measure that instead of being offended by her obscene gesture, Christ expressed immense delight in her ultimate act of self-abasement and obedience.

The next questions faced by Teresa were equally intimidating, given what was at stake. If she was indeed communing with God, what was she revealing about the divine? Were her messages truly orthodox, or tinged with heresy, or patently heretical? Could she be linked to any heresy in any way? Although any of the claims to mystical ecstasy made by Teresa could have aroused suspicion on the part of authorities, it was the similarity between her method of prayer and that of the Alumbrados—a homegrown Spanish heresy— that led the Inquisition to investigate her and to demand that she explain herself clearly in the autobiographical text that came to be known as the *Vida*. The Spanish term *alumbrado* means "illumined" or "enlightened." The Alumbrados were men and women who were hunted down by the Inquisition in the sixteenth century, ostensibly for observing certain methods of prayer and claiming to be illumined by the Holy Spirit or to be actually deified through their union with God.

The identity of the Alumbrados is a controversial issue.[11] Although there were various individuals who did indeed share common approaches to prayer and certain claims about their closeness to the divine, it seems clear to many scholars that the Alumbrado heresy was not as unified or organized as the Inquisition assumed. Consequently, experts still disagree on how to interpret the records kept by the Inquisition in its pursuit of the Alumbrados. Disagreement is strongest when it comes to the question of whether or not they all shared the characteristics and beliefs that the Inquisition ascribed to them. Were there really Alumbrados who believed that they could reach union with God and that this union divinized them and made them incapable of sinning? Were there Alumbrados who engaged in immoral behavior because of this antinomian belief? Did they all deny the existence of hell?

Regardless of how these questions are answered, no one can deny the fact that hundreds of individuals were pursued by the Inquisition and convicted of *alumbradismo* during Teresa's lifetime, and that many of those punished by the Inquisition had read some of the same devotional texts as Teresa and observed approaches to prayer very similar to hers. Moreover, not everyone suspected of alumbradismo was found guilty, and some of the individuals caught in the Inquisition's dragnet—such as Ignatius Loyola, founder of the Jesuit order[12]—later proved themselves to be leading figures of the Catholic Reformation. Distancing herself from these apparent connections was essential for Teresa, and this gave shape to the *Vida*. The key parallels with the Alumbrado heresy involved approaches to prayer and the outcome of those approaches. As the Inquisition saw it, the Alumbrados were far too keen on the methods recommended by Francisco de Osuna in his *Third Spiritual Alphabet*, one of Teresa's favorite devotional texts, particularly the practice of recogimiento and dejamiento, and the attainment of a prayer of quiet, a state in which the inner divine essence of the individual took over and did all the praying, wordlessly, removed from discursive or rational thought. The key question, then, was whether or not there was any substantive difference between the mysticism of the heretical Alumbrados and that of Teresa.

Teresa's *Vida* sought to provide the Inquisition and other ecclesiastical authorities with all of the information they needed in order to judge her orthodoxy. Although Teresa had much to reveal about the relation between the divine and the human in the highest states of prayer, none of her revelations proposed any of the teachings ascribed to the Alumbrados or to earlier mystical deviants, such as the fourteenth-century Free Spirit heretics. Another key account in the *Vida* that affirmed her orthodoxy, especially in contrast to the Alumbrados—who ostensibly denied any sinfulness in the higher states of mystical experience—is that which describes a vision she had in 1560, in which she not only saw the cramped niche she had earned herself in hell but also fully experienced the agony of being consigned to indescribable suffering in that stifling hole for eternity (32:1–7.173–75).

The Writing of the *Vida*

The most elemental fact to keep in mind as one reads the *Vida* is that it is written for an authority figure who is never mentioned by name but is constantly addressed throughout the text as "Vuestra Merced" ("Your Grace" or "Your Reverence"). The constant, inescapable intrusion of this nameless person in the text gives the *Vida* the feel of a long confession, or a plea for approval. The presence of "Vuestra Merced"—someone who is inspecting and judging—can make the reader feel as if Teresa is addressing him exclusively, or as if it is the reader who is being asked to pass judgment on her. This feature of the text raises certain basic questions. Who was this person? Why is he constantly addressed? What authority did he have? What does he have to do with Teresa and her text?

The name not provided by Teresa is that of García de Toledo, OP, subprior of Saint Thomas, the Dominican house at Ávila, who served as one of Teresa's confessors and advisors. His role in the writing of the *Vida* is considerable, and it has as much to do with the trust Teresa placed in him as with the pressures under which the text was written.

The men who requested her writing did so because they wanted to make sure that she was not deluded or intent on deluding others, or that she was not some heretic or demoniac. Although most of these men were close to her and very supportive rather than adversarial, especially in the writing of the two final versions, all of them would approach what she wrote with a hermeneutic of suspicion, and Teresa was keenly aware of this fact. In addition, Teresa knew that everything she wrote was subject to revision, perhaps even censure, and that her readers had the authority to hand her over to the Inquisition. We catch very clear glimpses of Teresa's constant self-awareness with every frequent interruption she addresses to "Vuestra Merced" throughout the *Vida*, asking for guidance and correction, pleading for leniency or forgiveness from her nameless superior, who obviously plays multiple roles as judge, spiritual advisor, confessor, and editor. In the case of the expression "Vuestra Merced," translated variously in English, but never accurately, Teresa's choice of words is revealing, for an exact translation is "Your *Mercy*," not "Your *Reverence*" or "Your *Grace*." Every time Teresa addresses García de Toledo, then, is she doing much more than calling his attention to potential imperfections in her prose? Might she be begging for mercy?

While it is undeniable that García de Toledo and the other readers who closely inspected her manuscripts were engaged in a collaborative project with Teresa, to some extent, they were also commissioned to assume an adversarial role, if necessary. So, although Teresa was engaged in a give-and-take with these men, and may have even hoped to influence their own spiritual lives, one must recognize that they were judges as well as mentors and that begging for mercy might have been on her mind now and then—or often—and that having to produce a text that can be classified as a "judicial confession" is far from an ideal context in which to write anything, much less a great religious book, or one that could fit comfortably in the category of autobiography.[13]

The *Vida* was written and rewritten over a period of eleven years, between 1554 and 1565, but most of it was penned in two bursts of feverish composition in 1561–62 and again in 1564, followed by the production of a final clean copy in 1565. The writing began in response to Teresa's mystical raptures, due to the fear that her confessors and superiors had about the nature of her claims and her method of silent, nondiscursive prayer, which made her seem too similar to the Alumbrados. Bit by bit, as she was commanded to supply her superiors with more information, Teresa constructed her *Vida* in five distinct stages, and each of these versions had different sets of readers. Although none of the early texts have survived, Teresian experts have been able to determine when the various drafts were written, for whom they were written, and by whom they were read.[14]

Teresa's first account was relatively brief, and it was written in 1554–55 as an examination of conscience (*cuenta de conciencia*) for her confessor Gaspar Daza and for Francisco de Salcedo, a devout "saintly gentleman" and close friend who had introduced her to Daza (23:6–7.127–28). Traditionally, *cuentas de conciencia* were written for one's confessor so he could get to know one better and tailor spiritual direction to one's specific character and needs. A second more detailed *discurso de su vida*, or account of her life, was penned in 1555 for Diego de Cetina, her first Jesuit confessor.

In 1560, Teresa penned another *cuenta de conciencia* for the Franciscan mystic and reformer Pedro de Alcántara. In addition, she wrote an account of her method of prayer for the learned Dominican professor of theology Pedro Ibáñez, who then ordered her to write a detailed narrative of her life and spiritual trajectory (11:8.72).

In 1561–62, while she was living in Toledo at the house of her close friend and patron, Luisa de Cerda, Teresa followed Ibáñez's orders and expanded on all of the previous accounts. The end result was the first full draft of the *Vida*, which she simply called "mi libro" or "my book." This text was then read by three Dominicans: García de Toledo, one of her confessors; the theologians Domingo Báñez and Pedro Ibáñez; and by the bishop of Ávila, Alvaro de Mendoza. Teresa also showed this version to a family friend, Inquisitor Francisco Soto y Salazar, who suggested that she send a copy to Juan de Ávila.

The final version of the *Vida* is an expansion of this 1561–62 text, and it was written in 1564 for García de Toledo. Upon finishing this version, Teresa made a copy in 1565 and sent it to Juan de Ávila, who found it much to his liking, but thought it should only be read by very few, due to its sensitive subject matter and the difficulties inherent in expressing ineffable experiences.

Although this process of composition and the long list of readers—a total of ten—obviously indicate that the *Vida* was something of a team project, experts tend to agree that the "Vuestra Merced" in the final version is García de Toledo. Of all of these manuscripts just mentioned, the only one that has survived is the last one: the copy made in 1565 for Juan de Ávila, which is now in the library of the palace of the Escorial.[15] Since the earlier versions are lost, we have no way of knowing how much censoring and revising took place along the way to that final manuscript copy or any way of discerning the role played by García de Toledo or any of her other readers. Experts surmise that all the various requests for revisions and expansions of what she had already written stemmed from a desire her readers must have had for greater clarity, especially on issues related to her mystical experiences, but we do not know and probably never will know how light- or heavy-handed the censorship or editing might have been. Another assumption commonly made is that in the final two versions of 1561–62 and 1564–65, Teresa's readers were much more interested in making sure that Teresa expressed herself in the most orthodox way possible than in censoring what she had to say. This is not to say, however, that the final version enjoyed a warm reception among all who read it.

Once Teresa finished writing that clean copy for Juan de Ávila in 1565, as she was in the midst of establishing her new Discalced Carmelite order, her *Vida* began to circulate among an ever-widening circle of people, some of whom had no personal connection with her. Troubles arose as soon as Alvaro de Mendoza, the bishop of Ávila, had a copy made for his sister, who, in turn, shared it with others who were curious about Teresa and, in turn, had more copies made. One of these unauthorized copies ended up in the hands of the powerful duchess of Alba and her daughter-in-law and a circle of their elite acquaintances, including the princess of Eboli, wife of one of King Philip II's advisors, all of them powerful individuals who had no theological training and had not received permission to read a text so highly charged with detailed descriptions of mystical raptures and other matters far beyond the ken of laymen and laywomen.

The unauthorized copying and distributing of Teresa's *Vida* greatly displeased Domingo Báñez, who had replaced García de Toledo as Teresa's confessor when García was sent to a post in the colonies of the Indies. Báñez knew what was in the *Vida*, for he had read the 1561–62 version. Keenly aware of the sensitive and highly technical nature of the material that was now being passed around by laypeople who knew little theology, Báñez requested that this new phase of uncontrolled circulation cease, even though he had no objections to the contents of the *Vida* itself. He had supported Teresa and her monastic reforms, and believed that her experiences were of divine origin, but he feared that the *Vida* would stir up too much controversy for Teresa and the church, especially if it were to be read by nontheologians. As he saw it, the best way to handle the *Vida* during Teresa's lifetime was to limit its circulation. We know that Báñez had no intention of locking up the *Vida* and hiding it from view but preferred to keep it under wraps, because he passed it on to some individuals he trusted, who would later testify that he had given them a copy with "great caution and secrecy."[16]

Despite the objections of Báñez, Teresa's *Vida* and other works continued to be copied and passed around. Teresa herself sometimes shared her writings with her fellow Carmelite nuns, some of whom helped to make copies that were clandestinely distributed.[17] But nuns were not the only ones involved in this process. One lay patron would later testify that he had paid for the copying and binding of several copies of the *Vida*.[18] One of Teresa's nephews made copies too,[19] and the countess of Camarasa testified that she had borrowed a copy from a Dominican nun in Toledo and then had a copy made for herself before returning it. This countess, Ana Félix de Guzman, precisely the kind of person that Báñez wanted to keep away from the *Vida*, was totally taken by it. Years later, she would say, "Without entrusting it to anyone, this witness carried it home herself, hiding it under her arm, and as she read it, she had it copied, because the peace that she felt in her heart when she read it was so great, that she did not want to be without it."[20] All in all, then, it is clear that the *Vida* and other texts written by Teresa were copied and shared by a diverse group of individuals that included secular and regular clerics, nuns from various orders, lay patrons, and members of the high nobility, some of whom belonged to the royal family and its inner circle. And it is also clear that despite Báñez's misgivings, many non-theologians seemed to appreciate the *Vida*, and to love it.

All of this clandestine copying and sharing of the *Vida* might have pleased Teresa and affirmed her inner conviction of its potential, but she remained painfully aware of the fact that none of this was supposed to happen, at least not until after her death. One Carmelite nun would later say that she remembered having seen Teresa "write one work and carry another under her arm" and that Teresa had said to her, "You will not see it in my lifetime, but I understand that after my death you will all benefit from it."[21] The copying, sharing, and carrying of books under one's arm had a slightly subversive edge, an edge that grew sharper and sharper as the copies multiplied and passed from hand to hand.

About ten years after Teresa's *Vida* began to circulate in manuscript form, some of Báñez's worst fears came true. First came the Inquisition trial of Bernardino Carleval, rector of the University of Baeza and a former confessor of Carmelite nuns, who was accused of alumbradismo in 1574. As the Inquisition dug into Carleval's past, one witness testified that he had heard Carleval speak about a book written by Teresa de Jesús that was full of "sublime revelations."[22] This bit of hearsay was enough to link Teresa with the Alumbrado heresy. Then came a direct accusation of alumbradismo from a resentful ex-novice in Seville. And then, as if that denunciation were not enough, a second accusation of alumbradismo was made in Castile by the princess of Eboli, a noblewoman with intimate connections to the royal court. The princess had long been a thorn in Teresa's side, demanding many favors in exchange for her patronage of a Discalced Carmelite convent in Pastrana. One of the favors she had received in 1569 was a copy of the *Vida*, which she circulated with abandon among acquaintances, even among her servants. Many disagreeable rumors about the contents of the *Vida* had spread from this circle of readers. In response to the princess's denunciation, which was acted upon much more quickly than the one from the ex-novice in Seville, the Valladolid tribunal of the Inquisition took up the task of inspecting the *Vida* in early 1575. Since the Inquisition did not have a copy, it commanded Alvaro de Mendoza, the bishop of Ávila, to surrender the one Teresa had given him.

Whether any inquisitors really suspected Teresa of alumbradismo remains an open question. But there is no doubt whatsoever that the cleric in charge of the Valladolid tribunal, Francisco de Soto y Salazar, was a friend of Teresa and her family, and that he had already read the *Vida* in 1564 and recommended that a copy be sent to Juan de Ávila. Soto tilted the scales further in Teresa's favor by choosing none other than her confessor Diego Báñez to render judgment on the *Vida* seized from the bishop of Ávila. After combing through the *Vida* once again and finding a few passages that he amended slightly, Báñez had this to say:

> I have examined this book very carefully, in which Teresa de Jesús . . . gives a plain account of all that goes on in her soul, so that she might be taught and guided by her confessors, and in all of it I have not found one thing that is bad doctrine, in my judgment; instead, there is much in it that

provides edification and advice for persons involved in prayer . . . This woman . . . even if she might be deceived, at least is not a deceiver, because she speaks so plainly of the good and the bad, with such great desire to be correct, that she makes it impossible to doubt her good intention.

Báñez also reiterated his earlier recommendation that circulation of the *Vida* be highly restricted, despite all of its many praiseworthy qualities. "I am resolved that this book should not be shared indiscriminately with anyone, but given only to learned men of experience and Christian discretion," he said. Eager to keep the *Vida* linked to its original intent, as a text written expressly for Teresa's spiritual guidance, Báñez added, "This book is very appropriate for the purpose for which it was written, that is, for this nun to give an account of her soul to those who are to guide her so that she not be deceived."[23] In other words, this was not a book that could or should instruct others since it was written by a woman who needed instruction herself.

Having taken Báñez's recommendations into account, the Supreme Council of the Inquisition ordered that every existing copy of the *Vida* be handed over to it. Only the duke and duchess of Alba were exempted from obeying this command. Whether or not everyone who had a manuscript did as they were told is a moot question. The immediate result of this decision was a curbing of all further copying and sharing, and the shuffling of all unreturned manuscripts to hiding places, for having a copy of the *Vida* in one's possession became a punishable offense. This ban would stay in place until 1587, five years after Teresa's death. During those five years, some additional copies were made before 1587, despite the Inquisition's ban on such activities. We know this because one of Teresa's favorite confessors, Jerónimo de Gracián, admitted that he had made some copies "for the monastics" in 1580, after he and Teresa were assured by the Grand Inquisitor, Gaspar de Quiroga, that he had found nothing wrong in the *Vida*. Nonetheless, even with such assurances from Grand Inquisitor Quiroga, those copies had to be made on the sly. Gracián later confessed: "I did not dare ask the Inquisition for permission, in order to avoid further controversy."[24]

While all copies of the *Vida* remained under this ban from the Inquisition, Teresa pressed on with her reforms and with further writing. In 1577 she penned a mystical treatise that gave more structure to her analysis of prayer and of the path to union with God. This text, *Moradas del Castillo Interior*, known in English as *The Interior Castle*, was in part intended as a substitute for her censored *Vida*, that is, as a manual for her nuns that distilled the mystical theology contained in the *Vida*, but circumvented some of the issues that had led to its sequestering by the Inquisition. Jerónimo Gracián would later take credit for the creation of this book, claiming that he had not only suggested it to Teresa but also ordered her to write it.[25]

During this trying time, as she wrote in whatever time she could spare, and as she traversed Spain establishing new convents, Teresa was not entirely in the dark about the fate of her *Vida*. Crushing as it was for her to know that the Inquisition had locked up her book, literally as well as figuratively, Teresa received indications that all was not lost. In February 1577, the second year of the *Vida*'s sequestration by the Inquisition, she wrote to her brother Lorenzo: "I've received some good news about my papers. The Grand Inquisitor himself is reading them . . . and he told Doña Luisa de la Cerda that there is nothing in them that they will have to concern themselves with."[26] Without a doubt, knowing that Gaspar de Quiroga approved of the *Vida* made Teresa feel a lot more secure about the future prospects for the *Vida*, as well as for her new order. After all, the Grand Inquisitor also happened to be the archbishop of Toledo and head of the whole Spanish church.

This knowledge emboldened her at exactly the same time that Gracián ordered her to write *The Interior Castle*. The fact that *The Castle* delves deeper into mystical theology and is more analytical in its approach to prayer and supernatural experiences than the *Vida*—and therefore somewhat less accessible or appealing to a wide reading public—may have much to do with the timing of the news she received from her friend and patron Doña Luisa de la Cerda, which not only freed her from fearing the wrath of the Inquisition but gave her enough of a boost in self-confidence to write less guardedly and to spread her wings, so to speak.

Teresa's Biographers

Focused as it was on her inner life of the spirit, Teresa's *Vida* could not fulfill the role of a traditional saint's *Life*, or hagiography, especially as her admirers pushed for her canonization. The rush to produce a suitable hagiography was inevitable. None other than Luis de León was commissioned to write such a book by King Philip II's sister, Maria of Austria. Having edited Teresa's manuscripts, and having worked so closely with her *Vida*, he was uniquely well suited for the job. Fray Luis was overtaken by death in 1591, however, before he could complete his work. His unfinished manuscript would have very limited circulation and no impact beyond clerical circles. But the demise of Fray Luis seemed to make little difference for one simple reason: someone else had already beaten him to the finish line.

In 1590, *The Life of Mother Teresa of Jesus* by Francisco de Ribera became an instant best seller. Its author was a Jesuit and former confessor of Teresa's who—like Fray Luis de León—also happened to die in 1591. Relying extensively on Teresa's *Vida*, as well as on his own acquaintance with her and her life, and his access to people who had been close to Teresa, Ribera wrote a gripping narrative that included many of the details found in the *Vida* and many others that were not, especially those that pertained to the last twenty years of her life, which are not covered in the *Vida*. Since his hagiography was translated and published in Latin, Italian, and French between 1601 and 1603, as Teresa's canonization process began to build up steam, Ribera was instrumental in helping expand and deepen support for that canonization as well as in increasing demand for Teresa's own *Vida* and her other writings. The appearance of Dutch and German translations in 1620–21, just before Teresa's canonization, also helped to increase devotion to her among Catholics who lived in close proximity to Protestants.

The success of Ribera's *Life* did not deter a Hieronymite priest, Diego de Yepes, from writing his own hagiography of Teresa. Like Ribera, he had served as confessor to Teresa. Unlike Ribera, he had also served as confessor to kings Philip II and Philip III, and was appointed bishop of

Tarazona in 1599. First published in 1606, as Teresa was well on her way to beatification and canonization, Yepes's *Life, Virtues and Miracles of the Blessed Virgin Teresa of Jesus*, was another instant best seller. Although some scholars argue that Yepes did not do all of the writing himself, and that his account drew perhaps a bit too much from Luis de León's unfinished manuscript, or perhaps from another unfinished manuscript by Julián de Ávila, Yepes has nonetheless won all the acclaim.[27] His hagiography is similar to Ribera's, and equally anchored in Teresa's *Vida*, but it is full of details that do not appear in either of those two texts.

Two other texts that proved less popular than those of Ribera and Yepes round out the number of hagiographies that extended the life of Teresa's *Vida*, drawing attention to it, expanding on it, and adding details not found in it. One of these, which appeared in 1609, was in Latin and aimed at a learned audience: *Compendium of the Life of the Blessed Virgin Teresa of Jesus*, by a Carmelite, Juan de Jesús Maria.[28] The other one appeared in 1611 and was written by Teresa's confessor and close companion Jerónimo de Gracián. Its title reflected baroque excess and revealed its purely hagiographic approach: *Declamation in which Is Covered the Perfect Life and Heroic Virtues of the Blessed Mother Teresa of Jesus.*[29]

All in all, then, these printed hagiographies can be considered extensions of Teresa's own *Vida*, as well as essential components of the cult that quickly developed around Teresa the saint, whose texts were counted among her many miracles and became highly prized avatars of Catholic identity in the baroque age throughout the Catholic world. King Philip II and his heirs to the throne of Spain might have kept their 1565 autograph of the *Vida* under lock and key in a "magnificent chest" at the Escorial and venerated it as a relic no less precious than one of her arms or fingers,[30] but thanks to the printing press and to editors, everyone could have a different kind of privileged access to the miracle of Teresa's *Vida*, and thanks to hagiographers, everyone could also place that miracle in its proper context and be affected all the more deeply by it and by Teresa's mysticism.

The Mysticism of the *Vida*

Teresa's *Vida* is a mystical treatise full of claims that many readers in our day and age would consider bizarre, insane, or fraudulent. Its central premise is as outrageous as all of the raptures and transports described within it: after all, this is a text that assumes—unquestioningly—that human beings can transcend the sensory material world and have intimate relations with the Creator of the universe. And it is precisely this seemingly preposterous aspect of the *Vida* that begs for attention, for to deal with it fully is to plumb what gives it structure and meaning.

Making sense of the mystical dimension of the *Vida* is not easy. The first and most immediate obstacle is Teresa's "gracious disorder," which can make even the most expert readers of mystical texts feel as if they are lost in the most complex of labyrinths. The second obstacle is the mysticism itself. Dealing with the first obstacle is relatively easy, especially in light of the challenges posed by the second one, so let us first focus on the *Vida*'s somewhat untidy outline.

The Structure of the *Vida*

Given that Teresa wrote her *Vida* for her confessors and spiritual directors over several years and that they suggested emendations, additions, and clarifications at different times during the writing process, it is not at all surprising that the text has an unusual structure and does not follow the standard pattern of an autobiography or a mystical text.

Teresa's *Vida* consists of forty chapters in which the narrative of her life is unevenly divided, with three times as many chapters devoted to the events of the eight most recent years of her life as to the first thirty-nine. Moreover, the entire text from start to finish is an interweaving of two distinct types of narrative, inseparably braided: one focused on the events of Teresa's life, the other focused on her life of prayer and her otherworldly experiences. These two narratives are interdependent: neither can stand alone nor make sense without the other. And this dual character gives the *Vida* a unique profile. As part history and part mystical treatise, the *Vida* not only tells the story of a remarkable life but also outlines and analyzes in great detail some of the most exceptional religious experiences any human being could claim. The history of the *Vida*'s reception, then, could not help but be as binary as its structure. In other words, the life of this book, that is, the history of its reception and interpretation, can be traced at two levels, as an autobiography—or autohagiography—and as a highly technical disquisition on prayer and encounters with the divine.

The *Vida*'s structure reflects its dual approaches and can be best understood as comprised of four distinct sections that intermingle its biographical and mystical elements. As is common in many religious autobiographies, the first section introduces the reader to the unconverted self, Teresa the sinner.

The first part of the book—chapters 1–10—is largely biographical, and covers her childhood, adolescence, early adulthood, and her life as a sickly and somewhat lackadaisical nun. This first section serves as a prologue for the following thirty chapters and also as contrasting background to them, and to the conversion experience that transforms the author from sinner into saint.

The second part of the *Vida*—chapters 11–22—is doctrinal and analytical rather than a narrative, and it is focused on prayer and the different levels of intimacy with the divine that can be attained through it. This highly introspective survey of Teresa's prayer life is an interruption to the narrative of her life, and serves as an essential primer on the mystical theology that permeates the rest of the book, which deals in great detail with the visions, locutions, and raptures that Teresa began to experience after her conversion in 1555.

The third part of the *Vida* stretches from chapter 23 to chapter 31. This section returns to narrative and provides a somewhat untidy account of Teresa's life as a mystic who is constantly encountering the supernatural while transitioning from a lukewarm nun into a monastic reformer. In chapter 23 Teresa tells the reader: "This is another, new book from this point forward—I mean another, new life." In other words, as she puts it, the life described in chapters 1–10 "was mine," and the life she will now begin to describe in chapter 23 is the one "God has lived in me" (3:1.126). This radical transition is not just a component of her mystical life but its very outcome, and the otherworldly experiences are therefore dealt with as having very worldly effects. In this section, Teresa describes various types of mystical experiences, including some of those that would forever be linked with her identity, and with the *Vida* itself. In addition, she describes the first steps she took toward reforming her Carmelite order, always with an eye firmly fixed on the connection that reform had to her prayer life and her extraordinary experiences.

Chapters 32 to 40—the fourth and final part of the *Vida*—focus on the years 1562 to 1564, from the time she leaves the Convent of the Incarnation and establishes her reformed Discalced Convent of Saint Joseph right up to the point when she is finishing the final draft of her autobiography. These chapters were probably added in 1564 to the first draft of the *Vida* written in 1561–62, at the suggestion of her confessor and chief reader, García de Toledo. Chapters 32 to 36 deal largely with narrative and focus on her early work as reformer. Chapters 37 to 40 bring the reader up to date on her unique inner life and provide details on the higher stages of prayer that she has been reaching during the writing of the *Vida*. Chapter 40 ends with a matter-of-fact statement addressed to García de Toledo, the immediate reader of the final 1564 manuscript: "This is the way I'm living now, my Lord and Father." No longer addressing him as "Your Mercy" (Vuestra Merced) but as "Lord and Father," Teresa closes her *Vida* with a direct reference to its nature and purpose as an act of obedience, self-examination, confession, and submission to authority.

The Context of Teresa's Mysticism

Every major religion on earth has had its mystics, that is, men and women who claim to transcend earthly existence and to experience higher realities. Normally, the other-worldly encounters of mystics reflect the beliefs of their own particular tradition. For instance, Buddhists tend not to immerse themselves in the New Testament, have visions of Christ, or experience union with the Christian triune God; and Christians tend not to pay attention to any of the teachings of the Buddha, believe in reincarnation, or yearn for ultimate fulfillment in Nirvana rather than in God. Historically, then, despite whatever similarities their lifestyles may share, such as practicing self-denial and praying ceaselessly, or having visions and trances, mystics tend to have tradition-bound experiences in which they encounter the ultimate reality that they have been conditioned to expect.[1] There have always been exceptions to this general rule, but Teresa of Avila was not one of them.

Teresa was a Catholic nun. Her religiosity was thoroughly Catholic and derived from a rich mystical tradition with ancient roots. Her immediate environment in sixteenth-century Spain, in the walled city of Ávila, and in her convents was Catholic to the core and unaffected by religious currents extraneous to Catholicism. The people who influenced her and the texts that shaped her piety were linked to those ancient roots, most surely, as were her expectations about ultimate realities, but she was most directly in tune with late medieval and early modern Catholic religiosity rather than with that of the distant Christian past. Moreover, having never ventured very far from her native Ávila before she embraced monastic life, Teresa's horizons were limited by local manifestations of that religiosity. Her local religion was firmly grounded in tradition, but also dynamic and in a state of flux: new approaches to spirituality gained ground steadily, but somewhat cautiously, in a climate of suspicion and of hypersensitivity to heresy. Ávila's massive walls could not keep it isolated from outside influences. As she admits, books were an essential part of her religiosity, and so were individuals who brought new perspectives to Ávila, such as the Jesuits. Consequently, to understand Teresa's mysticism, and, more specifically, how that mysticism is expressed in the *Vida*, one must first delve into the religious context that shaped her horizons.

Constant interaction between human and spiritual forces was a common expectation of traditional Spanish religion in Teresa's day, across all social strata. Everyday life pulsated with the possibility of the miraculous and otherworldly, and with an expectation of supernatural events. God, the saints, and the devil were always close at hand, on the other side of the permeable boundary that stood between the material and spiritual realms. Otherworldly realities were inseparable from much of daily life for peasant and noble alike, despite the undeniable and unavoidable presence of churlish skeptics and irredeemable agnostics. In Teresa's culture, monks, friars, and nuns were ostensibly poised to cross over to that other side, and their purpose in this life was to do just that, ideally, through their pursuit of moral and spiritual perfection. Undisturbed contemplation of God was supposed to be their ultimate goal.

Teresa's Books

Teresa's mysticism was shaped largely by the devotional texts she read, most of which had been written in the fourteenth to sixteenth centuries, but nonetheless distilled mystical traditions that stretched back to early Christian times. The oldest texts she read were a thousand years old: *The Confessions* of Saint Augustine and some letters of Saint Jerome, both of which had been recently translated into Spanish. Other texts that she mentions as influences in her spiritual development are *The Life of Christ* by Ludolph of Saxony (fourteenth century), the *Dialogue of St. Catherine of Siena* (fourteenth century), *The Imitation of Christ* by Thomas à Kempis (fifteenth century), *The Third Spiritual Alphabet* by Francisco de Osuna (sixteenth century), and *The Ascent of Mount Sion* by Bernardino de Laredo (sixteenth century).

Teresa openly acknowledged how much these books had influenced her, but she also claimed that much of what she experienced could only be directly attributed to God. When the Inquisition placed the Spanish translations of some of these texts on its *Index of Forbidden Books* in 1559, four years after her conversion, Teresa was saddened but unfazed. In the *Vida*, she recalled this event as a major turning point, after which books ceased to matter. "The Lord said to me, 'Don't be sad, I will give you living books,'" said Teresa, adding that after that point in time she had "very little or hardly any need for books" because "His Majesty Himself has been the true book where I have found all that is true" (26.6.142).

Much of the terminology employed by Teresa can be traced to her beloved books. One in particular, Osuna's *Third Spiritual Alphabet*, had provided her not just with terms but with approaches to prayer. Her use of terms such as "mental prayer," "meditation," "recollection," "prayer of quiet," and "prayer of union"—which can be found in Osuna's text—is much more than mere categorization. The terms, the methods and states they attempt to describe, and the experiences claimed by Teresa are all one and the same, indistinguishable from one another. What she learned, internalized, and acted upon is the very matrix of her mysticism and of the experiences described in the *Vida*.

The practice of "recollection" had ancient roots that reached back to the Desert Fathers of the early Christian era, but it could be traced to later advocates, such as the Rhineland mystics Meister Eckhart and his disciples Jan Van Ruysbroeck, John Tauler, and Henry Suso (fourteenth century) and their disciples Hendrik Herp and Denis the Carthusian (fifteenth century). Osuna and Laredo were both deeply indebted to translations of Herp and Denis the Carthusian published in Spain.

Mental prayer and the prayer of quiet had a long history too, also traceable to the Desert Fathers and to Dionysius the Areopagite, Saint Bernard of Clairvaux, and, more immediately, to the anonymous fourteenth-century English treatise *The Cloud of Unknowing*. It was also highly favored by the Brethren of the Common Life, a religious community with links to the Rhineland mystics, and also by Herp and Denis the Carthusian and Thomas à Kempis, the author of *The Imitation of Christ*, which Teresa knew under the title *Contempt of the World*.

Her use of "meditation" was not just something she picked up from Osuna but also from *The Life of Christ* by Ludolph of Saxony, who, in turn, was only passing on a long tradition of focusing on events in the life of Jesus and imagining oneself there, back in first-century Galilee or Judaea. It was also an imaginative exercise promoted in Teresa's own day by García de Jiménez in his *Book of Exercises for the Spiritual Life*, and, in turn, by Saint Ignatius Loyola in his *Spiritual Exercises*. Those young Jesuit confessors who were the first to assure Teresa of the divine origin of her otherworldly experiences based much of their advice on knowledge and experience derived from Loyola's *Exercises*.

Mental Prayer and Recollection

In addition to being an autobiography, a lengthy confession, and a mystical treatise, Teresa's *Vida* is also an instruction book of sorts, for much of what she has to say about her life of prayer is as prescriptive as it is descriptive and analytical. Identifying, enumerating, describing, and classifying different types and stages of prayer is an essential component of the book, and all of this sorting and analyzing—originally intended to provide her confessors with the details of her spiritual life—can also serve to guide others. As already mentioned, making sense of what Teresa is saying can be difficult due to her "gracious disorder." Yet, although the *Vida* is not a carefully outlined step-by-step instruction book, the text does contain a wealth of information that can be viewed as practical rather than strictly theological or biographical.

A good way to make sense of the *Vida*'s mysticism is to isolate its various components and to examine them individually. Doing so requires imposing a different order on the text than the one given by the author, and doing so carefully, on the text's own terms, without constant references to other texts of hers, especially *The Interior Castle* and *The Way of Perfection*, which were written later and incorporated mystical experiences that she had after the completion of the *Vida*. Once the components have been isolated, one can begin to examine certain key elements. First, one must deal with Teresa's mystical vocabulary, which was at once precise and vague. Second, one must engage with the issue of stages, or steps, on the mystical path to God. Third, one must sort out and examine the different kinds of experiences described by Teresa. Doing all this means grappling with her metaphors.

The entryway to mystical experience in the *Vida* is prayer. This is the most basic, most essential factor to consider. Although Teresa does speak of fasting, self-flagellation, the wearing of hair shirts, and other such corporeal penances as part and parcel of the mystical life, she emphasizes prayer much more than asceticism, and a great deal of the *Vida's* text is devoted to prayer. This could largely be due to the nature of the assignment given to Teresa by her confessors, which was to elucidate her life of prayer and her otherworldly experiences so they could determine whether or not she was actually dealing with divine realities. Teresa's asceticism was not in question, as far as we can tell, only her extraordinary prayer life.

Teresa's conversion in 1555 is linked to mental prayer, and asserts that it is "the door to those great favors" bestowed on her by God (8:9.62). As a nun, she was already engaged in a substantial amount of vocal prayer with her community, but this had never been enough to bring her to a transcendent state of consciousness beyond the material world. Save for one brief vision of Christ that she saw in 1538 with the "eyes of the soul"—in which he glared at her disapprovingly—Teresa had no otherworldly experiences before her conversion (7:6.54). As she saw it, all those years she spent in the convent as a "wicked creature" avoiding mental prayer had been fruitless.

Mental prayer is hard to define. In fact, it is easier to explain what it is *not* rather than what it is. Its main characteristics are silence, interiority, and its distinctness from vocal prayer. Unlike vocal prayer, which is recited out loud, mental prayer requires no spoken words and does not normally rely on set prayers, such as the "Our Father" or "Hail Mary" or biblical psalms. Descriptions of mental prayer vary, according to who is explaining it. As Teresa understood it, mental prayer is marked by a feeling of closeness with God. In her own words, it is "nothing else than a friendly relationship, a frequent private conversation with Him by whom we know ourselves to be loved" (8:5.61). For Teresa, mental prayer requires some personal effort: it is not a gift dispensed to the unwilling but rather a gift earned by choice and by deeds. Once chosen, and once entered into—as Teresa saw it—the benefits are so obvious and so plentiful that no one would want to turn away from it. A key to understanding what Teresa means by "mental prayer" is her insistence on its being a "conversation" or dialogue in which God talks back to the individual who is praying. It is an exchange initiated by humans to which God responds. In essence, then, it is a real crossing of the threshold that separates the mundane from the supernatural, and a necessary first step to further otherworldly experiences. Teresa was so convinced of the need for mental prayer and of its attainability that in her reform of the Carmelite order, she required her nuns to dedicate two hours a day to it. In the *Vida*, however, she provides no specific instructions on how to attain or practice mental prayer, other than to insist that it is only achieved by those who seek to practice it.

Instructions, and a more detailed analysis of mental prayer, would be provided by Teresa in another treatise, *The Way of Perfection*, which was written in two different versions between 1564 and 1569, also at the command of her confessors. This text was intended as a manual for Teresa's nuns: it was a how-to book, much more focused on outlining the various steps to be taken in mental prayer. In this text, she emphasizes the ineffability of this approach to God. Somehow, "without the noise of words," she says, the human faculties are suspended in mental prayer and "they bask in joy without understanding how they do so; the soul is set ablaze with love, and doesn't understand how it loves; it knows it enjoys what it loves, and doesn't know how it enjoys it."[2] This passage adds depth to what she had said in the *Vida* without contradicting it, but does not really make the meaning of mental prayer more exact.

Advocating mental prayer could be risky in Teresa's day, even though it was an ancient practice embraced by many revered saints. As stated earlier in chapters 1 and 2, mental prayer came to be associated with the Alumbrado heretics, who also espoused it. One of the charges made by the Inquisition was that Alumbrados favored mental prayer so much that they denigrated vocal prayer and all external ceremonies. Even worse, according to the Inquisition, the Alumbrados used mental prayer to achieve their highly prized states of recogimiento and dejamiento, which led to divinization and sinlessness.

Teresa did not learn about mental prayer from the Alumbrados, however, but rather from Francisco de Osuna's *Third Spiritual Alphabet*. Although Osuna taught Teresa that mental prayer led to recogimiento and dejamiento, and the attainment of a prayer of quiet, Osuna and Teresa assigned a very different meaning to these terms, and a different role for the concepts signified by them. For both Osuna and Teresa, mental prayer leads to spiritual and moral perfection, an intensification of one's appreciation of church rituals and sacraments, and ultimately to a virtuous life, not to the rejection of vocal prayer or external ceremonies, or to the development of an antinomian consciousness and a sinless divinized self, as among the Alumbrados.

As far as the two objectives of mental prayer were concerned—the attainment of recogimiento and dejamiento—Osuna and Teresa also disagreed with the Alumbrados. To begin with, in the case of Teresa, the concept of dejamiento, or self-abandonment, played no role at all in her mysticism, and does not need to be examined here. She used the term only once, in *The Interior Castle*, in reference to external poverty.[3] The concept of recogimiento, in contrast, was inseparable from that of mental prayer to both Osuna and Teresa, and played a central role in their mysticism, but in a way very different from that of the Alumbrados. To understand Teresa, then, one must grapple with that concept. Fortunately, its exact meaning is not as difficult to pin down as that of mental prayer.

In Teresa's *Vida*, "recollection" (recogimiento) is understood as an absolutely necessary inward turn and as the goal of mental prayer. The English word "recollection" does not really do full justice to its meaning in Spanish. The verb "recoger" means "to gather up," "pick up," or "collect," in the sense of bringing together or assembling things that are dispersed into one location. The full meaning of recogimiento as understood and employed by Osuna and Teresa is a movement from the periphery of the self to its center that seeks to bring together all of the disparate parts of the human self and concentrate them within the soul. Gathering up these scattered parts of the self requires withdrawing from the material world, for it is through the physical senses that the self becomes fragmented and scattered, and that the mind and soul get entangled in innumerable external distractions. In the state of recogimiento the soul's faculties are occupied entirely with God, while the five outward senses cease to matter and remain largely listless and unengaged.

Given that Osuna was influenced by the Rhineland mystics, who taught that God was most intensely present in the core of the soul, his understanding of recogimiento—and that of Teresa too—had a sense of motion to it, of gathering those bits of the self that were linked to the sensory world and plunging into that inner place where God dwelt in one's soul, that spot Meister Eckhart called the *seelengrund*, or ground of the soul. Thirteen years after she wrote the *Vida*, Teresa would turn this understanding of recogimiento into the central metaphor of her *Interior Castle*, and she would describe the path to God not as an upward ascent to heaven but rather as an inward journey to the deepest, inmost recess of one's soul. In the *Vida*, the central metaphor Teresa employs for the mystical quest is different, but the practice of that same inward, centering recogimiento is still an essential component of the text.

The Central Metaphor of the Four Waters

Grasping the meaning of recollection and its key role in the quest for God within oneself is essential for understanding the entire process of contemplation outlined by Teresa in the *Vida*, as well as for fully appreciating the central metaphor of the text. Recollection is actually part of the first of four steps in this quest for God—steps that are explained in the *Vida* by means of the metaphor of the four different ways in which a garden can be watered in a land as arid as that of Teresa's Ávila. The four methods represent four different steps in spiritual progress, symbolically represented by four increasingly less laborious and more efficient ways of watering a garden.

The first method is the most labor-intensive and time-consuming: drawing water from a well one bucket at a time. This is the first stage of the contemplative quest, which begins with vocal prayer and some meditation. The individual is very active, exercising his or her faculties and achieving progress through continuous effort.

The second method is that which employs a waterwheel with dippers attached to it and an aqueduct that conveys water to the garden. As the crank on the wheel is turned, water flows steadily down the aqueduct, with much less labor than the first method. This stage, she says, "already touches on the supernatural," and it is now that "the soul begins to recollect itself" and to realize that it is experiencing something that it "could not in any way attain by its own efforts." It is at this stage that the soul begins to experience the prayer of quiet, with which we shall deal presently (14:1–2.84).

The third method employs irrigation by means of a constantly running stream. It involves no human effort at all, beyond that of creating the irrigation system. Prayer at this stage crosses over into the realm of the supernatural fully, and here God "assumes the work of the gardener and lets the soul relax." Now the soul "flings itself totally into God's arms." This kind of prayer, says Teresa, is "a union of the whole soul with God," and one's joy is so intense "that sometimes it seems that the soul is about to leave the body, and, oh, what a blessed death that would be!" (17:1–5.96–97).

The fourth and final method is that of falling rain from heaven that "abundantly soaks and saturates the entire garden with water" (18:9.101). This stage of prayer and contemplation is pure bliss, infused by God, and involves no human effort. "In this state of prayer," says Teresa, "there is no feeling, but only enjoying, without any comprehension of what is being enjoyed." This ultimate stage is the "prayer of union," which shall also be dealt with presently. "It is obvious what union is," says Teresa. "It is two distinct things becoming one" (18:1–3.99–100).

At this highest stage, divinization takes place, but it is not at all of the sort that the Alumbrados were accused of professing. Teresa's divinization retains an ineffable yet real distinction between the soul and God. Once, while she was wondering what the soul did during these unitive fourth-stage ecstasies, Teresa heard God say, "The soul undoes itself totally, daughter, in order to get itself deeper in Me; she is no longer the one who lives, but I. Since it cannot fathom what it understands, it understands without understanding" (18:14.102). The "undoing" of the soul in this fourth stage—*deshacer* in Spanish—is not the same as "dissolving" or "dying," as some English translations have it, or any kind of annihilation, but rather a "remaking" or transfiguration of the sort mentioned by Saint Paul, which retains the integrity of the human self: "I no longer live, but Christ lives in me" (Galatians 2:20).

Mystical texts rely heavily on identifying, classifying, and enumerating different stages on the contemplative path, as well as types of prayer, and many such texts also subdivide each of the stages and prayers into different parts. The number of stages and substages could vary: three, four, seven, and twelve were the most common numbers employed. Quite often, mapping the stages and types of prayers and discerning the relation of the numbers in one text to those in another is not easy. Teresa was very familiar with this characteristic of mystical texts, and it shaped her own experiences as well as her writing. Consistency in numbering did not matter as much to her as classifying, or as finding the best metaphors, so while her *Vida* has four stages and the metaphor of the four waters, her *Interior Castle*, written thirteen years later, has seven stages and the metaphor of a castle with many rooms at different levels. These two texts complement each other in spite of their differences. Teresa does not contradict herself in the *Castle* but merely expands on what she had written in the *Vida*, much like an artist who paints different versions of the same scene or subject. Nonetheless, a certain tension runs through Teresa's works, including the *Vida*, because while she suggests that spiritual progress should not be measured on a hierarchical scale according to the kinds of "consolations" received from God, her texts are full of hierarchically arranged sets of numbers and metaphors that outline the progress of the soul on the contemplative path.

The Prayer of Quiet and the Prayer of Union

The prayer of quiet—which is attained at the second stage of the mystical quest and continues through the third—is infused contemplation, that is, a state in which God reaches out to the soul and makes his presence felt directly. This prayer is a gift, "a little spark given to the soul by God, as a sign or pledge that he is choosing it for great things," and since God gives the gift whenever he sees fit, the soul can do nothing to attain it (15:5.89). In this state, the soul enjoys an unearthly sense of peace and "a very great joy . . . and a most sweet delight" (15:1.87). It is called the "prayer of quiet" because the mind and soul are so overwhelmed by the divine presence that one is left speechless. As Teresa puts it, "Whatever the soul does during these times of quiet is only softly and without noise. By 'noise,' I mean searching around for many words with one's reason and discerning how to give thanks for this gift" (15:6.89).

The prayer of union, which is attained in the fourth and last stage, is also infused contemplation, but of a much more intense and higher sort, and Teresa stammers when trying to describe it. "I don't know how to explain the nature of this union—as it is called—or how it comes about," she says. "Mystical theology speaks of it, but I don't know what the proper terms are, and I can't understand what is meant by 'mind' or how this differs from 'soul' or 'spirit'; they all seem identical to me" (18:2.99). But while the spiritual and intellectual aspects of the prayer of quiet are difficult to describe, Teresa has less trouble with its physical effects, which are intense.

> With a very great and sweet delight the soul feels that it is fainting away almost completely, in a kind of swoon. It begins to lose breath and all bodily strength; it cannot even wiggle the hands without great pain; the eyes close involuntarily, or, if they remain open, they can hardly see anything; and if it tries to read, it can hardly spell out a single letter or recognize it . . . It hears, but cannot understand what it hears. It can apprehend nothing with the senses . . . Speaking is impossible, for it cannot bring itself to form a single word, and even if it could, it would not find sufficient strength to pronounce it; for all external strength vanishes, while the strength of the soul increases, so that it may the better enjoy its bliss. (18:10.101)

Teresa is not as precise about the duration or frequency of these unitive ecstasies as she is about their effects. She knows that "union" means the merging of two different things, and that the prayer of union brings the human self to the very edge of death in a paradoxical mix of spiritual bliss and bodily pain. But when it comes to details about the ineffable experience itself, she is always ready to admit that it is "a most difficult matter," and that it seems more impossible for her "to say something about it than to speak Greek" (18:7–8.100–101).

Mystical Phenomena

The *Vida* is full of accounts of Teresa's otherworldly phenomena: visions, locutions, trances, ecstasies, levitations, encounters with angels and demons, glimpses of heaven and hell, and intimate moments with God himself. In sum, the *Vida* is a journey to another dimension, a gripping narrative as full of marvels as Homer's *Odyssey*, which also happens to be about an exile straining to go home. It matters little that Teresa's goal is to reach heaven rather than Ithaca or any other spot on earth. Her story is that of an arduous, wonder-filled journey to the place she considers her true home, where her beloved awaits.

Due to the "gracious disorder" of the *Vida*, it makes little sense to impose a chronology on Teresa's otherworldly experiences, for she herself fails to do that and quite often admits that her own classification system is imprecise. So, instead of sorting out these accounts according to the order of Teresa's four stages of prayer or in relation to the different types of prayer involved, it is much better to deal with these accounts according to the type of experience.

Visions

Crossing the threshold of the realm of the senses involved seeing things that were not normally perceptible. For Teresa, seeing otherworldly realities was one of the most constant patterns of her mystical life, and she did not think of herself as deluded or insane. "That all this is merely imagined is the most impossible of all impossibilities," she said about her visions (28:11.152). Her visions were so constant and so intense and so *real*, in fact, that what she saw with her bodily eyes seemed like a dream or a "mockery" of what was genuinely real, and that she longed to die so she could get to that reality revealed in her visions (38:7.209). Yet, visions were the wildest of all wild cards in the religious climate of sixteenth-century Spain, for anyone who claimed to have direct access to the supernatural could be perceived as a fraud, or as demonically deceived, or as a threat to the hierarchical and sacramental order of the Catholic Church. Consequently, Teresa's accounts of her visions in the *Vida* were among the most potentially explosive of all issues.

Teresa had done enough reading in mystical texts to know that there were distinctions to be made concerning visions: some were corporeal and involved the bodily eyes, some were wholly spiritual and involved the eyes of the soul, others were imaginative and involved the eyes of the mind,[4] and yet another kind were intellectual and involved the mind itself. Visions had a hierarchy. Corporeal visions were the least trustworthy because they were the most susceptible to demonic deception. Since Teresa never claimed to have any such visions, they need no attention here. Spiritual visions were much more common for her, and so were imaginative visions, which were far more trustworthy than corporeal visions.[5] Teresa also claimed to have intellectual visions, which were the highest kind of all and the most delectable. In these visions God transmitted truths directly to her mind in an indescribable way, and she suddenly acquired a profound understanding of even the deepest mysteries, such as that of the Trinity. At times, however, it is difficult to tell what criteria Teresa is employing for distinguishing one kind of vision from another. It is also obvious that she was unable or unwilling to classify some of her visions, as in this passage concerning her visions of Christ:

> In some instances, it seemed to me that I was seeing an image, but many other times it seemed like it was Christ himself, depending on how clearly he wanted to show himself to me. Sometimes it was all too confusing: it seemed to be an image, not like drawings from this world, even the most accomplished kind . . . If it's an image, it's a living image, not a dead man, but the living Christ, and he reveals that he is both man and God . . . And sometimes he comes with such great majesty that no one can doubt that it's the Lord himself. (28:7–8.150–51)

Teresa also made it clear that her visions were beyond her control. "There is nothing one can do about them; our own efforts cannot make us see more or fewer of them or make them happen or not" (29:3.154–55).

Teresa had imaginative and intellectual visions of Christ, the Trinity, saints, demons, and dead people, or even heaven and hell. Some of the intellectual visions relayed intimate, ineffable knowledge of the deepest mysteries of the faith, such as the Trinity (27:9.145). Some imaginative visions were intense reifications of Catholic doctrine, such as the one in which she saw "a wonderful representation" of the humanity of Christ in the bosom of God the Father (38:17.211). Many visions conformed to Catholic iconography, while others were variations of it. Once, for instance, she saw the Holy Spirit floating above her in the form of a very large dove—larger than any she had ever seen—with wings "made of very resplendent, shiny little shells"

(38:10.209–10). When Christ appeared, he almost always manifested himself in his humanity, as Jesus, rather than as a disembodied second person of the Trinity, and she often classified these visions as imaginative because, as she understood it, such visions were better for revealing his physical self, while intellectual visions were better for communicating his divinity. Teresa had visions of the bloody, wounded, and crucified Christ, but most of her visions involved the resurrected Christ, gloriously embodied, radiant, and majestic. He was Christ the King, the Lord of all, and his beauty was sublime, beyond compare. Her visions of Christ were numerous, but problematic, at first. As previously mentioned, she had a hard time convincing some of her confessors that she was not being fooled by the devil, and they forced her to greet her visions with obscene gestures.

Those gestures she made reveal that Teresa's visions were not necessarily passive, as if she were merely looking at an image. They were often interactive, and some of them involved miracles. On one occasion, for instance, Christ took a crucifix from Teresa's hand and turned it into four "supernatural" precious stones that became a constant vision for her (29:7.156). The most famous of all of Teresa's visions—known as the transverberation—has already been mentioned in chapter 1. It was a fully interactive vision, and it involved an angel rather than Christ. Teresa says that it was rare to actually see an angel, for they were usually invisible. This heavenly being did much more than merely reveal himself: he speared her with a "long dart of gold," causing her indescribable bliss and pain simultaneously (29:13.157–58). This vision not only involved action, then, but also the strongest of reactions, making her moan out loud, and leaving her aflame with love for God and "a bliss greater than any that can be found in all of creation" (29:14.158).

Teresa also saw various saints. One vision she had of the Virgin Mary and her husband Saint Joseph is typical of others described in the *Vida*. On this occasion, Mary and Joseph vested her in a white garment and placed a gold necklace around her neck on which hung a cross bedecked with precious stones "incomparably different from those here below on earth." Though she could see Mary's "beautiful" face very clearly and observed that she looked very young, even girlish, she was unable to see Saint Joseph very clearly. "I *seemed* to see them ascending to Heaven with a great throng of angels," she also said, inserting a hint of doubt about her ability to fully comprehend what was happening (33:14–15.183). As was common with most of her visions, this one affirmed the correctness of her actions, for the Virgin Mary expressed great pleasure over the fact that Teresa had named her new reformed convent in Ávila in honor of Saint Joseph.

Teresa's visions could involve people around her, too. Once she saw the Virgin Mary vesting a Dominican priest with a white cope. In this vision the Virgin Mary informed Teresa that this priest was being rewarded for his support of the Carmelite reform, and that henceforth he would commit no mortal sins. And her visions extended to the afterlife as well. This same priest appeared to her several times after his death "in great glory" and told her "a number of things" (38:13.210). Sometimes she would see the souls of priests, monks, friars, and nuns ascending to heaven. She also claimed to have seen some Jesuits in heaven repeatedly, "with white banners in their hands" (38:15.210). Similarly,

Teresa reported seeing some souls ascend to heaven "from the depths of the earth" as her prayers and those of her fellow nuns freed them from purgatory (38:27–28.214). Teresa could see souls being taken to hell too, as in the case of one priest whose corpse was surrounded by demons who took turns dragging him about with large hooks before taking possession of his soul at his grave (38:24.213).

Teresa's visions raised questions in the minds of her confessors as they read the first draft of the *Vida*, and perhaps also piqued their curiosity, for there is a cluster of vision accounts in chapter 38, one of those that she was asked to add to the second draft. This chapter alone, from which all the examples above are taken, serves as a convenient summary of the range of her visionary experiences, which also included the devil.

The devil plays a key role in Teresa's *Vida*, but only as a foil to the power of God and to Teresa's confidence in her closeness to God. Her visions of demons are numerous and often detailed, but each and every one of them is an occasion for a victorious struggle and for letting her confessors know that she really had the upper hand. "I have hardly ever feared them," said Teresa about the demons she encountered. "Indeed, they seem to fear me. The Lord of all has firmly granted me power over them, and they are now no more of a bother to me than flies." Teresa's confidence in her own power over demons is like a golden shaft of light that pierces through the dark visions recorded in the *Vida*. "What harm can those devils do to me?" she asks, rhetorically. "If the Lord is all powerful, as I see that he is, and demons are his slaves, and I'm a servant of this Lord and King . . . Why should I not have enough strength to fight against all hell?"

Teresa could chase away demons by showing them a cross or by sprinkling them with holy water, and she boasted of her ability to taunt the devils, much like a cocky prizefighter. "For I believed I could easily vanquish them all with the aid of the cross; and I said to them: 'Come on, now, all of you, I'm a servant of the Lord and I want to see what you can do to me'" (25:19.139).

Teresa's bold taunting of demons assumes even more of a heroic swagger when contrasted with their appearance, which was always horrific and terrifying. The devil could be "a very abominable little black creature" or a flaming monster.

> Once, I was in an oratory, and he appeared at my left side in an abominable form. I took a close look at his mouth, especially, because he spoke to me, and it was horrifying. A great flame which was all bright seemed to come out from his body, without any shadow. In a frightful way he told me that I had really freed myself from his hands but that I'd be caught in them again. A great fear came over me and I made the sign of the cross as best I could, and he disappeared, but returned later. This happened to me twice. I didn't know what to do; I had some holy water there, and I tossed it in his direction; and he never returned again. (31:2–4.165)

At times Teresa does not distinguish between visions and actual physical assaults, or spiritual and mental disturbances that made her anxious. She says the devils could inflict "terrible interior and exterior pains and disturbances," or choke her, or cause her body, head, and arms to shake uncontrollably, or fill her with extreme anxiety. Her responses were physical too, and she put great trust in her two best weapons, the cross and holy water. Of these two, holy water was more powerful. "I know from experience that nothing works better than holy water to make the devils flee and not return. They flee from the cross too, but they return." In a passage that should have delighted her confessors, Teresa explained the power behind holy water: "I consider everything ordained by the Church to be so great, and I'm delighted to see the power of those words recited over the water" (31:4, 9.165–167). Sometimes, Teresa's protection came directly from God rather than through holy water. "At other times I saw a great throng of devils around me, and it seemed that a great brightness encircled me, and this kept them from reaching me. I understood that God was guarding me, so they couldn't get to me." When all is said and done, however, this power over demons was not some gift reserved for a rare few. Teresa carefully stressed that this power was accessible to all humans through their free will, and that choosing God over the devil was the key to vanquishing evil. "The devil's powers can only affect cowardly souls who surrender to them," she said, keenly aware that this was the right thing to say, for many reasons (31:11.168).

Teresa's otherworldly experiences were binary, that is, they opened doors to two transcendent realities: the divine or the demonic. When it came to divine experiences, her visions could take her to the ultimate reality of heaven or simply seem like visits from close relations within the walls of her convent. One of her visions of heaven—part of which involved no images—reveals few details and leaves much to the imagination: "I seemed to see the heavens open up, but there was no door such as I have seen some other times. There was revealed to me the throne which . . . I have seen on other occasions, and above it, another throne on which I understood the Divinity to be (I didn't see this, but knew it in some ineffable way)." Teresa not only admits that she cannot explain how she "saw" this, but goes on to say, "I discerned that all things that can be desired were there simultaneously, but I saw nothing. I was told—I do not know by whom—that all I could do there was to understand that I was incapable of understanding anything" (39:22.221).

This kind of infused knowledge beyond speech and images strains the bounds of comprehension, and Teresa's confessors knew that it had to be so. If the revelations had been more detailed and comprehensible, they would have been construed as fraudulent or demonic, for divine realities are essentially ineffable. The same rules apply to two of the grandest claims made by Teresa, which are found in the final chapters of the *Vida*. One of these is her claim to have grasped the reality of the Trinity itself, the highest of all mysteries: "Once . . . I was given a very clear understanding of the manner in which there can be only one God in three persons, and I was both shaken and consoled" (39:25.222). The other extreme claim is that she was able to comprehend the relation between God and everything that exists, including the human soul and all the sins committed by every human being. "Once, when I was in prayer, I saw very briefly how all things are seen in God and how He contains them all within Himself. It was all very clearly presented to me, but without any forms whatsoever. I don't know how to put it into words, but this vision has remained firmly imprinted upon my soul." In this vision, which was at once sublime and terrifying, she comprehended God as a "very clear diamond, much larger than the whole world," which "contains everything within itself" (40:9–10.225).

The opposite otherworldly reality to this was hell, and Teresa claimed to have gone there too, and her description of it is so graphic that it seems more fitting for a physical experience than some imaginative or intellectual extrasensory vision. One day, suddenly, "without knowing how," Teresa was thrust into hell, and she understood that God wanted her to "see the place the devils had prepared there" for her, and which she deserved for her sins. Unlike the common iconography that depicted hell as a communal pit, fiery and cavernous, crowded with all the damned and their demonic tormentors, the hell shown to Teresa was personal and solitary: a dark, hot, damp, foul-smelling, vermin-infested, cramped dungeon, accessed by a long, narrow muddy passage, where she would have to spend eternity in a hole in the wall that "looked like a small cupboard," enveloped in the blackest darkness. In this oven-like hole, it was impossible either to sit down or to lie down, and the walls "closed in on themselves and suffocated everything." The torment to be endured there was the exact opposite of the bliss to be enjoyed in heaven, and just as indescribable. "What I felt, it seems to me, cannot even begin to be exaggerated; nor can it be understood," she said. "I experienced a fire in the soul, impossible for me to ever describe what it is like. The bodily pains were so unbearable that despite my having suffered excruciating pains in this life and . . . even some, as I said, caused by the devil, these were all nothing in comparison with the ones I experienced there, fully aware as I was that they would go on without end and without ever ceasing."

All this horror, however, was as nothing when compared to the agony to be endured by the soul: "a constriction, a suffocation, an affliction so keenly felt and with such a despairing and tormenting unhappiness that . . . to say the experience is as though the soul were continually being wrested from the body would be insufficient, for . . . here it is the soul itself that rips itself apart." Teresa felt herself "burning and crumbling," but even worse was an "interior fire and despair" from which she knew there would never, ever be any relief.

As was the case with all her divinely given visions, even one as horrifying as this had a positive effect on her, for all visions were intended for a purpose. Suffering in hell for just an instant made Teresa realize that whatever suffering she endured on earth was slight—and easily tolerable—when compared to the suffering that awaited those condemned to suffer in hell for eternity. That insight, in turn, made her feel a deep compassion for all the damned, and especially for the "Lutheran" heretics who had been led astray. She asked, "Is there anyone who can possibly bear the sight of a soul in that supreme trial of trials that has no end?" This compassion also gave her even more reason to reform the Carmelite order, for the prayers offered by nuns wholly dedicated to contemplation would surely help to convert sinners and heretics, somehow (32:1–6.173–74).

Locutions

In addition to seeing and experiencing otherworldly realities or interacting with them, Teresa also described receiving messages directly from God, sometimes with words, sometimes wordlessly, sometimes as part of a vision, sometimes not. Teresa referred to these revelations as *este hablar*, which literally means "this speaking" or "talking." Although Teresa has no noun such as *locuciones* for this phenomenon, it is traditionally rendered into English as "locutions." These various kinds of locutions can come from outside the soul, or above the soul, or the innermost part of the soul. Intellectual locutions—like intellectual visions—are the most intense and cannot be faked by the devil. In this experience one learns in a manner that baffles the intellect. God does not employ human language, and one hears nothing externally or internally. Concerning those that involved words, she had this to say: "These words are very distinctly formed; but they aren't heard by the bodily ear. They're much more clearly understood, however, than any words heard by the ear, and it's impossible not to understand them, no matter how much resistance we may offer" (25:2.134). The most distinctive characteristic of these divine locutions, she says, is that they are transformative, for they affect the will and understanding, and always have a very positive effect on one's behavior. Locutions can also come from the devil, of course, but their effects are always negative, and this evidence—along with the disquiet and fear they produce—allows one to discern their demonic origin immediately.

Some locutions were messages for Teresa, many of them delivered at times of distress. Once, when she was unable to practice recollection and began to think that all of her visions had been illusions, Christ told her not to be troubled, and that there was much to be learned from such difficult moments. Christ could also reassure her repeatedly. "His Majesty says these words to me often, manifesting His great love for me: 'You're mine now, and I'm yours'" (39:21.221). Sometimes, locutions explain visions. At other times, locutions convey messages for Teresa to relay to other people.

Most of the significant locutions in the *Vida*, however, are those that reveal truths to Teresa that are beyond discursive reasoning or beyond the capacity of the intellect to comprehend.

Levitations

Teresa's mysticism had a physical component as well, for her otherworldly transports involved trancelike states, changes in her appearance, and other uncommon phenomena that her fellow nuns could not help but notice, and that they were all eager to make known to the world beyond the convent walls. The most extreme of these physical phenomena was levitation, that is, the suspension of the body in midair.[6] Addressing this issue in the *Vida* was required of Teresa, for she could not avoid what many around her had already reported numerous times: that she was often swept off the ground and stayed aloft in defiance of the laws of nature. Teresa's beatification and canonization inquests are filled with accounts by eyewitnesses who swore they had seen her suspended in the air, and heard her pleading with God for an end to such a "gift." They are not only numerous but detailed, and all speak of her resistance, as well as of the efforts made by her fellow nuns to pull her down.[7] Her own account of one such event is very similar to some of those recorded later, and we can safely assume that such events began to be reported by word of mouth before Teresa was commanded to write about them.

> Once, when we were together in choir, and I was kneeling
> and about to take communion, it disturbed me greatly [to

levitate], for it seemed to me a most extraordinary thing and I thought it would create quite a stir; so I ordered the nuns not to speak of it (for I had already been appointed prioress). At other times, when I have felt that the Lord was going to do the same thing to me (as happened once during a sermon . . . when some great ladies were present), I have lain on the ground and the sisters have tried to hold me down, but everyone has seen me enraptured anyway. (20:5.109)

Teresa's own analysis of this phenomenon is a cautious interweaving of opinions, questions, and statements of fact, in a voice that has both the ring of authority and a measure of deference. Differentiating between "rapture" and "union," she explains how the body reacts to different sorts of spiritual stimuli:

In these raptures it seems that the soul isn't animating the body, and thus you really feel the body cooling down as it loses its natural heat, with the greatest sweetness and delight. At this point, there is no way to resist, although in union, where we are on our own turf, resistance is almost always possible, albeit with great pain and effort. But with these raptures, normally, no such thing is possible. Usually, before you're aware of it or can do anything to help yourself, it comes like a strong, swift impulse; and you see and feel this cloud rising, or this swift eagle, sweeping you up with it on its wings. (20:3.109)

Two things stand out in this description: the fact that the body is affected by spiritual raptures, and that what it *feels* is an irresistible force, pushing it upward. What she says next is even more explicit about her own awareness of the effect of such raptures. Distancing herself from levitation, speaking of it as something involuntary and distracting, she affirms her limitations and her own awareness of the devil's wiles:

> You realize, and indeed see, that you are being carried away, and you know not where.... and you end up being carried away, whether you like it or not. Sometimes I dislike it so much that I would like to resist, and I do so with all my strength to do so, especially when I'm out in public, but also many times when I am all by myself and I fear I'm being deceived. (20:4.109)

Teresa also stresses the fact that what she has experienced is uncontrollable, precisely because it is a divine event—rather than demonic—and thus totally beyond her willpower or physical strength.

> When I tried to resist these raptures, it seemed to me that a tremendous force was lifting me up from beneath my feet, a force so powerful that I can't think of anything comparable, for it overcame me with a much greater intensity than any other spiritual experience, and left me feeling torn to shreds. (20:6.109)

Her interpretation of these raptures, then, is an affirmation of the hierarchical relationship between soul and body, and of the soul's superiority. At the very same time, it is also a confirmation of the inseparable bond between the spiritual and the physical.

Sometimes I've been able to resist, somewhat, but it has left me shattered and exhausted, like someone who has wrestled a mighty giant. At other times, though, I've been unable to resist, and my soul has been swept away, usually along with my head, without my being able to stop it; sometimes my whole body has been involved, too, and lifted off the ground. . . . One sees one's body being raised off the ground; and although the spirit pulls it along after itself willy-nilly, if one doesn't resist, it does so most gently, and one doesn't lose consciousness—at least, in my case, I've had enough sense left in me to know that I was being lifted up.[8]

And exhaustion was not the only side-effect of these raptures and levitations. Teresa also complained that they left her wracked with pain, as if all her joints had been pulled apart (20:12.III).

Whether or not Teresa defied the law of gravity is immaterial. The fact remains that she provided a logical explanation of a rare phenomenon that her culture accepted as possible, and that she did so in a way that avoided censure by her superiors. Her ability to confirm everything that needed to be confirmed in "holy" levitations is remarkable, especially in regards to the relationship between body and soul.

Concerning rapture . . . I say that it has left my body feeling very light many times, even weightless; sometimes so much so that I've been unable to feel my feet touching the ground. For, while the body is enraptured, it often feels dead, unable to do anything: it stays just as it was when the rapture seized it, whether standing, or sitting, or with the hands open or closed. Even though one rarely loses consciousness, I've sometimes lost it completely, but only rarely, and very briefly. (20:18.113)

Teresa's expert balancing act—her ability to claim the experience and distance herself from it all at once—prevented her from being condemned as a friend of the devil. She had already faced too many confessors who had interpreted her experiences that way, as demonic, so she had reason to be cautious. Perhaps even more remarkable than her annoyance and embarrassment in the face of such a divine favor is her bargaining with God himself. Unable to fathom what purpose levitation could serve, Teresa begs God to do away with it. Astonishingly, God grants her request.

> I begged the Lord earnestly not to grant me any more favors that had physical side effects; for I was weary of being constantly on guard, and His Majesty, after all, could grant me the same favors interiorly without it being known to anyone. It seems that in His mercy He deemed to answer my prayer, for up until now, I have never again received any such favors. (20:5.109)

What are we to make of this ambivalence? Perhaps this is as clear a testimony as we can have of the potential danger behind every levitation. Teresa focuses on the phenomenon as a painful distraction. She reckoned it to be a nuisance, and wanted everyone to know that she begged God to refrain from forcing her to hover at importune moments. But at the very same time she is also aware of its inherent value, as a sign of immediate contact with the divine. By distancing herself from levitation, and even claiming that God has freed her from it, Teresa paradoxically affirms her own humility and her special holiness. The best way not to be found guilty of "feigned sanctity" or of "inventing the sacred" was to convince the inquisitors that one did not seek to exalt oneself. Teresa summed up the value of levitation in precisely such a way, as a lesson in humility and selflessness.

> The effects of these raptures are truly great. One of the greatest is the manifestation of the Lord's mighty power. Since we are unable to resist His Majesty's will, either in soul or in body, and are not our own masters, we are forced to realize that there is One stronger than ourselves, however painful this truth may be, and that these favors are bestowed by Him, and that we, of ourselves, can do nothing whatsoever. This imprints in us great humility. Indeed, I confess that at first it produced a great fear in me, an awful fear. (20:7.109–10)

Despite all of these claims of humility, Teresa knew she was in a league of her own, so to speak. The very fact that she was asked to write about her extraordinary life had to make her conscious of her uniqueness. In addition, she probably suspected that she had acquired a reputation as a levitator, and that her accounts had the potential of surpassing all others. Teresa holds the rare distinction of levitating alongside someone else. At the Convent of the Incarnation in Ávila, tour guides will often point to the spot where she and John of the Cross both rose into the air simultaneously while they were discussing the Trinity. If the tour guide fails to mention it, one can always turn to the painting that hangs at that very spot, which immortalizes the event, showing John up in the air, sitting on his levitated chair, and Teresa kneeling behind the grille of the *locutorio*, with a text underneath that describes the scene.[9]

Ecstasy as Polemic

The *Vida* was not written as an anti-Protestant polemic, but, as it turned out, it served to reassert central Catholic beliefs that were being denied or contradicted by Protestants at the time. In many ways, the mysticism of the *Vida* could be interpreted as one of the strongest assertions of Catholic identity ever written, and also as a theological manifesto far more effective at challenging Protestant beliefs than any text written by a university-trained theologian. Of course, Teresa's theology was mystical rather than systematic, experiential rather than scholastic, but it was precisely those characteristics that gave it a uniquely powerful punch. The narrator of the *Vida* had no real understanding of Protestantism and could not argue against Protestants point by point with razor-sharp theological precision, but every page of her text screamed out as loudly as humanly possible: "Protestants are wrong, and my life proves it."

Teresa reified Catholicism, embodied it, made evident many of its truths. She denied so many Protestant beliefs and reaffirmed so many Catholic ones that trying to list them all would be foolish, especially in a brief study such as this one. The most important issues involved, however, can be easily identified. Protestants denied the attainability of moral and spiritual perfection; Teresa claimed she had aimed for it and achieved it. Protestants denied that one could have intimate, ecstatic encounters with God; Teresa claimed she had many such encounters. Protestants denied the value of asceticism and did away with monasticism; Teresa showed how effective monasticism was at leading human beings to their highest proper end. Protestants rejected Catholic ritual; Teresa embraced it and proved its efficacy. Protestants denied the existence of divinely given visions, locutions, and miraculous events such as levitation; Teresa was living proof of their existence. Protestants tended to be uncomfortable with the mingling of matter and spirit, or openly opposed to it; Teresa thrived on it. Protestants claimed that the Catholic Church was in the grip of Satan and the Antichrist; Teresa proved them wrong every time she chased away demons with holy water consecrated by that church.

Most significantly, Teresa affirmed that whatever she had accomplished could be aimed for and attained by anyone who set their mind and will to it, for humans had free will, and that free choice—aided by grace—actually determined one's relationship with the divine. In sum, her mysticism bristled with everything loathed by Protestants and stridently denied by them. In an age when rival Christian churches defined their identities as much by their differences, negatively, as by their beliefs, turning fine distinctions into weapons and constantly insisting that God was in the details of the differences, the mysticism of Teresa's *Vida* was the equivalent of a thermonuclear bomb in the Catholic arsenal.

In our own age, which is sorely lacking in mystics and highly skeptical of their outrageous aims and claims, the *Vida* is no longer any kind of weapon but is nonetheless a sharp-edged affront to doubters, and both a challenge and an inspiration for those who yearn for possibilities beyond our ken, especially that of eternal bliss and of fore-tastes of it in the here and now, which require abundant self-denial.

Mysticism for All

Teresa did not intend her *Vida* to become a polemical weapon—that function was imposed on it by others—but she certainly did intend for it to become a pedagogical and apostolic tool. Despite all the mistrust surrounding her text and all suspicions of error surrounding it, there are clear in-dications that Teresa imagined a wide posthumous audi-ence for the *Vida*. Its most obvious audience would be her Carmelite sisters and other monastics, naturally, but Teresa had already seen the interest shown in it by devout lay-people, and one must assume that she must have also had such readers in mind. This extension of mysticism beyond convent walls, which could be called "democratic" or "egal-itarian," was somewhat revolutionary. It was not a revolu-tion begun by her, as evidenced by the flood of mystical texts published under the direction of Cardinal Jiménez de Cisneros around the time of Teresa's birth, but it was an egalitarian spiritual revolution she gladly joined and bravely moved forward. Encouraging monastics and lay-men and laywomen with no theological education to em-brace a life of prayer and to aim for the highest reaches of contemplation was something truly modern, made possible by the printing press and other factors, economic, social, and political, as well as spiritual. The *Vida*, then, can be seen as mysticism for the masses, as a modern text, a manual for universal conversion, rather than just an account of one nun's conversion and of its effects on her.

But how was Teresa's *Vida* received by her contemporaries and by the next few generations? What was its impact? It is to this subject that we must now turn.

The Life of the *Vida*, 1600–1800

After Teresa's death in 1582, as word began to spread about miracles attributed to her, the Inquisition's ban on her texts became increasingly untenable. If Teresa was indeed a saint, then how could anything that she had written be kept under lock and key? The first significant change in the status of the *Vida* came in 1586, a mere four years on the road toward her seemingly inevitable canonization, when the General Chapter of the Discalced Carmelites approved the publication of her complete works. In 1586 the empress Maria of Austria, King Philip II's sister, who had been deeply affected by reading the manuscript of the *Vida* owned by the duke of Alba, helped speed up the publication process, and the Royal Council (Consejo Real), Spain's second highest authority, commissioned Luis de León as editor. Friar Luis was an Augustinian and a prominent theologian and professor of biblical studies at the University of Salamanca who had been denounced to the Inquisition twice but emerged from these ordeals with a burnished reputation for orthodoxy and holiness. He worked quickly, collating various manuscripts of most of Teresa's texts, checking for additions, alterations, and errors made in transcribing, and amending some of the spelling in her manuscripts. As he confessed later, this was not an easy task.

I have labored in reading and examining her writings . . .
And I have also compared copies with the originals that I
had in my possession for many days, and I have restored the
texts to their own purity, exactly as the Mother left them
written in her own hand, without changing their words or
substance, as did many of the transcriptions that were in
circulation, which had deviated greatly from the originals
due to the carelessness or the disrespect and wrongheaded-
ness of some scribes.[1]

The *Vida* was first published together with most of her
major writings at Salamanca in 1588. Within the thousand
or so pages of this first edition of her *Obras*, one could find
the *Vida*, *The Moradas* (*The Mansions*, or *The Interior
Castle*), *The Way of Perfection*, some of the *Relations*, the
Maxims, and *Exclamations*. The only major text missing
from this edition was the *Foundations*, which was deemed
too sensitive because many of the individuals mentioned in
it were still alive.

From start to finish, then, it took the *Vida* thirty-four
years to make it into print. And for twenty-two of those
years, it lay dormant in the final draft that was eventually
published in 1588. We have no way of knowing how much of
what Teresa wrote about her life of prayer in those eleven
years of composition (1554–65) was altered by the suggestions of the men who read all the various drafts, much less of
what was fine-tuned when she wrote the two full drafts of
the final version between 1561 and 1564. We can only guess,
since the only manuscript to survive is the clean copy she
penned in 1565 for Juan de Ávila, which was the end product
of a process of revision during which Teresa carefully

followed the editorial suggestions of her various supervisory readers. That manuscript has only fourteen very minor corrections, some of which can be identified as being in Teresa's own hand, a few others that can be attributed to Domingo Báñez, and a few more that might be from Juan de Ávila.

We have no expressions of discontent from Teresa herself about the process of composition and no hint of frustration about the editorial suggestions of her male superiors. Closely supervised and mentored as she was during the writing of the *Vida*, we can only assume that she negotiated, adapted, and accepted suggestions for revision with a mixture of frustration and gratitude, and that the 1565 autograph in the library of the Escorial is something truly hers, in every way, no matter how many alterations and revisions were required along the way. Her editors had a difficult role to play, at once subservient and authoritarian, for they were as overawed by Teresa as they were intent on ensuring that she express herself in the clearest way possible.

Consequently, despite all the unknown revisions, that final version of the *Vida* is no less "authentic" or "genuine" than any best-selling or prize-winning book published today. Editors and authors still have to negotiate, just as Teresa and her advisors and inquisitors did. Inquisitions may come and go, but good editors still do remain an author's best and final line of defense against their own limitations.

Initial Reception

After 1582, the *Vida* quickly became linked to Teresa's apparent holiness and the process of her canonization. As her first editor Luis de León put it, with so many signs of her saint-hood being manifest, and "the miracles she worked every day," not publishing her writings would have been an "insult to the Holy Spirit."[2]

Four separate inquiries were undertaken over a span of nineteen years. First came a thorough "Informative" inquest in 1591–92, directed by the bishop of Salamanca, in whose diocese she had died. A second Informative inquest was directed by the papal nuncio in Spain, Camilo Gaetano, in 1595–97. The third inquest ("Remissory" *in genere*, 1604) and the fourth inquest ("Remissory" *in specie*, 1609–10) were both directed from Rome, under papal supervision. More than four hundred individuals, most of whom were Carmelite nuns, were interviewed throughout Spain as part of this process.[3]

Much to the delight of her promoters, Pope Paul V beatified Teresa in 1614. This rank of *beata* allowed the faithful to venerate her as "Blessed Teresa" and to seek her intercession. In Spain, this event was greeted with many public celebrations that included processions, sermons, literary contests and feasts, theatrical productions, dances, bullfights, and fireworks. The feasting included some of the leading literary figures of the day. The poet Luis de Góngora contributed one of his celebrated romances for the celebrations in Córdoba, titled "On the Seed Fallen," in which he praised her as the "glory of our nation," who "has written so much, and so well." Miguel de Cervantes, the author of *Don Quixote*, wrote a sonnet titled "On the Ecstasies of Our Blessed Mother Teresa de Jesús," and read it at the court of the duke of Alba, in close proximity to the chapel where Teresa's incorruptible corpse was buried. Some of the sonnet's erotically charged lines focus intensely on Teresa's divine encounters.

> It is just that you should enjoy Heaven
> in divine ecstasies,
> on all the paths through which
> God knows how to lead a soul
> so He can give as much of Himself as she can take in
> and even more, stretch her, dilate her, and enlarge her,
> and with his gentle love
> join her to Himself and enrich her.[4]

Eight years later, in March 1622, Pope Gregory XV completed the canonization process by elevating Teresa to sainthood. This momentous event gave rise to even more elaborate celebrations in Spain, and to theatrical productions based on the *Vida*, some penned by the top playwrights of the day, including the prolific Félix Lope de Vega, who wrote two plays, one titled *Mother Teresa de Jesús* and the other titled *The Life and Death of Santa Teresa de Jesús*. As Lope de Vega saw it, Teresa the Spanish nun had become a truly Catholic saint, a universal exemplar:

> In lands, isles and seas, now
> incense is kindled,
> temples are readied for you,
> and altars are erected.[5]

This reference to temples and altars was no exaggeration, although the plays are loaded with plenty of hyperbole. In 1615, seven years before her canonization, Teresa had already been hailed as the greatest virgin in all of Christian history and "the Queen among all the Brides" of Christ. Several sermons preached after her beatification likened her to the Virgin Mary, and one of them suggested that Teresa's reception into the heavenly court was nearly as grand as that of the Mother of God. Two other sermons identified Teresa as the woman described in the book of Revelation, chapter 12, with the moon under her feet and a crown of twelve stars—an image traditionally linked to the Virgin Mary and, more specifically, to her Immaculate Conception.[6]

Spain was not the only place where such effusive praise and veneration could be found. By the time that the English recusant Abraham Woodhead published his translation of Teresa's *Vida* in 1671, Teresa's universality was sealed, and so was her role as a perfect embodiment of the Catholic Reformation and "defender of the true faith." Woodhead's preface to the *Vida* makes all of this very clear:

> So great was her Zeal of his Honour, and grief for the great injuries and affronts, that our Lord suffered, in those times, from the Huguenots, or Lutherans as she calls them, then much prevailing in the Southern parts of France, demolishing the Churches and Altars, and Violating all Sacred persons, and things, That she saith she, not able, as being a woman, and that of no worth, to do him other Service, erected those her new Foundations, chiefly for this end, to endeavour with continual Prayer, and right Penances, performed therein, to appease the Divine wrath for the great sins of Christendom, and to implore his assistance to the Catholick Clergy, and all other Defenders of the true Faith; and to procure the Conversion of so many unfortunate Souls, seduced into such gross impiety.[7]

Lingering Opposition

Teresa's canonization did more than spawn plays and poems that relied on the *Vida* and exposed a wider public to elements of its narrative; it also elevated the *Vida* to a special status as a divinely inspired text. But the ascent of the *Vida* to this zenith was not as smooth and inevitable as its promoters had made it seem. Few of those clerics, playwrights, and poets who celebrated Teresa's sainthood showed awareness of the full extent of the opposition that she had faced in her day, or of how much effort the Inquisition had put into suppressing the circulation of the *Vida*. Moreover, hardly any of those who sang Teresa's praises in 1614 or 1622 mentioned the strenuous opposition to Teresa that persisted for some years after her death, or of the efforts made to have the *Vida* condemned by the Inquisition as a heretical treatise shortly after it was first published.

Opposition to Teresa's *Vida* had remained strong in some circles, even after miracle accounts began to surface in the wake of her death in 1582. It stands to reason, then, that opposition actually intensified after the publication of the *Vida* and other titles in 1588, for the printed text could now reach thousands of readers rather than mere dozens. Even worse—in the minds of those who suspected Teresa of error—translations of her *Vida* could now cross borders and infect Catholics in other nations where it was harder to control heresy than in Spain.

A remarkable feature of the campaign launched against Teresa and her writings is that it moved along a track parallel to that of the beatification and canonization process. This anti-Teresa campaign began in 1589, before the beatification inquests were launched, and it kept pushing for the condemnation of Teresa as a heretic until 1598 in four distinct phases, while the canonization inquests moved forward. The first phase was occasioned by the publication of Luis de León's *Los Libros de la Madre Teresa de Jesús* in 1588, which made the *Vida* available to a wide reading public, lay as well as clerical. This phase involved denunciations to the Inquisition, which forced that tribunal to take another close look at Teresa's work. The second phase began in 1591, followed by a third phase in 1593, and a fourth phase in 1598, all of which also involved additional denunciations. The number of individuals involved was small, but their status and persistence made their challenge potentially formidable.

The man who led the first charge in August 1589 was Alonso de la Fuente (1533–92), a Dominican friar, theologian, and itinerant preacher who had spent more than seventeen years ferreting out Alumbrado heretics in the south of Spain, denouncing them to the Inquisition, working as a *calificador* (examiner) for that tribunal, and bringing them to trial. Fray Alonso was convinced that the Alumbrado heresy had its roots in Rhineland mysticism—in John Tauler and Henry Suso, disciples of Meister Eckhart—and in all the devotional texts derived from this tradition, including those favored by Teresa that advocated recollection, the prayer of quiet, and the prayer of union. In other words, Fray Alonso saw nothing but alumbradismo in Teresa, and, to make matters worse, he identified her writings as imbued with a virulent strain of that heresy that could be cleverly disguised as orthodoxy. Having once denounced Juan of Ávila's text *Audi Filia* to the Inquisition for its heretical tendencies, Fray Luis had no qualms about also denouncing Teresa's work.

The worst thing about Teresa's alumbradismo, charged Fray Alonso, was its deceptive nature, for it could easily lure innocent, well-intentioned, devout people into error and allow them to remain undetected. Fray Alonso pulled no punches in his accusations: "This book . . . has the venom of heresy within it, so secretly expressed, so well disguised, so smoothly varnished, that those who are ignorant as well as those who are subtlest of theologians in the world can use it as a sealed and closed manual or as scripture read in the dark of night, unnoticed by Catholic ears." His denunciation also lashed out at the publisher for promoting Teresa's work as inspired by the Holy Spirit. Fray Alonso alleged that the only inspiration Teresa could have received was from "an evil angel, the same one who fooled Mohammed and Luther and all other heresiarchs." Moreover, he argued that the most convincing proof of the book's demonic derivation was Teresa's broaching of subjects that "exceeded the capacity of any woman."[8]

Aware of Fray Alonso's zeal and of the high number of denunciations he had made against Alumbrados in the past, the Inquisition assigned one of its *calificadores* to review the charges made against Teresa and pass judgment on their validity. The report of this anonymous *calificador*, submitted in November 1589, cleared Teresa of any of the errors ascribed to her by Fray Alonso, concluding that all of the accusations were groundless. Undeterred by such a verdict, Fray Alonso submitted four additional denunciations between late 1589 and the spring of 1591, singling out other issues for condemnation. Meanwhile, in June 1590, the Inquisition had also received another denunciation from Antonio de Sosa, an Augustinian friar who agreed with Fray Alonso.

Given this rash of denunciations, the Inquisition turned over the case to two highly regarded *calificadores*, Juan de Orellana, a Dominican friar who had met Teresa years before, and Antonio de Quevedo, an Augustinian friar. Orellana was the first to submit a verdict on the three books he read—the *Vida*, *The Interior Castle*, and *The Way of Perfection*—and it was very negative. Orellana argued that Teresa was wrong about the highest degrees of prayer, especially on the issue of the soul's union with God, which—as he saw it—was explained in heretical terms as a total loss of human agency. Due to this great ancient "error," which he traced to the early days of Christianity, and to a multitude of smaller errors he found scattered throughout her texts, Orellana recommended that Teresa's books be banned. Quevedo, in contrast, judged Teresa's books to be free of error and heresy, and, in addition, recommended that they remain accessible to everyone, even layfolk, for there was nothing in them that could confuse or harm anyone.

Whether or not the Inquisition deliberately chose to ignore this case due to the death in 1592 of the principal accuser, Fray Alonso de la Fuente, or due to the difference of opinion between their two *calificadores* is immaterial. The investigation froze at this point, with no decision being reached, and the case lay dormant until the summer of 1593 when a distinguished Dominican theologian, Juan de Lorenzana, submitted yet another denunciation of Teresa's books to the Inquisition, charging that they were full of errors and doctrinal "venom."

Lorenzana had met Teresa in 1568. At that time he had not found her dangerous, but, as he explained to the Inquisition, his interest in her was piqued anew by her published texts and by the disagreements about her orthodoxy that circulated in clerical circles. Deciding to judge for himself, he immersed himself in Luis de León's edition of Teresa's works, only to discover that they were full of errors and worthy of censure. In addition, he also found many theological errors in Ribera's hagiography of Teresa and recommended that it be banned along with all her books. The Inquisition responded by asking Juan de Orellana—who had already condemned Teresa two years earlier—to review her books once again and submit a more detailed analysis of their content. Orellana's second report was even more critical of Teresa than his first. In sum, he found her books to be full of "very pernicious deception," and recommended that they be banned, along with Ribera's hagiography, in order to "protect good people who desire to be spiritual from being deceived."[9]

The accusations of heresy leveled by Lorenzana and Orellana were serious indeed, but seem to have been shelved. Five years after they had been made, the Inquisition had not yet passed judgment on these accusations. In addition, it had made no effort to stop the publication of Teresa's works. The silence of the Inquisition was deafening. In the meantime, as the rush toward Teresa's beatification and canonization moved along, those who spotted errors in her work fell silent too, until early 1598, when one final accusation of heresy was delivered to the Inquisition by Francisco de Pisa, a professor of Sacred Scripture and dean of the Toledo cathedral. Pisa had probably met Teresa more than once in Toledo, during her various visits to that city, but much like Lorenzana, who had also met her and found nothing to be alarmed about at the time, he picked up Luis de León's edition of Teresa's works years later only to be horrified by the content of these texts, especially the *Vida*. Pisa was so enraged by the heresy he perceived in Teresa's *Vida*, in fact, that he could not bring himself to finish reading it. Seeing nothing but alumbradismo in Teresa, and dismissing her as "an uneducated woman" who refused to be guided by her learned confessors, he advised the Inquisition to remove all of Teresa's texts from circulation and to prevent the publication of any more editions. He also suggested that the Inquisition take a closer look at Ribera's hagiography too, because it portrayed Teresa as a divinely inspired saint and glorified her heretical teachings.[10]

Pisa's accusations fell into the same void as all those that preceded it. The punctiliously obsessive Inquisition filed his *memorial* along with all the others, preserving them for posterity, but doing nothing more than that. Since no records were archived of whatever discussions might have taken place concerning this case, all we know is that the Inquisition simply refused to take sides on this controversy. Its lassitude in this case was unusual, for sure, and out of character, but not too puzzling.

To question the holiness of Teresa or the orthodoxy of her texts was to swim against an overpowering current. The identity and status of the naysayers made no difference, for they were few in number. Given the colossal momentum behind Teresa's canonization at that time, which was driven by both church and state, it was simply impossible to cast doubt on her holiness and orthodoxy. Teresa had quickly claimed a very special place in the mentality of late sixteenth-century Spain, not just as a saint but also as a national heroine. Relegating all complaints about Teresa to a dark corner of an archive was all that the Inquisition could do. On rare occasions, such as this one, it listened and nodded politely, and sat on its hands.

Six years after Pisa's denunciation was filed away in the Inquisition's archive, Teresa was beatified and his charges of heresy instantly became null and void. Eight years after her beatification, Teresa was proclaimed a saint, and by then the *Vida* and its author were well on their way to playing an enormously significant role in Spain and beyond—a role none of her accusers would have thought correct or possible.

Patroness of Spain and International Figure

Separating Teresa from her *Vida* is impossible when it comes to assessing the role she came to play in Catholic culture, especially after her canonization in 1622, for her impact on Catholicism was inextricably tied to the events described in the *Vida*. Her impact at home, in Spain, was immense and unique, and beyond Spain too, for very few other Spanish saints became as international as Teresa. Only Ignatius Loyola, founder of the Jesuits, and Francis Xavier, the great Jesuit missionary, can compete with Teresa in this regard, but it could be argued that Teresa's global reach is more remarkable an achievement due to the fact that the Discalced Carmelite order she founded was dwarfed in terms of size and global reach by the Jesuits, who made a concerted effort to promote the veneration of Ignatius and Francis in the churches they built and manned on five continents. Ignatius and Francis became global Jesuit saints, first and foremost— representatives of their very large and influential order. Teresa, in contrast, became a global saint who transcended her relatively small Discalced Carmelite order. Teresa's international reach, then, can be attributed in great measure to her *Vida*, and to the impact that text had on the Catholic world, both directly and indirectly.

At home, Teresa actually became more than a saint, for she was quickly turned into an avatar of *españolidad*, or Spanishness, rivaled only—perhaps—by the fictional character of Don Quixote. This is most convincingly evidenced by the fact that in 1627, a mere five years after her canonization, King Philip IV proclaimed Teresa patroness of Spain, an honor she was to share with Saint James, or Santiago, who had held that title for centuries. Raising Teresa to the same status as one of the twelve apostles—who also happened to be the patron saint of the Reconquista that drove out the Moors—was as high an honor as could be bestowed on anyone in Spain. One of the sermons preached in Madrid when this proclamation was made summed up the public's attitude, as well as its awareness of Teresa's global reach: "Everything about this saint is Spanish: her life, her death, her holiness, her religious order, her miracles, her teachings, and the fame she has earned throughout the world, all of these are Spanish."[11]

Teresa's new status rankled some, nonetheless, especially the privileged members of the military order of Santiago, which spearheaded its protest through the pen of one of their own, the great writer Francisco de Quevedo. In his two polemical texts, *His Sword for Santiago* and *A Brief for the Patronage of Santiago*, Quevedo voiced two major objections to Teresa's new rank: first, he argued that Saint James had a unique role to play as patron of the Reconquista and defender of the nation; second, he questioned the wisdom and propriety of assigning such a manly role to a woman. Yet none of those who objected to Teresa's new role, including Quevedo, dared to question her sanctity or her "Spanishness." Eventually, Quevedo's side would gain the ear of Pope Urban VIII and convince him to decree in 1630 that Saint James was the sole patron of Spain. This reversal, however, did little to tarnish or lessen Teresa's standing as an exemplar of everything Catholic and Spanish.[12] In the twentieth century, during the Spanish Civil War, this sentiment would be revived with a vengeance, and its endurance would be made manifest in unexpected ways.

Editions and Translations

In Spain, the publication of her texts and the growth of her cult went hand in hand. The first step took place in 1586, a mere four years after her death, when the General Chapter of the Discalced Carmelites approved the publication of her complete works.

As previously mentioned, the first edition of her *Obras*, edited by Fray Luis de León, was published at Salamanca in 1588. This vernacular Spanish edition of the *Obras*, which had some omissions, errata, and incorrect punctuation, was reprinted in 1589, then for the next one and a half centuries, various editions were published in other Spanish cities and locations under Spain's rule, in Portugal, the Netherlands, and Italy, as follows:

Zaragoza 1592, 1615
Madrid 1597, plus at least thirteen printings, 1607–1793

Naples 1604

Brussels 1604, plus six printings, 1610–1753

Barcelona, 1606, plus three printings, 1680–1724

Valencia 1613, plus three printings, 1623–49

Lisbon 1616, 1628, 1654

Antwerp 1630, 1649

In 1645, due to constant reports of transcription errors in Luis de León's edition from expert readers of Teresa's autographs, the Discalced Carmelite order decided to embark on a new edition of Teresa's works and assigned the task to one of its own, Francisco de Santa Maria, who had written a history of the Discalced reform. Several Carmelites worked on this new edition, which was published in Madrid in 1661. Nonetheless, errors continued to be caught by those who inspected Teresa's manuscripts, so in the mid-eighteenth century, the Discalced Carmelites prepared yet another new official edition. The friar assigned this task was Andrés de la Encarnación, who, after diving into Teresa's original manuscripts, detected more than seven hundred errors in the second edition of the *Vida* alone and thousands more in other works (twelve hundred in the *Foundations*). He also rediscovered many letters to publish for the first time. His edition would roll off the presses in 1752, and again in 1778 and 1793.

Outside of Spain, Teresa became one of the most widely venerated and widely read Catholic saints of the early modern age. As one of her translators put it, Teresa's books proved so "beneficial to all sorts of Readers; whether those already Spiritual, and Holy, or those as yet involved in great Imperfections, and Sin," that it became imperative to have them "translated into most Modern languages."[13] Her universality and that of the *Vida* can be easily perceived in the high number of translations that flowed from European presses between 1599 and 1800. Despite the fact that we do not yet have a definitive list of editions of Teresa's texts in translation, the figures that can be gleaned from available data are impressive and speak for themselves:

Number of languages: 8
Number of translations (excluding anthologies): 47
Number of editions (excluding anthologies): 107
Number of anthologies: 67
Total number of editions (including anthologies): 174

The *Vida* itself was the first of Teresa's texts to be translated and published abroad. That translation was into Italian, and it first appeared in 1599. Soon thereafter, translations of the *Vida* in other languages began to flow from presses in other countries: Latin (Mainz, 1603); Flemish (Brussels, 1609); English (Antwerp, 1611); French (Douay, 1629); and German (1700).

These translations of the *Vida* were not the only ones available, however. Abroad, just as in Spain, the *Vida* also reached the hands of many readers through translated editions of Teresa's collected works (*Obras*), in all of which the *Vida* was always included. In some cases, such as in that of France, the first translation of the *Vida* appeared in the first edition of the French *Obras* (Paris, 1601). In other cases, such as Latin and German, it was the other way around, and the first translation appeared as a stand-alone text. In one case— that of Polish—the only translation published was in the *Obras* (Cracow, 1664). The figures available for translated editions of the *Obras*, all of which included the *Vida*, also speak for themselves:

French: 4 translations, 13 editions
Italian: 3 translations, 13 editions
German: 1 translation, 5 editions
Flemish: 1 translation, 2 editions
Latin: 1 translation, 1 edition
English: 1 translation, 1 edition
Polish: 1 translation, 1 edition

Another indication of the popularity of Teresa's *Vida* is the fact that it had multiple translators in various languages, and that many of them were not Carmelites. Working up a new translation of a text that has already been translated is a sign of intense interest in an author, and of a desire to get to the precise meaning of that author's words; capturing the full meaning of the original is deemed essential. As the old Italian wisecrack "traduttore, traditore" has it, to translate is to betray, so it is not too surprising that some translations of the *Vida* were considered defective in some way, and in need of improvement, because what she had to say mattered a great deal to many.

The total number of translators is at least seventeen, including those who produced the text of the *Vida* alone and those who translated it as part of Teresa's *Obras*.

In French, the *Vida* had at least six translators: Guillaume de Chèvre, a Carthusian (Paris, 1601); Jean de Brétigny, a Carthusian (Douay, 1629); Elisée de Saint Bernard, a Carmelite (Paris, 1630); Cyprien de la Nativité de la Vierge, a Carmelite (Paris, 1644); Robert Arnauld d'Andilly, a

Jansenist (Paris, 1670); and Abbé Martial Chanut, a Carmelite (Paris, 1691).

In Italian, it had three translators: Giovanni Francesco Bardoni, an Oratorian (Venice, 1636); Marco di San Giuseppe, a Carmelite (Venice, 1689); and Carlo Sigismondo Capece (Venice, 1729).

In English, it had three translators: William Malone, a Jesuit (Antwerp, 1611); Tobie Matthew (London, 1623); and Abraham Woodhead (London, 1671).

In Flemish, it had at least three translators: an anonymous Jesuit (Brussels, 1609); Elias of Saint Teresa, a Carmelite (Antwerp, 1632); and Servatius of Saint Peter, a Carmelite (Ghent, 1697).

In Latin it had two translators: Anthony Kerbech, an Augustinian (Mainz, 1603); and Matthias Martinez van Waucquier (Cologne, 1626–27).

The *Vida* and the Expansion of the Discalced Carmelite Order

In addition to spreading throughout Europe in translations, the *Vida* became international due to the fairly rapid spread of the Discalced Carmelite order, which made its presence felt throughout Catholic Europe and the Iberian colonies overseas. Wherever the Discalced Carmelites went, devotion to Teresa and her writings followed. The first Discalced Carmelite convent to be established outside of Spain was that of Genoa in 1584. By 1650, fifty-six houses for men and women would dot the Italian peninsula, all independent from the Spanish Discalced Carmelites, but all equally devoted to Teresa and her teachings. In France, which was recovering from the Wars of Religion and still full of Protestants, the order's first convent was established in Paris in 1604, and the second and third in Pontoise and Dijon in 1605. Not long thereafter, other convents would be founded in Amiens, Bordeaux, Toulouse, and Limoges, and also in the war-ravaged Low Countries, in Brussels, Louvain, and Mons. In 1616, a convent for exiled Englishwomen was also established in Antwerp.

These new outposts of Teresa's order signaled the beginning of a tremendous expansion of the Discalced Carmelites into far-flung locations in Central and Eastern Europe, as far north and east as Lithuania, and also across the Atlantic in the New World. From 1611 till the end of the seventeenth century, one or two new convents were established every year, and in each of those, Teresa was not only read and venerated by its members but also by the local layfolk who came into contact with them. In fact, many translations of Teresa's works can be attributed to the efforts of her Carmelite disciples in locations beyond Spain. And in all of these locations, the methods of prayer recommended in the *Vida* were practiced, and the mystical phenomena described therein continued to surface. When Abraham Woodhead described Teresa's legacy among her Carmelite nuns, nearly ninety years after her death, he found it unnecessary to differentiate between the effects caused by Teresa herself and her *Vida*:

> Many also there were of her Spiritual Daughters in the
> Monasteries she founded, that, by these her Directions,
> arrived to several Degrees of Prayer Supernatural ... The

favours which our Lord doth in these Monasteries are so great, that they astonish me: for, He conducts them all by Meditation; and some attain to perfect Contemplation; others are advanced so far, as to arrive to Extasies, and Rapts; to others our lord doth Favours of another kind, bestowing on them likewise Revelations, and Visions, such as, it is manifestly discerned, do proceed from God. There is never a one of these Monasteries at this day, wherein are not found either One, or Two, or Three such [Spiritual Daughters].[14]

Although Teresa's writings became popular throughout Europe in the seventeenth century, it was in France that they had the most dramatic impact, for they influenced a new generation of reformers and mystics whose legacies were as diverse as they were long-lasting. Among those who were deeply affected by Teresa's writings, and especially by her *Vida*, Pierre de Bérulle, Francis de Sales, John Eudes, and Vincent de Paul would play the most significant roles. None of these men were Carmelites, and all of them founded different religious orders too, but they were influenced by Teresa, and each in his own way passed on various elements of her mystical theology to succeeding generations.

Barbe Avrillot, better known as Madame Acarie (1566–1618), a married woman who would eventually become a Discalced Carmelite nun and a mystic in her own right, was the first link in this chain of Teresian disciples that would one day come to be known as the "French School of Spirituality."[15] And it was through the fiery text of Teresa's *Vida* that this first link was forged. Madame Acarie encountered Teresa through the *Vida* thanks to the 1601 translation of

Jean de Quintanadoine, Sieur de Brétigny,[16] the son of a Spanish father and French mother, who was so impressed by the Discalced Carmelite convent in Seville when he visited it in 1582, and by the work of Saint Teresa, that he felt compelled to translate it into French.

Shortly after reading Brétigny's translation of the *Vida*, Madame Acarie began to claim that Teresa was visiting her from beyond the grave, and that in these apparitions Teresa ordered her to establish Discalced Carmelite convents in France. As a noblewoman who invited influential reformers to her salon, Madame Acarie was well placed to introduce other elites to the *Vida* and to tackle the challenge issued to her by Teresa. In 1602 she convinced her cousin Pierre de Bérulle (1575–1629), an energetic newly ordained priest, and Francis de Sales (1567–1622), bishop of Geneva and a preacher at the court of King Henry IV, to help her bring the Discalced Carmelites to France. After receiving permission from Pope Clement VIII—who was approached by de Sales—Bérulle brought some Spanish Discalced Carmelites to Paris and established a Discalced convent in 1604, and then, in the following twenty-five years, he established forty-three additional Carmelite houses, an average of nearly two per year. Bérulle himself established a new order, the Oratory, which had an enormous influence on the reform of the French clergy, and he also authored a number of mystical texts deeply rooted in Teresa's mysticism, all of which stressed the central importance of self-abandonment, of experiencing the reality of the human and divine Christ, and of a loving union with God. Madame Acarie joined the Discalced Carmelites in 1613, after the death of her husband, took the religious name of Marie of the Incarnation, and was well known for her ecstasies, her miracles, and her stigmata. The personal contacts made by her and by Bérulle, through which the influence of Teresa's mysticism was passed on to the so-called French School of Spirituality, produced spectacular results, principally because their focus on the mystical life—much like Teresa's—stressed action in the world as much as contemplation.

Their close associate Francis de Sales not only served as an exemplary bishop while barred from his see of Geneva, the epicenter of Calvinist Protestantism, but also authored two of the best-selling devotional treatises of his age, *Introduction to the Devout Life* (1608) and *Treatise on the Love of God* (1616), both of which were influenced by his own constant reading and rereading of Teresa, to whose writings he had been introduced by Madame Acarie and Bérulle. In addition, de Sales helped establish a new religious order for women, the Sisters of the Visitation, which was initially led by the noblewoman Jeanne de Chantal. De Sales, in turn, passed on the Teresian influence to Vincent de Paul (1581–1660), founder of the Daughters of Charity and of the Congregation of the Mission, and John Eudes (1601–80), founder of the Order of Our Lady of Charity and of the Congregation of Jesus and Mary.

At about the same time that these leading reformers of the French Catholic Church were putting their Teresian mystical zeal into action, a lay brother of the Discalced Carmelite community in Paris who performed menial tasks, Lawrence of the Resurrection (1614–91), expanded Teresa's influence to new dimensions. Lawrence, who was too uneducated to rise above the rank of lay brother, developed a simple and appealing approach to prayer inspired by Teresa's mysticism, especially her emphasis on cultivating a constant awareness of the presence of God, which she had summed up by saying that "the Lord walks among the pots and pans" in the kitchen as well as in the choir stalls. Lawrence's approach and his inner composure so impressed his brethren that his bits of wisdom were collected and turned into a book after his death by Joseph de Beaufort, vicar general to the archbishop of Paris. This book, titled *The Practice of the Presence of God*, which was published repeatedly and underwent many translations, also somehow made its way into some Protestant circles in the eighteenth century and gained a wide readership, especially after John Wesley, the founder of Methodism, embraced it and recommended it. To this day, it is still read by many Protestants, even conservative evangelicals, some of whom are unaware of its connections to Teresa and the Carmelite mystical tradition.

Wayward Disciples

Teresa's influence, as well as that of her *Vida*, did not always flow in a positive direction in the eyes of the Catholic Church. In religion, more so than in other human endeavors, the interpretation of any text is a wild card, unpredictable and always potentially susceptible to unexpected twists and turns, often of an ironic sort. Consequently, despite all of the acclaim and veneration earned by Teresa and her *Vida* in Catholic culture, some of her interpreters ended up on the side of heresy rather than orthodoxy. The two most significant of these wrong turns were the theological and devotional movements known as Jansenism and Quietism.

Jansenism was a reformist movement within early modern Catholicism that focused primarily on theological and ethical issues rather than mysticism, but nonetheless had an odd connection to Teresa, her *Vida*, and other books of hers. The theologian who gave rise to this movement was Cornelius Jansen (1585–1638), a Dutch theologian from the University of Louvain who was also bishop of Ypres. Jansen's chief interest was the relation between the human will and divine grace. In 1640, his massive posthumously published study of Saint Augustine's theology of grace, titled *Augustinus*, won him a substantial following, and before long, a powerful movement arose within the Catholic Church that bore Jansen's name and occasioned the "Jansenist" controversy, the most serious rift among Catholics since the advent of the Protestant Reformation.

Jansenism's links to Teresa were not to be found in Jansen or his theology, however, which stressed the damage caused to humanity by original sin and advocated a rigorous puritanical ethic. The connection to Teresa was to be found most intensely in the Cistercian abbey of Port-Royal-des-Champs, a convent in France that became the epicenter of Jansenism, where several key figures were highly devoted to Teresa and very fond of her *Vida*. The most significant of these Teresians at Port-Royal was its abbess, Jacqueline-Marie-Angélique Arnauld (1591–1661), who, after reading Teresa's *Vida*, *Way of Perfection*, and *Foundations* began to reform her convent in 1609 along Teresian lines, emphasizing strict enclosure, poverty, and silent prayer. In fact, so much emphasis was placed on Teresa at Port-Royal by its abbess Angélique that her fellow nuns began to refer to her as "the Teresa of our order." In 1625, when Angélique opened another reformed convent of

Port-Royal in Paris, she immediately visited the Discalced Carmelite nuns of that city, all of whom began to call her "Madre Teresa" because of how much she resembled their sainted reformer, not just in spirit but also in physical appearance.[17] In addition, Angélique's oldest brother, Robert Arnauld d'Andilly (1589–1674), a distinguished writer who would later spend his final years at the abbey of Port-Royal as a hermit, produced one of the most widely read translations of Teresa's works, including the *Vida*.

The nuns' devotion to Teresa at Port-Royal was eventually eclipsed by the Jansenist theology of several individuals who became associated with their convent, most notably, two of Angélique's brothers, the above-mentioned Robert Arnauld and Antoine Arnauld (1612–94), and Jean du Vergier de Hauranne (1581–1643), better known as the Abbé of Saint-Cyran, a friend and close associate of both Pierre Bérulle and Cornelius Jansen who became spiritual director of the nuns at Port-Royal-des-Champs and its satellite convent in Paris. Under Saint-Cyran's direction and Antoine Arnauld's presence, Jansen's theology soon overshadowed Teresa's mysticism, and Port-Royal became to Jansenism as Rome was to Catholicism, Wittenberg to Lutheranism, and Geneva to Calvinism.

Yet, Teresa's *Vida* continued to be required reading for many Jansenists, including one of its most brilliant adherents, the mathematician, scientist, inventor, and philosopher Blaise Pascal (1623–62), who took up residence at Port-Royal, along with his sister Jacqueline, and raised Jansenist polemics to great heights. In addition to inventing the world's first calculating machine, proving the existence of air pressure, devising probability theory, and having a very

Teresian mystical experience that changed his life, Blaise Pascal published a scathing satire in 1657 entitled *The Provincial Letters*, which skewered the chief opponents of Jansenism, the Jesuits, and arguably did more to publicize the Jansenist cause than any other text. Pascal not only read Teresa's *Vida* but made several references to her in his unfinished defense of the Christian religion, which was posthumously published as the *Pensées* (Thoughts), a philosophical tour de force that would influence a wide spectrum of thinkers for the following three centuries, including the existentialists of the twentieth century.

The Jansenist controversy was as convoluted as it was lengthy, and most of its history has nothing to do with its Teresian roots at Port-Royal, which quickly became invisible. Jansenism troubled the Catholic Church for more than a century, and, in the process, also became a political issue in France as Jansenists began to oppose the absolutist claims of the French monarchy. In 1705, bowing to pressure from King Louis XIV, Pope Clement XI issued the bull *Vineam Domini*, in which he condemned Jansenism, and in 1713, a second and more detailed condemnation would follow in the bull *Unigenitus*. The end of Jansenism had already been signaled in the death of the abbey of Port-Royal, anyway, which was abolished by Pope Clement in 1708, emptied of its nuns in 1709, and demolished in 1710. To confirm the utter error linked to this wayward abbey—once a hotbed of Teresian mysticism—the remains of those buried there were removed, too, including those of its own "Teresa," the abbess Jacqueline-Marie-Angélique Arnauld.

The demise of Jansenism coincided with another fray that focused on the relation between human and divine nature and had some affinities to Teresa's mysticism, though this controversy was much smaller in scale and impact. This dispute concerned Quietism, a mystical movement restricted to a relatively small number of men and women, but marked by concerns that linked it to other major theological disputes that shook early modern Catholicism.

Quietist adepts were accused of believing that in the higher reaches of the mystical quest, the perfected human soul that had achieved self-annihilation was absorbed by God and ceased functioning as an independent self. This was the "quiet" in Quietism: a total self-surrender in which God took possession of one's mind and will and one no longer needed to talk to God in prayer because God and the soul were now finally united and the praying was really done by God. This mysticism had deep roots in Catholic tradition, but it also echoed previously censured movements, such as the heresy of the Free Spirit (fourteenth to fifteenth century) and Spanish *alumbradismo* (sixteenth century). Naturally, the link to Teresa was there too, not just because of her teachings on the prayer of quiet but because she had herself been suspected of being an alumbrada.

The chief proponent of Quietism was a Spanish priest in Rome, Miguel de Molinos (1628–97), whose treatises *The Spiritual Guide* and *A Brief Treatise on Daily Communion* (1675) were initially approved by Catholic Church authorities and published and translated numerous times. Accusations of heresy began to be leveled against Molinos in the late 1670s, despite his popularity, and his opponents eventually convinced Pope Innocent XI to condemn him in 1687, in the bull *Coelestis Pastor*. Molinos admitted his errors and was imprisoned for the remaining ten years of his life.

Although Quietism attracted a following, it was limited to the spiritual elite and never had much of an impact on the Catholic Church as a whole. Nonetheless, Quietism took hold of one remarkable woman in France who kept the movement in the public eye through her writings and her connections at the court of Louis XIV: Jeanne-Marie Bouvier de la Motte-Guyon, a widow better known as Madame Guyon (1648–1717), who created a tight circle of followers, including the archbishop François Fénelon (1651–1715), but ended up being condemned, silenced, and imprisoned in the infamous Bastille of Paris for seven years. But her persistence in promoting the principles of Quietism, which had roots in Teresa's mysticism, especially as expressed in the *Vida*, would eventually pay off beyond the confines of Catholicism. Her greatest influence, ironically, would be among Protestants who picked up her writings, especially the Quakers. The Protestant disciples of Madame Guyon—and indirectly of Teresa—would signal a seismic shift within certain branches of the Protestant tradition in the eighteenth century, a shift toward a growing appreciation of the mystical tradition rejected by the major reformers of the sixteenth century.

Unlikely Disciples

Madame Guyon's transmission of Teresian mysticism to Quakers may seem odd, but it is not unique. Despite the fact that some of her hagiographers viewed Teresa as God's answer to Luther, she had a way of crossing the boundaries that separated Catholics from Protestants, and translations of her *Vida* had something to do with that, because they made her texts available in regions where Catholics and Protestants lived near each other, such as parts of France, the Netherlands, and Germany, or places where a Catholic minority could make its texts clandestinely available, such as England. Although it is extremely difficult to quantify the effect of Teresa on Protestants outside of Spain, there are various cases that make the existence of that effect obvious, such as that of Madame Guyon and the Quakers. Another prominent case is that of the English poet Richard Crashaw (1613–49), who converted to Catholicism after reading *The Flaming Hart*, the second English translation of the *Vida*, penned by Tobie Matthew in 1623.

The son of a Puritan minister, Crashaw was educated at Pembroke College, Cambridge, and ordained as a clergyman in the Church of England. Despite his father's virulent anti-Catholicism, Crashaw gravitated toward the Catholic sensibilities of High Church Anglicanism, which ran strong at Pembroke College, where he held a fellowship after his graduation in 1634 and also served as curate of the college's chapel. In the midst of rising Puritan agitation and civil war, Crashaw left his post at Pembroke College and fled to France in 1644, where he openly embraced the Catholic Church. While living in exile, in extreme poverty, he published *Steps to the Temple* in 1646, a collection of religious and secular poems in Latin and English. Three years later, he died unexpectedly after being appointed to a clerical post at the Shrine of the Holy House of Loreto in Italy. In 1652 his English religious poems were republished in Paris in 1652 under the title *Carmen Deo Nostro* (Hymns to Our Lord). Three of Crashaw's best-known and most highly regarded English poems honor Teresa and rely heavily on the *Vida* for their imagery: "A Hymn to the Name and Honour of Saint Teresa," "An Apologie for the Fore-going Hymne," and "The Flaming Heart." Some interpreters of Crashaw consider these the most sublime of all his poems.

Within this trilogy, which is filled with references to Teresa's mystical ecstasies, Crashaw's poem "The Flaming Heart" has the most direct reference to the *Vida* and its life-altering potential. Crashaw was directly inspired not only by Teresa's text but also by an image or illustration of the trans-verberation, as indicated in the poem's full title: "The Flaming Heart upon the Book and Picture of the Seraphicall Saint Teresa (As She is usually Expressed with a Seraphim Beside Her)." Much of this poem is about the challenge of rendering something as ineffable as Teresa's ecstasy into an image, and many of its lines chide the artist for not fully comprehending his subject.

> O most poor-spirited of Men!
> Had thy cold pencil kist her pen,
> Thou couldst not so unkindly err
> To show us this faint shade for her

Crashaw asks, "Painter, what didst thou understand?" Throughout much of the poem, then, Crashaw seeks to reverse the imagery of the "poor spirited" artist, transferring the agency of the wounding to Teresa herself. "Give her the dart," he says, "for it is she . . . shoots both thy shaft, and thee." Dwelling on the theme of self-abandonment, Crashaw sums up his own desire to mirror God-filled Teresa, seamlessly entwining God, Teresa, and her *Vida*, imploring this triune entity to effect his mystical self-emptying and his union with the divine:

By all the Heaven thou hast in him
(Fair sister of the Seraphim!)
By all of Him we have in Thee;
Leave nothing of myself in me.
Let me so read thy life, that I
Unto all life of mine may die.[18]

The transverberation is a recurring theme in all three of these poems, with a special focus on the "dart" with which the angel pierces Teresa's heart. The metaphorical references to Cupid and his arrows are deliberately emphasized by Crashaw in his "Flaming Heart" poem, where he speaks of "Love's whole quiver," and also, in a different way, in his "Hymn to Saint Teresa," where the paradoxical coincidence of pain and bliss, wounding and healing, death and life are explicitly linked to the bridal imagery of the Song of Songs, that most erotic of biblical texts:

Oh, how oft shalt thou complain
Of a sweet and subtle pain:
Of intolerable joyes:
Of a death in which who dyes
Loves his death, and dyes again,
And would forever so be slain,
And lives and dyes, and knows not why
To live, but that he thus may never leave to dy.
How kindly will thy gentle heart
Kiss the sweetly-killing dart!
And close in his embraces keep
Those delicious wounds, that weep
Balsam to heal themselves with.[19]

The image of the transverberation that Crashaw folded into this poetry was no superficial element of the life of the *Vida* but rather one of its most distinctive characteristics, for few other religious autobiographies or mystical treatises have attracted as much attention from artists as the *Vida*. It could be argued that the *Vida* had an additional life beyond its text, and so intense a life, in fact, as to demand an entire book-length study rather than one brief chapter in a small book such as this. (Imagining the *Vida* in art is the subject of chapter 5.)

For now, what needs to be said about the life of the *Vida* after Teresa's death and canonization is this: The papal condemnation of Quietism in the late seventeenth century had a somewhat chilling effect on Catholic interest in mysticism and in the *Vida* for a century or so, but it could not snuff it out altogether. When all is said and done, as long as monasticism survived, along with Catholicism, so did mysticism and a continuing interest in Teresa and her *Vida*. The rising tide of skepticism and secularism that swept through Western culture in the eighteenth century did more to reduce the *Vida*'s popularity than any other factor overall, but even that seismic shift in attitudes away from religion known as the Enlightenment ultimately failed to eclipse religion or mystical inclinations.

Teresa's *Vida* was always more than a text. It was a key element of a saint's cult. The manuscript autograph was itself a holy relic, one of the most valuable among the seven thousand or so relics at the royal palace-monastery of the Escorial. And in baroque Catholicism, relics alone were not sufficient for any saint's cult, especially a saint as highly revered as Teresa. Images were essential too, so let us now turn our attention to that subject.

The Life of the *Vida* in Art

Given the vivid imagery found throughout Teresa's *Vida*—much of which mirrored traditional Catholic iconography—and given the high value placed on sacred art by the Council of Trent, it is not at all surprising that her text acquired a visual dimension soon after it was first published, or that it inspired artists to create some of the most emblematic images of the Catholic Reformation and the baroque age. Rather than being deterred by Teresa's own admission of the inadequacy of her metaphors, or by the challenge of depicting events that involved a realm beyond the senses, patrons and artists alike showed great eagerness to express the inexpressible visually, precisely because Teresa's rare ability to engage with that extrasensory supernatural realm was perceived as a resounding affirmation of Catholic beliefs and Catholic identity.

Moreover, the link between the *Vida* and religious art was intrinsic, something that stemmed from Teresa's own descriptions of her supernatural experiences. Teresa had a "pictorial imagination," that is, a penchant for visual metaphors and figures of speech that relied on vivid imagery. Her visually oriented figures of speech, which number more than 420 in the *Vida*, are a key element of the entire narrative.[1] Moreover, Teresa also had an intense cognitive and affective relationship with religious imagery, as evidenced by the fact that she often describes her own visions as being "just as in a picture," and admits that she was so "fond of pictures" that she could not understand how anyone could genuinely love God, *el Señor*, without them (9:6.65). Teresa also ascribed spiritual power to images, as in the case of her own conversion to the mystical life, which was sparked by an image of the "gravely wounded" Christ (9:1.63). The link between physical images and Teresa's visions is so intense, in fact, that some art historians have argued that her visions were derived from works of art.[2]

Early Depictions of Teresa

Given this commingling of image, experience, and narrative in the *Vida*—which often makes it impossible to distinguish any one of these essential elements from the other two— and given the fact that representations of mystical ecstasies quickly became a very popular subject for artists, especially in Spain, Italy, and the Spanish Netherlands,[3] it was only natural for Teresa's text to evoke visual representations and to serve as an inspiration for many a patron of religious art as well as for many an artist. One might say that Teresa's ecstasies were a "perfect" subject, and that no ecstasy of hers was more perfect than the transverberation. In the baroque age, it has been argued, "the ecstatic look and the ecstatic attitude speak the clearest religious dialect."[4]

This natural extension of Teresa's narrative beyond mere literature to the realm of the visual arts took many forms, repeatedly, in engravings, paintings, and sculpture. Some of these images were wedded to the text, as illustrations of its content; some of them served as a translation from the verbal to the visual (a much-needed function in an age with low literacy rates); and some of them served a religious function, as avatars of the sacred and objects of veneration. And, as is common with all images—especially religious ones—much of this art served multiple functions at once.

The earliest illustrations to appear in the first few printed editions of Teresa's works were portrait images, used as frontispieces.[5] Teresa's only genuine portrait was by Juan de la Miseria, a Discalced Carmelite friar, for which she posed in 1576 when she was sixty-one. Although this portrait remained in the Convent of Saint Joseph in Seville, where it was created, the image was copied various times in drawings and paintings, and these reproductions, some of which were less faithful to the original than others, eventually established a fixed representation of the "authentic" Teresa. Ironically, Teresa herself was not pleased by the portrait that influenced all subsequent renderings of her likeness. According to legend, her immediate response had been to say, "May God forgive you, Fray Juan, for you've made me look ugly and bleary-eyed"[6] (see frontispiece).

Teresa's objections aside, Juan de la Miseria's portrait gave the world the only glimpse it would ever have of her true likeness. Fray Juan's portrait depicted Teresa at prayer, her hands clasped in an easily recognizable gesture of devotion, but other details in this portrait, which identify Teresa as a supernaturally gifted saint, may have been added later: an image of the Holy Spirit in the form of a dove hovering directly beside her face; a narrow phylactery, or banner, that surrounds Teresa's head, with the Latin inscription *Misericordias Domini in Eternum Cantabo* (I will sing of the Lord's mercy forever);[7] and the legend "B.V. Teresa de Jesús," which identifies her as a "blessed virgin" (*beata virginis*), and could not have been included too long before her 1614 beatification.[8]

Obviously, attributes such as these, normally reserved for the most eminent doctors of the church,[9] would be immensely difficult to justify in any portrait of a living person, regardless of their reputation for holiness, especially after the Council of Trent set clear guidelines for sacred art in 1563, in its twenty-fifth session. Nonetheless, the dove representing the Holy Spirit—a sign of Teresa's closeness to God and of her orthodox authority—would henceforth become one of the chief iconic elements in all visual representations of Teresa. And this key element was no mere contrivance. It was a depiction of a supernatural encounter described by Teresa in the *Vida*:

> Once, on the vigil of Pentecost, I went after Mass to a very secluded spot . . . and began to read about this feast in the Carthusian's *Life of Christ*. As I read about the signs that can be received by beginners, proficients, and perfect to let them know if the Holy Spirit is with them, it seemed to me, when I had read about these three states, that—so far as I could understand—by the goodness of God, He was with me constantly . . . While I pondered this, I was seized by a strong impulse without my knowing why. It seemed as if my soul wanted to leave my body . . . And as this was happening, I saw a dove above my head, very different from those here on earth, for it didn't have feathers like theirs,

but its wings were made of very resplendent, shiny little shells. It was larger than a dove; I seemed to hear the rustling of its wings, and the fluttering lasted for as long as it takes to recite one Ave Maria. (38.9–10)

Although the dove added to Fray Juan's portrait did not exactly resemble the unearthly one described by Teresa, that image was in essence the first visual depiction of any of Teresa's visions. And this image made its way into print and universality as soon as Luis de León published his 1588 edition of Teresa's *Obras*, which included an engraving based on it, with the same iconic attributes. Subsequent Spanish editions of the *Obras* would include similar versions of this image.

The first depiction of Teresa that diverged slightly from Juan de la Miseria's portrait appeared in the 1599 Italian translation of the *Vida*, in which the unknown artist added a quill pen and an inkwell as a way of emphasizing her role as an author. This same detail appeared in the image of Teresa in the hagiography by Diego de Yepes, first published in 1606. The significance of this iconographic feature would prove to be immense, for the quill pen began to appear in other images fairly rapidly, and would eventually become a regular identifying attribute in most images of Teresa— along with the dove—especially those crafted specifically for purposes of veneration.

Turning the *Vida* into Images

As her fame increased and her beatification and canonization process moved forward, however, the printing of mere portraits of Teresa proved insufficient. Apparently, many thought that a life as full of extraordinary events as hers merited depiction in greater detail, and that no text could provide as many details of her encounters with the supernatural as the *Vida*. It stands to reason, then, that in 1613, as part of the effort to promote Teresa's sainthood, the *Vida* was brought to life visually, in a graphic hagiography consisting of twenty-five loose-leaf engravings, titled *Vitae Beatae Virginis Teresiae a Iesu*. Printed in Antwerp—then under Spanish rule and a center for publishing Catholic texts—these engravings were the handiwork of two Flemish artists, Adriaen Collaert (1560–1618) and Cornelis Galle (1576–1650). The project was conceived of and promoted by two of Teresa's closest associates and disciples, her confessor Jerónimo Gracián de la Madre de Dios and Ana de Jesús Lobera, prioress of the Discalced Carmelite convent in Brussels, both of whom were wholly committed to promoting the beatification and canonization of Teresa and to making her many supernatural encounters as well known as possible.[10]

The concept of a graphic hagiography was somewhat new at the time, but derived from one of the key objectives of the hagiographic genre: that of inspiring veneration as well as imitation of the saints. Capturing events from a saint's life in imagery had long been a central characteristic of medieval Catholic iconography, but the reach of sacred icons had been limited to churches, chapels, and the dwellings of powerful elites. After the invention of the printing press, however, religious art could be widely distributed in engravings and brought within the walls of the homes of all the faithful. In a very real way, then, graphic hagiographies could assume the function of *libri pauperum*, that is, of books for the poor and illiterate, in ways unimaginable to Pope Gregory the Great, who coined that term in a very different context a millennium earlier.

Getting Galle and Collaert to produce a highly condensed graphic version of Teresa's *Vida* was a major achievement for Teresa's promoters, for these two artists had published an immensely popular graphic hagiography of Ignatius Loyola in 1610.[11] Loyola, the founder of the Jesuit order, was also on his way to canonization, along with Teresa, and the popularity of Galle and Collaert's engravings had proven that there was a demand for visual versions of saints' lives and that such a medium was perfect for promoting and increasing the veneration of any holy man or woman on the way to canonization.

The twenty-five Collaert-Galle engravings visualized significant events in the life of Teresa, especially those that involved her mystical encounters with the supernatural. Although a few of the engravings depict events found only in the hagiographies of Ribera and Yepes or in oral accounts from Carmelite circles, the vast majority of them are drawn straight from the *Vida* itself, especially from chapters 38, 39, and 40, and, in addition, the very brief Latin captions below the images often contain paraphrased quotations from it. In essence, then, these engravings are an abridged illustrated version of the *Vida*. Letters written by Ana de Jesús while the engravings were being produced indicate that she was largely responsible for selecting the events depicted by Collaert and Galle, all of which highlight Teresa's unique relationship with the divine.

Seven of these engravings would prove very influential in the development of Teresian iconography. Two of these seven images rendered supernatural phenomena that had a physical dimension and could have been observed by her sisters in the convent: one depicts her brandishing a cross at demons (even if they could not see the demons, her sisters could have seen her waving the cross); the other captures her levitating several feet off the ground in the presence of ten eyewitnesses. Four other engravings attempted to visualize Teresa's most extraordinary mystical experiences, which could not have been observed by anyone: her "conversion" while venerating an image of the suffering Christ; her encounter with Christ in which he said, "You're mine now, and I'm yours"; her vision of the Trinity; and her transverberation at the hands of an angel. The seventh of these most significant engravings portrays Teresa as a divinely inspired writer guided by the Holy Spirit, quill pen in hand, the heavens opening above her, a stack of her books covering most of the writing table. Of these seven images, the one that would eventually come to represent the essence of Teresa's mysticism would be that of the transverberation, and we will return to this definitive image presently.

Galle and Collaert's engravings proved so popular that a second edition was published the following year, 1614, to coincide with celebrations of Teresa's beatification. In 1622, when Teresa was canonized, two more editions were published. In 1630, another edition appeared, and, decades later, yet again, one more in 1677. The impact of this series of engravings on the cult of Saint Teresa and on artists throughout the Catholic world was immense, and it could be argued that its depictions of events described in the *Vida* expanded the reach of the text in ways that its author and her confessors could have never imagined, even as far away as the New

World. Among these American artists, the best known are José Espinoza de los Monteros, whose series of sixteen paintings from 1682 still hang in the Carmelite convent of Cuzco, Peru, and another series of paintings created by an unknown disciple of his in the 1690s for the Carmelite convent in Santiago, Chile.[12]

Multiple illustrations derived from events described in the *Vida* appeared in some hagiographies too, and in anthologies of Teresa's writings. One of the most richly illustrated of these was the *Vita effigiata di S. Teresa Vergine*,[13] published in Rome in 1655, which has been attributed to the Discalced Carmelite friar Alesio Maria della Passione. This illustrated book, which contained thirty-six engravings, along with a seventy-five-page account of Teresa's life, and an anthology of Teresa's poems, prayers, and sayings, would be published again in 1670, with thirty-six additional engravings, many of which depicted her mystical experiences. Its illustrations differ from those of Collaert-Galle, not only in style but also in content, for the events depicted vary to a considerable extent, and many of those in both editions of the *Vita effigiata* are drawn from sources other than the *Vida*. The popularity of this work prompted the publication of a French-language edition in 1670, which contained the same illustrations as the Roman edition of 1655.[14] Then, once again, in 1716, another work entitled *Vita effigiata della serafica vergine S. Teresa di Gesu* was published in Rome, this time with no text at all—returning to the format of the Collaert-Galle editions—but rather with seventy-one engravings by the Flemish artist Arnold van Westerhout, some of which were reinterpretations of the illustrations in the 1655 *Vita* published by Alesio Maria della Passione.[15]

The exact number of early modern engravings of scenes from Teresa's *Vida* has never been definitively tallied, but such a tally is ultimately unnecessary. What matters the most is that the *Vida* became visual, and that printed images of her extraordinary life spread far and wide all over the Catholic world, increasing devotion to Teresa as a saint, and inspiring artists to produce more images of her. Above all, the engravings—unlike paintings and sculptures—had an incredibly wide reach, and they helped make Teresa and some of her mystical experiences avatars of Catholic identity.

The Symbolic Power of the Transverberation

Engravings printed by the thousands might have reached more people than any image in a chapel, but those unique and spatially bound renderings of events from Teresa's *Vida* were significant too, as objects of devotion and symbols of Catholic identity. Paintings of Teresa began to be commissioned even before her beatification in 1614, mostly by Discalced Carmelite convents. Images of her mystical experiences proliferated quickly, and in 1622, at her canonization ceremony in Rome, a banner depicting her ecstasy of the transverberation hung in Saint Peter's Basilica.[16] After her canonization, the number of paintings produced began to grow and to extend beyond Carmelite circles. The commissioning of sculptures was less common, but one sculpture in particular eventually attracted so much attention that it eclipsed all other depictions of Teresa, especially after the invention of photography: Gianlorenzo Bernini's rendition of the transverberation, commissioned by the Cornaro family for their burial chapel at the Discalced Carmelite church of Santa Maria della Vittoria in Rome.

When it came to rendering the transverberation, Bernini was a relative latecomer. For various reasons—which will be analyzed presently—by the time that Bernini began to create his version of the transverberation in 1647, this ecstasy was already a highly favored subject among artists and the most frequently rendered of all of her mystical experiences. And long after Bernini finished the project in 1652, on the seventieth anniversary of Teresa's death and the thirtieth of her canonization, the transverberation continued to be depicted by artists around the world more often than any other event in Teresa's life.[17]

But why was it that this particular ecstasy attracted so much attention and became so emblematic of Teresa's mysticism and Catholicism, even to the point of being celebrated as a liturgical feast day in the Catholic Church every August 26? Tracing the development of this image over the decades that preceded Bernini's reification of Teresa's encounter with a wounding seraph should help explain why this ecstasy became so emblematic. And analyzing how this particular ecstasy was rendered over time, after Bernini, should also shed light on the visual impact of all of Teresa's ecstasies and of the *Vida* as a whole.

Of the many images of the transverberation ever made, some are better known than others, such as Bernini's, and many have remained in relative obscurity. Some images have had more of an impact than others, too, and have served as templates for other depictions, many of which are copies or slightly different versions. Regardless of how the event is rendered, all images of the transverberation reify three themes of central significance in early modern Catholicism: love, ecstasy, and martyrdom. Let us turn to some of the most significant of these images, not as an attempt at cataloging but rather at gaining some perspective on the various ways in which the text of the *Vida* was repeatedly brought to life.

The earliest depiction of Teresa's transverberation was one of the twenty-five loose-leaf engravings of Collaert and Galle's *Vitae Beatae Virginis Teresiae a Iesu*, published in Antwerp in 1613, in anticipation of her beatification (fig. 1). This engraving is attributed to Adriaen Collaert, who chose to embellish the scene by adding the presence of four additional angels around Teresa and by depicting Jesus Christ and the Holy Spirit directly above her halo-ringed head. Collaert captures the instant just before the angel plunges his long dart into Teresa's heart. The setting is a nondescript, yet architecturally formal indoor space, with two leaded windows and a balustrade that resembles an altar rail, with no altar anywhere in view. The weapon has a flaming arrowhead-shaped tip and is long enough to look like a spear but has arrow-like fletching at the back end. Teresa leans back, slightly off balance, her arms wide open in expectation of her imminent wounding, her eyes open but upturned, with the irises barely visible under her eyelids, in a trancelike state. One of the four angels supports Teresa's back, keeping her upright. In the upper center of the image, encircled by glowing clouds, Jesus is depicted bare-chested, at a smaller scale, to suggest the distance being bridged between heaven and earth, his muscular arms wide open, his gaze focused directly on Teresa's upturned eyes, while a dove representing the Holy Spirit hovers between him and Teresa.

This engraving was reproduced numerous times by various publishers, and it also provided a template for many

FIGURE 1. Adriaen Collaert, 1613. From *Vitae Beatae Virginis Teresiae a Iesu*, in Adriaen Collaert, *Vita S. Virginis Teresiæ a Iesv* (1630). Digitized by Boston Public Library, https://archive.org /details/vitasvirginister00coll.

subsequent depictions of the transverberation, including some in Spain's overseas colonies. Collaert's image was seminal, but due to the vagaries of the printing process, sometimes the orientation of the image would be reversed.[18]

The following year, Bernardo Strozzi (1581–1644), a Genoese artist who spent much of his career in Venice, completed one of the earliest paintings of the transverberation (fig. 2).[19] While it is probable that Strozzi might have relied on Collaert's engraving, his version of Teresa's ecstasy is no copy. The only two figures in Strozzi's painting are Teresa and the cherubim, in an indistinct space, neither indoors nor outdoors, neither on earth nor in heaven. There is no celestial vision or hierophany, and Strozzi's Teresa—unlike Collaert's—has no halo. The background is devoid of heavenly figures and comprised entirely of sharply contrasting clouds, half of them dark, directly over Teresa, the other half surrounding the winged cherubim, bathed in a glowing, golden light. The angel wields a long spear, which is touching Teresa's chest, about to penetrate it, with no flame on its tip. Teresa is not supported by another angel but leans with her left elbow on some object that looks like a wooden chest, upon which stands a slender crucifix, flush against the edge of the painting. Mouth agape, arms bent at the elbows with her palms upturned, Teresa fixes her gaze on the crucifix with upturned eyes. Strozzi's rendering gives the impression that Teresa is in a state of shock rather than rapture, but there is no mistaking the message that the pain about to be endured by her is linked to the pain of the crucified Christ, in which she longs to share, and that her violent ecstasy is a form of martyrdom. Unlike Collaert, who heavy-handedly depicted Christ manifesting himself from heaven, along with the Holy Spirit, Strozzi chose to limit the divine presence to the crucifix. Despite the inclusion of an angel in the scene, Strozzi's Teresa is more earthly than Collaert's.

Around the time of Teresa's canonization in 1622, new images of the transverberation were produced. Among the most significant and influential were two Flemish engravings by Anton Wierix III, one similar to Collaert's version and faithful to the text of the *Vida*, the other radically different in all respects. In the earlier of these two engravings, which partly resembles Collaert's, Wierix captures the

FIGURE 2. Bernardo Strozzi, 1614. *Estasi di Santa Teresa* oil on canvas, 111 × 90 cm (43.7 × 35.4 in.). The Room of Aurora or Flora, Museo di Palazzo Reale. With the Permission of the Ministero dei Beni e delle Attività Culturali e del Turismo—Palazzo Reale di Genova.

moment when the angel is about to wound a kneeling Teresa. In this rendition, the foreground is littered with flowers and the background is replete with heavenly beings (fig. 3). The dart-wielding angel stands to Teresa's left, one hand on her arm, the other wielding a weapon that looks like a large arrow, with a flaming tip and fletching at the back end. Four smaller angels hover around and above Teresa. Two of them keep her upright, one holding her right arm and her back, the other holding her up by her shoulders; the other two drop flowers on Teresa from on high. Peeking out from billowing clouds, four more angels reveal their heads, serving no discernible role. At the top center, ringed by clouds, emitting rays of light—the largest and brightest of which reaches all the way down to Teresa—God the Father opens his arms wide as he gazes intently on the scene below. Unlike Collaert and Strozzi, Wierix chooses to internalize Teresa's ecstasy. Her head surrounded by a glowing nimbus, her arms open wide, Teresa stares vacantly into the distance rather than at Christ or an image of him. A Latin inscription from the Song of Songs at the bottom refers to the flower-strewing angels and makes the central bridal theme of the image as obvious as possible: "Sustain me with flowers, surround me with apples, for I am wounded by love" (*Fulcite me floribus, stipate me malis: quia charitate vulnerata ego sum*). By adding this text, Wierix ensures that his image be interpreted as a spiritual marriage feast in which the angels act as acolytes of sorts. And by choosing a Latin text that reads "I am wounded" (*vulnerata sum*) rather than "I languish" (*langueo*)—as does the normative Vulgate version of the Bible—Wierix also ensures that the theme of martyrdom is clearly perceived.[20]

Wierix's second engraving strays from Teresa's text substantially and represents the themes of ecstasy, love, and martyrdom in a very different way (fig. 4). In this engraving, which is set in a landscape, with a city far away near the horizon, there are no weapon-wielding cherubim. Instead, it is the Christ Child—assisted by the Virgin Mary and Saint Joseph—who does the wounding, with a bow and arrow, just like the pagan Cupid. And instead of capturing the instant just before Teresa is wounded, Wierix depicts Teresa leaning back at a steep angle, with an arrow protruding from her chest. His bow loaded with a second flame-tipped arrow, additional arrows strapped to his waist in a full quiver, gently steadied by Saint Joseph, the Christ Child aims at the fallen Teresa, who looks more dead than ecstatic, while the Virgin Mary holds yet another arrow in her hand, ready to hand it to her son for a third shot. As in previous renderings, Teresa's body is being supported by angels, this time three in number. A choir of angels sits on clouds, up in heaven, playing musical instruments, while two angels in flight approach Teresa, one about to place a crown of roses on her head—a bridal symbol—and another bearing a palm frond in his right hand, a symbol of martyrdom. Up in heaven, at the apex, God the Father sits on a cloud, his right arm extended, and beneath him, riding a wide shaft of light beams, the dove symbolizing the Holy Spirit flies toward Teresa. In this peculiar rendering of the transverberation, Wierix ignores Teresa's text, but in the process he manages to highlight more themes than preceding images, including his own. Here, the entire Trinity is present, along with the Holy Family, making God the explicit agent of the mystical wounding; the link between mystical ecstasy and death is

S. VIRG. ET M. TERESA A IESV.
Fulcite me floribus, stipate me malis:
quia charitate vulnerata ego sum. Cant. 2.

Anton. Wierx fecit et excud.

FIGURE 3. Anton Wierix, 1614–22. Engraving, overall: ½ × 2¾ in.
(11.4 × 7 cm). Harris Brisbane Dick Fund, 1953. The Met,
Accession #53.601.19(143).

dramatically portrayed in a very obvious way; and the love and martyrdom themes are much more explicit, with the Christ Child playing Cupid.

What are we to make of this peculiar image, especially of its fusing of themes and its blending of Christian and pagan motifs? To begin with, the image needs to be understood as a highly allegorical rendering of Teresa's text, deeply encoded with visual cues that reify the full Catholicity of Teresa's ecstasy, and, as such, it needs to be decoded as an emblem rather than as a depiction of a historical event. Emblems are heuristic devices: carefully crafted symbolic pictures that aim to convey meaning visually, on multiple levels. In other words, they are densely encoded visual puzzles. Emblems had medieval antecedents but began to gain popularity as a pictorial and literary genre in the sixteenth century— thanks largely to the printing press—and became all the rage in the seventeenth, especially in the Netherlands, where Anton Wierix lived.[21] Emblems could be secular or religious, or both at once, and they often blended ancient classical motifs with Christian ones in an attempt to convey moralistic lessons. They could be found in public spaces as well as in books. At early modern royal funerals, for instance, emblems were thickly embedded into the ceremonies, and lengthy descriptions of their meaning were often published afterward.[22] There were also religious emblems and emblem books, which were meant to serve as pictorial aids to prayer and devotion, and they were made to be pored over and meditated upon.[23] Wierix himself was quite adept at creating and publishing emblems.[24]

Wierix could expel the angel from the transverberation and replace him with a Cupid-like Christ Child because he

Sᵗᵃ· Virgo TERESA Carmelitarum Excalceatorum fundatrix.

Quid parentes tela datis   Quærit ab hoc necis sortem,
In amantem incitatis   Imo putat esse mortem,
Vitæ Sagittarum?   Dum negat interitum.

Anton. Wierx fecit et excud.

FIGURE 4. Anton Wierix, 1622–24. Engraving, sheet: 4¾ × 3⅛ in. (12.1 × 7.9 cm). The Elisha Whittelsey Collection, The Elisha Whittelsey Fund, 195. The Met, Accession #51.501.6213.

was deeply into emblematic expression, and sought to convey *meaning* rather than *fact*. And the meaning he tried to convey in this second engraving of his could not have been any clearer, especially for an audience familiar with emblems: Teresa's transverberation was convincing proof of her sanctity and of the truth of the core teachings of the Catholic Church. The fact that his Christ/Cupid was copied numerous times over several generations, even in faraway Spanish America, suggests that Wierix had indeed tapped into some essential vein in Catholic symbolism.

At roughly the same time, in 1629, Guido Cagnacci, who was commissioned to paint an altarpiece for a Carmelite church in Rimini, inserted into his version a pair of angels who are staring at each other, as if amazed at what they are doing, one holding up a swooning Teresa, the other wounding her with a long dart (fig. 5). The wounding angel seems to be pausing, his fingers gingerly pressed on the dart, his other hand palms up. The tip of the burning dart has already penetrated Teresa's chest, and its flames singe her habit. Teresa has collapsed totally, her hands limply crossed. Her eyelids and lips barely open, Cagnacci's Teresa seems to hover somewhere between ecstasy and death.

Fast-forward to Rome in 1647. The great sculptor Gianlorenzo Bernini, who is being shunned by Pope Innocent X after years of service to previous popes, is commissioned by Cardinal Federico Cornaro (1579–1653) to create a burial chapel for him and his family in the left transept of the relatively undistinguished Discalced Carmelite church of Santa Maria della Vittoria. Cardinal Cornaro asks Bernini to sculpt an image of the transverberation for the chapel altar and life-size images of himself and some of his family

FIGURE 5. Guido Cagnacci, 1629. Detail of *Santa Teresa e Santa Maria Maddalena de' Pazzi, 1629–1631*. *La Pala dei Carmelitani*. San Giovanni Battista, Rimini, Italy. The Picture Art Collection / Alamy Stock Photo.

members for both sides of the chapel, depicting them as spectators to Teresa's ecstasy. Bernini takes on the job and makes history.

It could be argued that Bernini's *Ecstasy of Saint Teresa* is not just the most remarkable baroque sculpture but also the most daring, and also the best known. So much has been written about his depiction of the transverberation that it would be foolish to attempt even a brief summary of that literature, let alone provide a detailed analysis of the image itself. Masterpieces tend to challenge the limits of language, as do mystical experiences.

Bernini's rendering is at once very faithful to Teresa's text and also highly imaginative and metaphorical (fig. 6). The fact that this rendition is three-dimensional distinguishes it from all previous paintings and engravings, but experts agree that Bernini was well aware of some previous images and made deliberate choices of his own in response to them. All that one can see in his transverberation is Teresa and the wounding angel, as in Strozzi's painting. Gone are the heavenly host and all three persons of the Holy Trinity. A lone Cupid-like cherubic angel with one bare shoulder and a slightly mischievous smile holds a slender metal arrow in his hand, and there is no flame on its tip. His weapon is still at some distance from Teresa's body, and it is not aimed at her heart but rather at the lower part of her abdomen. Teresa floats on a cloud, her bare left foot dangling over its edge, as in a spasm, and the folds of her habit all awry, as if in a writhing fit of motion. Her left arm dangles limply, her palm resting on the clouds rather than open to the angel. She is not anticipating a painful wounding; she is already enraptured. Her face says it all. Mouth

FIGURE 6. Gianlorenzo Bernini, 1647–52. *The Ecstasy of Saint Teresa*. Altar Cornaro Chapel, S. Maria della Vittoria, Rome, Italy. Hercules Milas / Alamy Stock Photo.

half agape, lips fully flushed, eyelids loosely shut, Teresa expresses nothing but an ecstatic swoon.

Many interpreters have deemed this image to be overtly erotic. In Bernini's own day, an anonymous pamphlet complained that he had "dragged that most pure Virgin down to the ground" and transformed her "into a Venus who was not only prostrate, but prostituted as well."[25] In the late twentieth century, French psychiatrist Jacques Lacan would famously declare that anyone could tell that Bernini's Teresa was experiencing an orgasm, and art historian Irving Lavin would write, "Whether or not Teresa was hysterical or Bernini vulgar, the [sculptural] group evinces a physical eroticism, that well-meaning apologists do wrong to deny."[26] Franco Mormando's recent assessment is blunt: "The reason for the popularity of Bernini's Teresa is not merely artistic or religious, it also, let's be honest, has a lot to do with sex."[27] Such interpretations notwithstanding—and all subtlety aside—Bernini's Teresa reifies all of the central themes his predecessors aimed to convey symbolically, with consummate baroque metaphorical confidence: love, ecstasy, martyrdom, and the superiority of Catholicism.

Moreover, Bernini captures with exquisite genius an essential characteristic of Catholic belief inherent in the transverberation itself and all depictions of it: the coincidence of opposites. Teresa is a virgin experiencing a nuptial encounter with Christ; she is ecstatic, suspended between heaven and earth, evincing pain and bliss simultaneously, physically as well as spiritually; and she is dying a martyr's death, but yet very much alive, perhaps more alive than ever. Teresa's strange ecstasy is a mirror image of Mary the virgin who is impregnated with God incarnate, of the suffering Christ who brings eternal bliss to all humans, and of the dying Christ who rises from the grave and lives eternally embodied. Throw in a weaponized angel for good measure—because Teresa's text makes it necessary to do so—and you add yet another mirroring coincidence of opposites, in double reverse: a reference to the angel who stops Abraham from carrying out the sacrificing of his son Isaac, which had been commanded by God, as a test of faith. Teresa is a sacrificial victim, a martyr for sure, who is at once slain and spared by God through the agency of one of his angels.

After Bernini, all depictions of the transverberation—despite the brilliant artistry of many of them—seem to pale in comparison. Such a judgment is subjective, of course, and based on the amount of attention received by Bernini's masterpiece in the relatively recent past. Many depictions of the transverberation continued to be produced for four more centuries, especially in the seventeenth and eighteenth. Some of the best among them matched Bernini's ability to convey essential Catholic beliefs and values, but perhaps none were able to surpass his artistry or the notoriety of his suggestive masterpiece. But since this is a study of Teresa's *Vida*, the book, rather than of depictions of it, and since most representations of the transverberation produced after Bernini followed patterns set by the first few artists who tackled the subject, it is best at this point to narrow our focus.

One convenient way of summarizing all subsequent depictions of the transverberation is to subdivide them into three groups and mention some of the most distinctive examples in each of these categories. First, there were those renderings that followed the pattern set by Collaert, with

FIGURE 7. Josefa de Óbidos, 1672. *The Ecstasy of Saint Teresa of Ávila.*
Igreja (Church) Matriz de Nossa Senhora da Assunção, Cascais, Portugal.
UtCon Collection / Alamy Stock Photo.

depictions of Teresa surrounded by various angels and other
heavenly figures. In this category, one can list the renditions
of the following artists: Josefa de Óbidos (1672), one of the
very few women artists to interpret Teresa's ecstasy, who
made the flame at the tip of the dart prominent (fig. 7);
Carlo Cignani (1688), who filled his canvas with angels in
motion; Lucas Jordan (1688) and Peter Van Lindt (late seventeenth century), who limit the divine presence to the Holy
Spirit, in the form of a dove; Francesco Fontebasso (mid-
eighteenth century), whose angel wields the smallest of all
darts; Michelangelo Unterberger (1750), who involves all

three persons of the Trinity and whose Christ holds a cross larger than Teresa; Giuseppe Maria Colignon (1825), who included Saint John of the Cross, along with the Holy Family and many angels, and depicted Teresa kneeling on a manuscript copy of her *Vida*; and Jérôme-Marie Langlois (1836), whose dart-wielding angel is much taller than Teresa.

Then there were those artists who emulated Strozzi's painting, as well as Bernini's sculpture, and limited the event of the transverberation to Teresa and the wounding angel, or a small number of other angels. Among these, one can list Francisco Camilo (1664), whose angel wields a very long and narrow flame-tipped weapon; Nicola Fumo (1725), whose polychromed wood sculpture depicts the angel as a small cherub wounding Teresa from above; Antonio Viladomat (eighteenth century), whose painting is but one of scores of very similar depictions of a swooning Teresa being approached by the angel over her right shoulder; Pompeo Batoni (1743), whose boyish angel looks as if he is performing delicate surgery on a worried and definitely unecstatic Teresa; Giuseppe Bazzani (1750), whose brawny angel looks as if he is about to rape a drugged Teresa (fig. 8); and José Gutiérrez de la Vega (1825), whose angel interrupts Teresa at her writing table.

Lastly, there were artists who chose the emblematic approach of Wierix and portrayed Teresa as wounded by an arrow shot by a Cupid figure, either the Christ Child or an angel. Of these, a few stand out: Antonio de Pereda (1642), whose Christ Child is nearly indistinguishable from Cupid, save for the nimbus around his head and the blue globe of the earth upon which he stands, aiming his arrow at an ecstatic Teresa who is about to be crowned with roses by a

FIGURE 8. Giuseppe Bazzani, 1745–50. *Ecstasy of Saint Teresa*. Szépmûvészeti Múzeum, Budapest, Hungary. Art Collection 2 / Alamy Stock Photo.

cherub; Gregorio de Ferrari (1690), whose winged Cupid-like angel cannot be mistaken for the Christ Child, and whose dead-looking Teresa—an arrow protruding from her chest—is joined in her ecstasy by Saint Francis of Assisi and Saint Francis Xavier; and Antonio Mohedano in Spain (1650), Juan Rodríguez Juárez in Mexico, and Marcos Zapata in Peru (eighteenth century), who painted replicas of the Wierix engraving.

After the mid-nineteenth century, depictions of the transverberation began to wane drastically, along with depictions of mystical ecstasies as a whole, a peculiar development that merits more attention than it has received. All in all, however, Teresa's *Vida* had a significant impact on Catholic art for nearly three centuries, and continues to do so up until our day, at a devotional level, as any Internet search for images of Saint Teresa will quickly reveal.

What are we to make of this intensely visual dimension of the *Vida*, and especially of its role in the shaping of Teresa's legacy within the context of Catholic piety and identity? The answer may not be too surprising for anyone who already understands—as Teresa did—that to be a good Catholic after the advent of Luther meant that one had to be as different as possible from Protestants and skeptics.

Imagining the Unimaginable

The extremity of Teresa's mystical ecstasies—the outrageousness of her divinized self, so near to God himself—might have unnerved some clerics in her own day who were accustomed to tamer sorts of mysticism and unaccustomed to female assertiveness, but she and her contemporaries were living in new and difficult times in which Catholics needed a good measure of outrageousness.

Iconoclastic Protestants could not help but be horrified by visual depictions of Teresa's life. Everything about her was so wrong, so awfully and so unimaginably despicable. To depict scenes so ungodly and to venerate them was all the proof any good Protestant needed of the fact that the institution they called the "church of Rome" was indeed possessed by Satan.

And—polemics aside—what could have been more useful to Catholics than images of Teresa's life and of her miracles and ecstasies? She embodied their beliefs and identities in so many ways, and those images of her outrageously audacious encounters with the divine could perfectly fulfill the role assigned to sacred art by the Council of Trent:

> Let the bishops diligently teach that by means of the stories of the mysteries of our redemption portrayed in paintings and other representations the people are instructed and confirmed in the articles of faith, which ought to be borne in mind and constantly reflected upon; also that great profit is derived from all holy images, not only because the people are thereby reminded of the benefits and gifts bestowed on them by Christ, but also because through the saints the miracles of God and salutary examples are set before the eyes of the faithful, so that they may give God thanks for those things, may fashion their own life and conduct in imitation of the saints and be moved to adore and love God and cultivate piety.[28]

In sum, for many Catholics—especially those who were illiterate—the visual Teresa was perhaps more significant than the textual Teresa, and seeing her *Vida* more useful than reading it. If images were indeed the *libri pauperum*, or books of the poor, as Pope Gregory I declared nearly a thousand years before the publication of Teresa's *Vida*, then she has certainly had a larger audience staring at depictions of her transverberation than reading about it, not only among Catholic rustics in the preindustrial age, but long after it too, down to our own day, among the devout as well as among cultured secular elites for whom the veneration of art has become a cozy sort of piety.

From Enlightenment to Modernity

Skeptics, Seekers, Psychoanalysts, Fascists

New Age, New Challenge

"The seeker after truth must, once in the course of his life, doubt everything, as far as possible."[1] So said René Descartes in 1644, in his *Principles of Philosophy*. To understand the fate of Teresa's *Vida* during much of the eighteenth and nineteenth century, one need only read that one sentence, or its axiomatic version, which became a battle cry for many educated elites: *de omnibus dubitandum* (everything must be doubted).

As Teresa embodied the Catholic Reformation, Descartes embodied a negative reaction to it. Reared by a Catholic family and educated by Jesuits, this genius who invented analytical geometry and calculus chose to exalt doubt over faith, and in doing so challenged not only Catholicism but also Protestantism and all belief. Yet, in many ways he was as much a man of his age as the editors and translators who cranked out editions of the *Vida*, and as the patrons who commissioned paintings and sculptures of the transverberation. The seventeenth century was a transitional age, full of contradictions, in which witch burnings vied for attention with the rise of modern empirical science.[2]

The skepticism so keenly promoted by Descartes had been fermenting for well over a century before he was born, at multiple levels. The broadest and deepest level of non-conformity with church teachings was the indifference and freethinking skepticism of the common folk, of which nearly every clergyman complained, both Catholic and Protestant. As the records of the Spanish Inquisition and Geneva Consistory reveal, a deep-seated resistance to the normative theology and ethics of all churches could be found across a broad spectrum, caused by ignorance, apathy, disdain, and the vicissitudes of a life on the edge of mere subsistence.

A second type of nonconformism, closely related to the first, was that of elite freethinkers. Clergy in all churches of the Reformation era complained of such types. Francis de Sales (1567–1622), the Catholic reformer who would become titular bishop of Geneva, also singled out a type of learned libertine for censure, and warned the faithful to "guard against bad books" and not to read that "infamous Rabelais and certain other writers of our era who make a career out of doubting everything, of despising everything and making fun of the maxims of antiquity."[3] François Rabelais (1494–1553), a humanist Catholic cleric and one of the literary giants of the French Renaissance, would come to be known, among other things, for uttering as his final words on his deathbed, "I go to seek a great Perhaps" and "ring down the curtain, the farce is over."[4]

A third type of disbelief, bound closely to the second, was also elitist in nature and linked to the recovery of classical pagan ways of thinking that were intrinsically at odds with Christianity. A case in point is that of a single Epicurean text recovered in the fifteenth century: *On the Nature of Things*, a poem by Lucretius, written about two generations before the birth of Christ. This text, which had been lost for nearly a millennium, was discovered in a remote monastery and set into circulation by the humanist Poggio Bracciolini (1380–1459). Until then, Lucretius had been known only through descriptions by other ancient writers. Once he was brought to light again, however, Lucretius found disciples who thought that he had a lucid and rational understanding of reality superior to that of Christianity, and utterly incompatible with it.[5]

Voices were raised in Teresa's lifetime against the growth of Epicureanism and atheism, among both Catholics and Protestants. In 1564, shortly after she had finished writing the *Vida*, a Reformed Protestant pastor and a close associate of Calvin would warn that "the number of epicureans and atheists is much greater than anyone thinks." He would also complain that these atheists did not believe in "anything at all," and submitted everything to doubt, creating a personal religion for themselves that consisted of nothing more than "opinions that torment human brains."[6]

During the seventeenth century, skepticism and unbelief would continue to grow, and traditional Christian beliefs would erode within the ranks of the learned elite. Among the leading lights of this new age, a strident materialism prevailed. Julien Offray de La Mettrie would argue against the existence of the soul in his *Man the Machine* (1747). Paul Heinrich Dietrich, Baron d'Holbach, would attack Christianity as an impediment to the moral advancement of humanity and argue that there was "no necessity to have recourse to supernatural powers to account for the formation of things."[7] David Hume would raise skepticism to new levels and ridicule theistic beliefs, especially in his *Natural History of Religion* (1757) and *Dialogues Concerning Natural Religion* (1779). Even those "enlightened" elites who clung somewhat tenuously to belief in a deity, such as Immanuel Kant, denied the possibility of having any meaningful religion beyond an ethical code in his *Religion within the Limits of Reason Alone* (1793). The "enlightened" approach to religion would perhaps be best summed up by Thomas Paine in his *Age of Reason*: "My own mind is my own church. All national institutions of churches . . . appear to me no other than human inventions set up to terrify and enslave mankind, and monopolize power and profit."[8]

The tenor of this era needs to be taken into account as a significant element of the cultural context into which Teresa's *Vida* entered in its second and third century in existence, when its significance was challenged in new ways.

The Curious Life of the Post-Baroque *Vida*

During the seventeenth and eighteenth centuries, the *Vida* had a complex and bifurcated life. In various ways, the text continued to exert considerable influence within Catholic culture, claiming a prominent place in Catholic devotional life and assuming a new polemical edge vis-à-vis rising skepticism and secularism. On the other side of the battle lines, however, among those who were religiously indifferent or aggressively skeptical, the *Vida* received scant attention, or none at all, since explicit dismissals of the *Vida* were deemed unnecessary. Dismissing traditional Christianity or religion as a whole was the main concern for self-anointed progressives of all stripes, most of whom tended to vent their spleen on much larger issues than the mystical raptures of nuns.

This bifurcated life of the *Vida* extended for a century and a half, roughly between 1650 and 1800. During the first half of the nineteenth century, the life of the *Vida* entered a new phase, during which it seemed to slip into relative obscurity. Save for a French edition of the *Vida* in 1843 and a Spanish edition of the *Works* published in 1844, no new editions of the *Vida* appeared at all between 1800 and 1850.

Identifying what caused this dramatic drop in publications is challenging, but not altogether impossible, especially if one considers some of the most salient characteristics of this time period. In addition to contending with the rise of skepticism and secularism across Europe as a whole, traditional religion had to face the challenges posed by the upheavals of the Industrial Revolution and the extreme political and social turmoil caused by the French Revolution and the Napoleonic Wars. In Catholic areas especially, anticlerical and antireligious sentiment also began to increase.

In France, between 1789 and 1815, and most intensely during the Reign of Terror and the campaign to "de-Christianize" the nation in the 1790s, all church institutions were devastated, and many clergy imprisoned or guillotined, including the sixteen nuns of the Discalced Carmelite convent of Compiègne.[9] In Spain between 1798 and 1841 the Catholic clergy were gradually stripped of their property and privileges by successive governments. In the 1830s the state even suppressed the Discalced Carmelites and other religious orders.

Carmelites were one of the religious orders that were hardest hit during this turbulent era, and the numbers alone prove it. Before the outbreak of the French Revolution, the Carmelite order had thirteen thousand members worldwide, dispersed over fifty-four provinces. By the end of the nineteenth century, the order had shrunk to 727 members in a mere eight provinces. Since Carmelites were the leading promoters of Teresa's texts, is it that surprising that the *Vida* should have seemed moribund or even dead for so many decades?

As it turned out, however, the *Vida* was neither mortally wounded nor dead. It was merely hibernating, so to speak. Beginning in the mid-nineteenth century, presses throughout the world began to crank out new editions, at first haltingly, but then steadily at an ever-increasing rate, up until the Second World War. Then, in the postwar era, with the advent of the atomic age in the world at large and the reforms of the Second Vatican Council in the Catholic Church, the *Vida* sprang back to life with more vigor than ever before.

France was the first to bring the *Vida* out of hibernation in the nineteenth century, with a new edition in 1843. But Spain quickly regained its leadership role, with at least seven editions of Teresa's *Obras* and one edition of the *Vida* between 1844 and 1882. In the English-speaking world, two new translations of the *Vida* appeared, one by John Dalton in 1851 and the other by Henry James Coleridge in 1881.

In the twentieth century, the pace of publication speeded up considerably, especially after 1950, with so many new editions in Spanish that it is difficult to track them all, and new translations in several languages, including French, Italian, German, English, Flemish, and Portuguese, some of which have gone into multiple editions. In English alone, in the twentieth century, the *Vida* attracted no fewer than five translators: David Lewis (1911), Edgar Allison Peers (1944), J. M. Cohen (1957), and Kieran Kavanaugh and Otilio Rodriguez (1976). In the twenty-first century, the *Vida* continues to enjoy a robust publishing history in various languages, including yet another new translation in English by Mirabai Starr (2007), and the first ever in Chinese (2015).

Given the increased secularization of Western culture in the twentieth and twenty-first centuries, which makes that of the nineteenth century seem like child's play in comparison, what could account for this dramatic upsurge in the *Vida*'s popularity? By all reasonable measures of secular hegemony, the *Vida* should be dead by now, most surviving copies confined to the bookshelves of Catholic zealots who hanker for hair shirts and the Latin Mass of the Council of Trent. But that is not at all the case. Far from it.

One of the most surprising twists in the modern history of the *Vida*—perhaps the most astounding of all—is how it became attractive to a most unlikely assortment of strange bedfellows, many of whom despise one another, or at least would feel uncomfortable if asked to gather for tea in the same room—even in a very, very large room.

Seekers

First, let us consider the most traditional readers, her natural audience: the seekers, those women and men who are drawn to Teresa the saint and mystic because they venerate her and ache to follow in her footsteps. Teresa speaks to them directly through the *Vida*, as if she were still alive, across time and space. What she says in the *Vida* is not only true and totally real, as they see it, but also applicable to them. Some are even converted by the text, or so moved by it that their lives are never the same after reading it. A complete list of such faithful devotees—all sorts of monastics, priests, seminarians, and layfolk from all walks of life—would be long indeed, and impossible to compile. A few such devoted readers have become well known, and some have helped to popularize the *Vida* and to expand its reach.

One of the most remarkable of these devotees was a Discalced Carmelite nun, Thérèse of the Child Jesus and the Holy Face, better known as Saint Thérèse of Lisieux, or simply "The Little Flower." Thérèse was born in 1873, entered the convent at age fifteen, and died of tuberculosis in 1897. Her life was cut short at an early age, but in those brief twenty-four years, she lived an exemplary life, as much of a sign of contradiction to the secularists, skeptics, and atheists of her day as Teresa of Avila was to Protestants three centuries earlier. Her monastic name was a tribute to Teresa of Avila, and to two icons very dear to Teresa—a statuette of the infant Jesus and the image of Christ's face miraculously imprinted on the Veil of Veronica. Thérèse read the *Vida* and was deeply affected by it. Following in Teresa's footsteps, she embraced a Christocentric life of prayer and experienced ecstasies and visions, though to a lesser extent than her namesake.[10] Thérèse's best-known teaching, known as "the little way," which had an immense influence on twentieth-century Catholic piety—involved focusing on the small, insignificant, mundane tasks and assigning them great spiritual significance. As Thérèse put it:

> The most trivial work, the least action when inspired by love, is often of greater merit than the most outstanding achievement. It is not on their face value that God judges our deeds even when they bear the stamp of apparent holiness, but solely on the measure of love we put into them.[11]

This "little way" was nothing new among Discalced Carmelites. It was a core teaching of Saint Teresa, expressed in various ways throughout her texts, including the *Vida*, but perhaps most winsomely summarized in her quip "The Lord walks among the pots and pans in the kitchen, helping you both interiorly and exteriorly."[12] Thérèse would get all the credit for her "little way" in the twentieth century, despite its origins in Teresa's *Vida* because, like Teresa, she also wrote a spiritual autobiography, published posthumously in 1898 as *The Story of a Soul*, that took the Catholic world by storm, becoming a best seller in many languages. That autobiography would eclipse Teresa's *Vida*, due largely to its relative brevity, the devotional fervor surrounding its author, and its historical setting in the turbulent, skeptical present rather than the distant past. Credited with many miracles, Thérèse was canonized in 1925, and then quickly became one of the most popular Catholic saints, rivaling Saint Francis of Assisi and Saint Teresa of Avila herself. In 1997, Pope John Paul II would declare her a doctor of the church, bestowing on her the same rare honor as Teresa of Avila, even though Teresa had written much, much more and accomplished considerably more than her. In many ways, this recognition of Thérèse's significance—despite her meager publications—was a confirmation of the popularity of her "little way" and of the influence of Saint Teresa and her *Vida*.[13]

A very different kind of seeker who was deeply influenced by the *Vida*, and helped to create interest in Teresa among non-Catholics, was Evelyn Underhill (1875–1941), an Anglican laywoman who became a pioneer in the modern study of spirituality. A prolific author and untiring speaker with pronounced Catholic sensibilities, Underhill was the first woman invited to lecture Anglican clergymen,[14] as well as the first woman to lead spiritual retreats in the Church of England. Underhill's most influential book, *Mysticism*, first published in 1911 and still widely read more than a hundred years later, drew substantially from Teresa's *Vida*, quoting it extensively and including scores of references to it as representative of the most significant features of Christian mysticism. Out of its many salient features, two stood out as audacious and somewhat prescient of cultural shifts that would later emerge: her unabashed respect for mysticism as something positive rather than some pathological delusion, and her wholehearted ecumenical embrace of elements of Catholicism previously rejected by Protestantism.

Underhill's accomplishments were somewhat paradoxical, for while she heightened her culture's appreciation of tradition, she also overturned convention in various ways. First, as a layperson (in an ecclesiastical as well as academic sense) she dared to write and publish about the devotional heritage of Western Christians with commanding authority, eventually becoming more influential than many of those clerics and scholars who had long dominated the field. Second, as a woman she helped to change gender stereotypes in

a most disarming way, long before it was expected, principally through her renown as writer and teacher, and as a
great admirer of Teresa and other women mystics. Third, as
an Anglican she dared to think and pray ecumenically long
before it was fully acceptable, reaching back to the Catholic
heritage of the Church of England, and engendering an appreciation among Protestants for much that they had previously rejected and ignored.[15] Fourth, as a believing Christian living in an increasingly secular and materialistic
culture, she chose to call attention to the world of the spirit
and to teach about the human capacity for the divine and
supernatural. Fifth, as an erudite and astute analyst of higher
states of human consciousness, Underhill would also play an
important role (as we shall see below) as an eloquent oppo-
nent of psychological analyses of mysticism.

A third seeker greatly influenced by Teresa's *Vida* was the
German Jewish philosopher Edith Stein (1891–1942), who
converted to Catholicism in 1922 after reading Teresa's *Vida*
and eventually became a Discalced Carmelite nun in 1934,
taking the name Teresa Benedicta of the Cross. A disciple of
the phenomenologist philosopher Edmund Husserl, she
would publish several books on metaphysics, epistemology,
and philosophy of the mind, but her academic career was
hampered by discrimination, even though her mentor Husserl considered her intellectually superior to his other disciple, Martin Heidegger, now widely regarded as one of the
greatest philosophers of the twentieth century. After earning
her doctorate in 1916, Stein had difficulty finding a professor-
ship because she was a woman. Then, after the Nazis rose to
power, she was forbidden to teach because she was Jewish. In
1942, despite the fact that she had become a Catholic and a

nun, Stein was sent to the extermination camp at Auschwitz, where she was killed in its gas chambers, alongside her sister, who had also converted to Catholicism. Fifty-six years later, Pope John Paul II would canonize her as a saint and martyr, and pronounce her copatron of Europe, alongside Saint Catherine of Siena.

Edith Stein had been a seeker for truth since her teenage years when she abandoned the Jewish faith of her pious parents and became an atheist. Throughout her undergraduate and graduate schooling, she had continued that search for truth as a philosopher but gradually opened her search to include religion. In 1921, while visiting a friend, a chance encounter with the *Vida* changed her life. "I picked at random and took out a large volume," she would say later. "It bore the title *The Life of Teresa of Avila, written by herself.* I began to read, was at once captivated, and did not stop until I reached the end. As I closed the book, I said, 'That is the truth.'"[16]

Stein's influence on philosophers and theologians has increased steadily since her murder at Auschwitz, especially after the posthumous publication of her *Finite and Eternal Being* in 1950 and its translation into various languages. As a Discalced Carmelite nun, Stein wrote much that related to Teresa, including a summary of the *Vida,*[17] but her interests were so wide-ranging and her output so prolific that she cannot be pegged solely as a mystical writer or an expert on Teresa. Stein's *Collected Works* in German fill twenty-seven volumes.[18] These texts have a very wide audience and have also attracted considerable attention from feminists, ethicists, and political theorists.[19]

Dorothy Day (1897–1980), another seeker greatly influenced by Teresa's *Vida*, was an American journalist, writer, social activist, and founder of the Catholic Worker movement. Reminiscing about her early years as a free-thinker involved in radical leftist causes, she would later say in her own autobiography, "My radicalism at that time was confined to conversations and week-end beach parties with Communist friends."[20] As in the case of Edith Stein, Day discovered Teresa's *Vida* accidentally during a phase in her life when she was drawn to religion but still could not make any leap of faith. In Day's case, she stumbled onto the *Vida* while reading another book in which it was repeatedly mentioned and negatively assessed, *The Varieties of Religious Experience* by William James. Her curiosity piqued, Day picked up a copy of the *Vida* and her life was never the same again, for after reading it she felt ready to make her leap of faith and to join the Catholic Church in December 1927.

What attracted Day to Teresa above all was Teresa's impetuosity and her constant focus on her own imperfections. She was also awed by the way in which Teresa's mysticism caused her to be very active in the world. As she put it, "I had read the life of St. Teresa of Avila and fallen in love with her. She was a mystic and a practical woman, a recluse and a traveler, a cloistered nun and yet most active. She liked to read novels when she was a young girl, and she wore a bright red dress when she entered the convent." And, again, as had happened with Thérèse of Lisieux and Edith Stein, Day found Teresa so inspiring that she felt compelled to appropriate her name in some way, as an unwed mother: "There were other delightful little touches to the story of her life which made me love her and feel close to her. . . . So I decided to name my daughter after her."[21]

A tireless crusader, Day wrote constantly for the newspaper she had cofounded, the *Catholic Worker*, interweaving theological issues with social, political, and economic concerns. She also oversaw or inspired the creation of hundreds of settlement houses and farming communes, took part in civil rights marches, and promoted pacifism with uncommon energy. All in all, Dorothy Day came to represent religiously inspired social activism and Catholic involvement in public affairs. She also embodied the empowerment of the laity and of women in a rigidly hierarchical church run by male clerics.

Despite frequent calls from Catholic conservatives for a formal church censure of Day, and despite her famous quip "Don't call me a saint, I don't want to be dismissed that easily,"[22] she was nominated for sainthood soon after her death. And thanks to the support this nomination received from American bishops in 2012, she can now be addressed as a "servant of God," a title applicable to all who are in the first step of the long and complicated process of canonization.

Psychoanalysts and Other Diagnosticians

While some modern seekers and devotees found great inspiration in Teresa's *Vida*, a very different circle of readers was attracted to it as a rich source of pathologies to examine, both physical and psychological.

Eighteenth- and nineteenth-century skeptics who viewed mysticism and all other forms of religious "enthusiasm" negatively, as something to be dismissed and eradicated, tended to ignore Teresa's *Vida*. With the development of the new science of psychology in the late nineteenth century, an area of inquiry in which religious experiences became a subject of greater interest, Teresa's *Vida* gained a new audience. As one might expect, initial psychological studies tended to view mystical ecstasies as symptoms of mental illness and to conceive of the role of the psychologist as that of a diagnostician who could identify the pathologies involved. Ironically, this skeptical, materialistically based approach was not much different from that of the sixteenth- and seventeenth-century inquisitors who sought to discern whether the mystical claims of anyone—male or female, young or old—were due to mental illness rather than encounters with demonic or divine beings.

Early psychological interpretations of Teresa's *Vida* were superficial and highly dismissive. Pioneering French neurologist Jean-Martin Charcot (1825–96) was among the first men of science to peg Saint Teresa as an "undeniable hysteric." Other medical authorities followed suit. In his *Psychopathia Sexualis* (1866), Richard von Krafft-Ebing not only dismissed mystics as hysterics—a pathological condition he linked to nymphomania—but also famously argued that "sexual feeling is really the root of all ethics . . . and religion." Focusing intently on Bernini's transverberation sculpture, and undeterred by the fact that Bernini's Teresa was made of marble, he diagnosed her as "sinking in a hysterical faint."[23] Similarly, in their *Studies in Hysteria* (1893–95), Josef Breuer and his disciple Sigmund Freud relied on the *Vida* for their diagnosis of Teresa as a highly functional but mentally ill genius who could be considered "the patron saint of hysterics."[24] Breuer and Freud would soon thereafter part ways, as Freud began to assign an increasingly prominent role to sexuality in the development of hysteria, but their diagnosis of Teresa's mysticism as a psychological disorder set the tone for many subsequent psychoanalytic appraisals of the *Vida*.[25]

Few within the nascent field of psychology dared to challenge such disparaging diagnoses, but in his 1901 Gifford Lectures at the University of Edinburgh, published the following year as *The Varieties of Religious Experience*, American philosopher and psychologist William James fearlessly called into question all scientific disregard for the positive dimension of mystical experiences. "One may truly say," argued James, "that personal religious experience has its root and centre in mystical states of consciousness."[26] A physiologist by training, and a self-described pragmatist, James was not willing to dismiss religion as bunk, or dangerous, and he focused on the positive effects that mystical experiences had on certain historical figures, such as Teresa of Avila, who stands out prominently in his book. One should not assume that mystics are mentally ill, James argued. On the contrary, he said, "[t]hey offer us hypotheses . . . which we may voluntarily ignore, but which as thinkers we cannot possibly upset. The supernaturalism and optimism to which they would persuade us may, interpreted in one way or another, be after all the truest of insights into the meaning of life."[27]

James had read the *Vida* carefully, and his arguments in defense of the positive effects of mysticism often rely on examples from it. Like Breuer and Freud, he praised her ability to engage with the world. Nonetheless, his pragmatic assessment of the ultimate value of her accomplishments was not entirely positive:

> Saint Teresa . . . had a powerful intellect of the practical
> order. She wrote admirable descriptive psychology, pos-
> sessed a will equal to any emergency, great talent for poli-
> tics and business, a buoyant disposition, and a first-rate
> literary style. She was tenaciously aspiring, and put her
> whole life at the service of her religious ideals. Yet so pal-
> try were these, according to our present way of thinking,
> that . . . I confess that my only feeling in reading her has
> been pity that so much vitality of soul should have found
> such poor employment. In spite of the sufferings which
> she endured, there is a curious flavor of superficiality
> about her genius.[28]

Ultimately, James was unimpressed with the social and ethical utility of establishing seventeen convents. And he was
also repulsed by some aspects of Teresa's character that he
deemed to be characteristic of a "typical shrew," that is,
someone who is totally self-absorbed and highly manipula-
tive. Her shrewishness was proven, as he saw it, by "the bus-
tle of her style, as well as of her life," which was nothing but
"voluble egotism" and status seeking. Even worse, James
concluded, Teresa was clever enough to fool her contemporaries into mistaking her egocentric wiles for sanctity:

> In the main her idea of religion seems to have been that of
> an endless amatory flirtation—if one may say so without
> irreverence—between the devotee and the deity; and apart
> from helping younger nuns to go in this direction by the
> inspiration of her example and instruction, there is abso-
> lutely no human use in her, or sign of any general human
> interest. Yet the spirit of her age, far from rebuking her, ex-
> alted her as superhuman.[29]

Negative assessments such as this did not suppress interest in mysticism as something positive. It could be argued, in fact, that the work of James, Breuer, Freud, and other psychologists actually helped devotees of Teresa to gain strength, not in numbers, necessarily, but at least in their convictions and in their ability to express them. Nothing proves this assertion more dramatically than Evelyn Underhill's masterpiece, *Mysticism*, published a year after the death of James, which was a detailed and highly lucid response to the negativity of the psychologists. "Contemplative genius," argued Underhill, need not be diagnosed as mental illness. Underhill blasted away with mordant wit at the blindness of the psychologists of her day: "They have not hesitated to call St. Paul an epileptic, St. Teresa 'the patron saint of hysterics'; and have found room for most of their spiritual kindred in various departments of the pathological museum." In the process of trying to free mystics from the pathological museum of the psychologists, Underhill provided seekers like herself—including Edith Stein and Dorothy Day—a grammar of dissent. Over and against their materialist and physiological frame of reference, Underhill proposed a metaphysical and spiritual one, at once logical and poetic:

> Mysticism . . . is the name of that organic process which involves the perfect consummation of the Love of God: the achievement here and now of the immortal heritage of man. Or if you like it better—for this means exactly the same thing—it is the art of establishing his conscious relation with the Absolute.[30]

Underhill's work would inspire many to take seriously the claims of mystics such as Teresa, and more than a hundred years after its publication, her *Mysticism* remains a constant point of reference, especially among scholars.

But Underhill's claims for the reality of that "Absolute" could scarcely curb the self-confident, materialistic approach of the psychologists. Throughout the twentieth century, and well into the twenty-first, professional and armchair diagnosticians have continued to mine Teresa's *Vida* for psychopathological gold. The prevailing attitude in the medical and scientific professions toward anyone who claimed experiences of the sort described by Teresa was best summed up in 1935 by the atheist mathematician and philosopher Bertrand Russell: "From a scientific point of view," he quipped, "we can make no distinction between the man who eats little and sees heaven and the man who drinks much and sees snakes. Each is in an abnormal physical condition, and therefore has abnormal perceptions."[31]

Russell's sarcasm sheds light on an undeniable fact: similarities between psychoses and mystical trances suggest that physical disorders might be the cause of both phenomena. Consequently, since the *Vida* describes Teresa's many somatic ailments in detail, it was inevitable that pathologists in disciplines other than psychology would attribute her raptures to physical rather than mental or emotional causes. One diagnosis that gained substantial attention was that of temporal lobe epilepsy, some symptoms of which match physical and mental conditions of raptures described by Teresa.[32] Whether her ecstasies were attributed to epilepsy or some other neurological cause, all such diagnoses shared a common assumption: that the extrasensory events described in the *Vida* were hallucinations produced by natural physiological causes within the human brain rather than by encounters with supernatural realities or with anything one might call the Absolute.[33] Such assumptions have been tested in laboratories, especially with a device dubbed the "God Helmet," which was developed by inventor Stanley Koren and neuroscientist Michael Persinger to study the effects of magnetic stimulation in the temporal lobes of the brain. According to Persinger, his God Helmet has induced mystical experiences in many of his subjects, and his experiments have led to the creation of a new field of scientific research that calls itself "neurotheology," which focuses on the neurophysiology of religious experience.[34] Although some experts in the scientific community have yet to accept the validity of this research, it continues to attract attention, most probably because it seems to confirm the basic materialist assumption that mystics are freaks of nature rather than links to the supernatural.[35]

Another twentieth-century search for a physiological cause of Teresa's mysticism involves hallucinogenic drugs. Although no one has yet suggested that Teresa's ecstasies were chemically induced, attempts have been made to compare the ecstasies and visions of the *Vida* to the parallel experiences of subjects in LSD-assisted psychotherapy. This research has questioned the assumptions of the psychoanalysts as well as that of the neurophysicists, positing that Teresa's "convulsions" were not hysteria or some other sort of "degenerative psychopathology" but rather a very positive and healthy progression of the self to "higher states of consciousness" through prayer.[36] In other words, these researchers who have carried out controlled empirical experiments with LSD have questioned the dominant materialism of the scientific community—while employing psychotropic substances as mystical catalysts—and arrived at spiritual conclusions similar to those of Evelyn Underhill.

The alluring charm of God Helmets and psychedelic drugs notwithstanding, neurological etiologies have yet to trump psychological ones in the case of Teresa, especially when it comes to issues of sex and gender, which became a major cultural obsession in the latter part of the twentieth century, a fixation so intense that it became a defining trait of the age itself. In this area, one of the most prominent psychoanalysts to turn his attention to Teresa's *Vida* was Freud's disciple Jacques Lacan (1901–81). His interpretation of Teresa was not based on any reading of the text of the *Vida* itself, however, but rather on a cursory perusal of Bernini's sculpture of the transverberation. Lacan, a demigod of sorts in French intellectual circles in the second half of the twentieth century, wielded enormous influence in many fields beyond psychoanalysis, including philosophy, linguistics, and critical theory, especially post-structuralism. Lacan employed Teresa's ecstasies as proof positive of a "fact" he had discovered as a psychoanalyst: that women inhabit a sphere of cognition outside language. In his lecture "God and the Jouissance of Woman," he argued that Teresa had experienced "supplementary jouissance," that is, a kind of rapture that surpasses that of sexual orgasm, but which women are unable to fully comprehend or explain. "You only have to go and look at Bernini's statue in Rome," he said, "to understand immediately that she's having an orgasm, there is no doubt about it. And what is her *jouissance*, her orgasm from? It is clear that the essential testimony of the mystics is that they are experiencing it but know nothing about it."[37]

Not surprisingly, Lacan's sexualized psychoanalysis of Teresa was vehemently rejected by feminist scholars and writers who refused to be cowed by his exalted stature. Two of his most formidable opponents were Luce Irigaray and Julia Kristeva.

Three decades younger than Lacan, and a former disciple of his, the feminist psychoanalyst, philosopher, and polymath Irigaray dismissed Lacan's interpretation of Teresa in her book *Speculum of the Other Woman*, arguing that the mystical realm is not beyond female cognition but rather "the only place in the history of the West in which woman speaks and acts so publicly."[38] As a counterpoint to Lacan's notion of jouissance, Irigaray employed some dense jargon of her own, including the neologism "la mystérique," which was central to her complex feminist deconstruction of Freudian and Lacanian psychology. Although perhaps only comprehensible to a small number of specialists, Irigaray's critique of Lacan also represents a trenchant repudiation of the interpretation of mystical experience as a pathology and an oblique meditation on the integrity of Teresa's *Vida*.

Julia Kristeva, a Bulgarian émigré to France, is another highly respected feminist author who delves into psychoanalysis, philosophy, semiotics, and literary criticism. Her most recent novel, *Teresa, My Love: An Imagined Life of the Saint of Avila*, seeks to integrate past and present through the character of a French psychoanalyst who becomes obsessed with Teresa. Kristeva interweaves her own autobiography with fiction, history, and psychoanalysis, turning her "imagined" life of Teresa into a diagnostic critique of present-day Western culture and society.[39]

In her earlier work—which is embedded in her novel—Kristeva's psychoanalyzing of Teresa is as riddled with psychojargon and neologisms as Irigaray's, and equally inaccessible to anyone unacquainted with Freud and Lacan or with recent trends in semiotics and literary theory. What emerges out of the thick fog of theoretical argot is a Teresa who has escaped from the "psychic tomb" of melancholy in which all mystics find themselves. Employing concepts such as "Imaginary Father" and "the abjection of the mother"—which she sees as essential to understanding the development of the human psyche—Kristeva argues that Teresa succeeded in overcoming her melancholy because of the healing potential inherent in Christian symbols, especially those of the Virgin Mary as "ideal mother" and God as "Oedipal and symbolic father." Kristeva proposes that Teresa's mysticism was not a mental illness but rather a means to a goal, a way to overcome male hegemony and achieve Lacanian jouissance, that is, "the direct re-experiencing of the physical pleasures of infancy and of later sexuality."[40] What this jouissance might be in metaphysical terms is not at all clear, but it is most definitely not the same as Teresa's "God" or Underhill's "Absolute," since it is not really an encounter with a higher reality. Nonetheless, it is still something positive rather than psychopathological.

Fascists

Among the various twists and turns in the life of the *Vida* in the twentieth century, one of the oddest was its appeal to Spanish Fascists. How and why did Fascists come to view

Teresa as one of theirs? To fully understand this odd coincidence of opposites, one must first come to grips with the
turmoil of the Spanish Civil War of 1936–39 and the role of
religion in this conflict.

By 1936, Spain was intensely polarized. On the left side of
the political spectrum, an amalgam of anticlerical parties
viewed Spain's Catholic Church and religion in general as a
nefarious component of an unjust status quo. Included in
this coalition were various factions of Communists, Social-
ists, and anarchists. On the right side an odd assortment of
traditionalist parties clung tightly to Catholicism as the
lynchpin of national identity and social and political order.
The Right included monarchists, democrats of various sorts,
and Fascists. As this polarization intensified throughout the
1920s and early 1930s, Centrists dwindled and lost political
power, leaving Spain sharply divided between an aggressive
Left bent on transforming Spain and ridding it of religion
and an increasingly defensive Right intent on resisting any
such change. Since both the Left and the Right were fragmented, comprised as they each were of parties with differ-
ing views, the issue of religion rose in significance as a unify-
ing factor for both sides. Just as the common loathing of
Catholicism helped keep leftists together, despite their
many disagreements on other issues, the defense of Catholicism became one of the chief goals of the Right, and one of
their tightest bonds.

After the outbreak of open war between the Left and the
Right in July 1936, the rightists (referred to alternatively as
Nationalists or Fascists), who made Catholicism a defining
characteristic of their cause, chose Saint Teresa as their patron saint. This evocation of Teresa as an avatar of Spanish

Catholic identity had actually begun long before the Civil War, due to the increasing threat posed to traditional Spanish Catholicism by secularists in the course of the nineteenth century. In 1882, the three-hundredth anniversary of Teresa's death brought forth a revival of interest in her work and legacy, and marked the beginning of a modern appropriation of Teresa as an icon of Spanish identity.[41] Prominent intellectuals who linked Teresa to the national character in different ways included the novelist Leopoldo Alas, better known as "Clarín" (1852–1901); the writers and critics Emilia Pardo Bazán (1851–1921), José Martínez Ruiz, better known as "Azorín" (1873–1967), and Blanca de los Ríos (1862–1956); and the philosopher Miguel de Unamuno (1864–1936). Among those who interpreted Teresa as representative of some sort of national—even genetic— mystical genius, none was perhaps more influential than the polymath Marcelino Menéndez y Pelayo (1856–1912), who argued that Teresa represented a distinctly Spanish philosophy linked to mysticism that was "the highest and most sublime philosophy" of all.[42] Another scholar who exalted the "Spanishness" of Teresa over and against "incorrect" interpretations by foreigners was the Claretian priest José Dueso. As he saw it, Teresa should be required reading for Spaniards, for the "manly" virtues and "iron temper" she embodied were a perfect antidote to the "feeble and effeminate character" of early twentieth-century society.[43] In sharp contrast, the historian Américo Castro proposed in 1926—two decades before Teresa's Jewish ancestry was rediscovered—that the "Spanishness" of Teresa's *Vida* could be traced to Jewish and Muslim influences, especially the attitude of *vivir desviviéndose* (living in disagreement with oneself), a trait he identified as a defining characteristic of Spanishness.[44]

With boosters such as Menéndez Pelayo and Dueso, the nationalizing of Teresa intensified among Spanish Catholics, especially in the face of growing political instability. In 1922, the venerable University of Salamanca awarded Teresa an honorary doctorate, declaring her a "genius of our race," and an archdeacon of the cathedral of Ávila proclaimed her a patron of Spanish military personnel.[45] In the early 1930s the cult of Teresa as a nationalist racial avatar continued to grow. About the same time, a biography of Saint Teresa by Gabriel de Jesús appeared, *La Santa de la Raza*, meaning "saint of the Spanish race."[46] This peculiar assignation, which was based on total ignorance of her Jewish ancestry, turned Teresa into the patroness of a distinct race, and gained favor with Franco and his Fascists as they conducted their war against Republican Rojos (Reds). In 1939, Silverio de Santa Teresa—who would eventually become superior general of the Discalced Carmelites—sealed the acceptance of this unique title by publishing *Saint Teresa of Jesus: Supreme Synthesis of the Race*. A tireless promoter of Teresa as an ideal figure, Silverio de Santa Teresa had earlier published another book that would influence Fascists, titled *Saint Teresa: Model of Christian Femininity*.[47]

Such heavy-handed promotion of Teresa as the embodiment of Spanishness and of all the traditional values rejected by the leftists might have gained less traction had something most unusual not occurred that linked Franco to Teresa physically, turning him into her most fervent devotee. The bizarre events in question, which involve a severed hand of Saint Teresa, seem to foreshadow the so-called magical realism that would later become the hallmark of Latin American literature.

Back in the late sixteenth century, when Saint Teresa's incorruptible corpse began to be carved up by relic seekers, her left hand had been sent to Lisbon.[48] Three centuries later, due to anticlerical hostility in Portugal, that hand, encased in a silver jewel-studded reliquary, was taken in 1910 to the Discalced Carmelite convent at Ronda, in southern Spain. In late 1936, when Republicans seized that town and ransacked every church and chapel, they found this relic, but instead of destroying it, as they had done with innumerable others, they crammed it into a suitcase along with other loot—some jewelry, a lacquered box full of gold, some crucifixes, and 110,000 pesetas—and took it to Málaga. When Franco's troops drove the Republicans from Málaga in early 1937, they were very surprised to find this suitcase in a general's office. Very quickly, Teresa's hand was sent to Franco, who claimed it for himself. A sermon preached in Salamanca when Franco received Teresa's hand employed the rhetoric that would continue to be used by the Fascists for decades:

> As Teresa is the Mother of spiritual people, she is also *La Santa de la Raza* (Saint of our race) . . . Teresa's magisterial spirituality is a reflection of Spain's spirituality . . . and of the heroic spirit of our Reconquista, our discovery of America and our civilizing of it, our role in the Council of Trent and the Battle of Lepanto . . . She is watching over Spain from Heaven, and this is why her hand has been brought here providentially, to Salamanca, which is now the heart of Spain, where her Caudillo [Franco] resides,

carrying on the struggle to preserve Christian spirituality and civilization.[49]

Two months later, Silverio de Santa Teresa would publish an article titled "The Hand of the Saint Redeemed from Bolshevik Slavery," in which he promoted Teresa's new political role, emphasizing the miraculous power she was lending to the Fascist cause through the hand that was now in Franco's possession. As he saw it, Teresa's hand had already dealt a blow to the "Bolsheviks" and freed herself so she could assist Franco's Fascist army:

> Saint Teresa refused to perform the miracle of blinding the thieves to prevent them from stealing her relic so that she could perform an even bigger and more opportune miracle, that of [a] slap in the face (forgive the expression) to General Villalba, and making him flee from Málaga so it could fall quickly to our troops and she could join us.[50]

After taking the city of Madrid on Saint Teresa's birthday (28 March 1939), Franco petitioned the bishop of Málaga for permanent custody of the saint's hand. Franco's letter to the bishop said that he had "a fervent devotion to the most Spanish of saints," and that he had perceived Teresa's constant protection in all his battles. "Surely," continued the petition, "the Mystical Doctor, one of the greatest glories of our nation, who used to order her nuns to pray for those who governed Spain (as I believe they still do), would be immensely pleased to have her hand next to the Caudillo who has proposed—with God's help—to forge a new Spain that will be as great as the empire-building Spain of the Saint's own day." The bishop granted Franco's request,[51] saying:

Your Excellency should indeed keep the hand so you may continue to express your fervent devotion to it in the intimacy of your home . . . and so this venerated hand of the great Spanish Saint can continue to guide your steps in peace-building, just as it guided them with so much good fortune during the recent war.[52]

For the rest of his life, up until the day he died, Franco would keep the relic near him, and even travel with it. He would also turn Teresa into a Fascist, literally, naming her an honorary general in his army, and awarding her a medal, which was attached to the reliquary containing her hand. A visitor to Franco's office was once surprised to find him signing death sentences while seated at his desk, sipping hot chocolate, with Teresa's hand next to him near his elbow.[53]

Creating a Fascist Teresa was not entirely Franco's doing. Among Spanish Fascists, devotion to Teresa ran high, but the piety they cultivated was utilitarian and it had more to do with the political realm than with the sacred or supernatural. A salient example of this pragmatic Fascist piety— and one of the oddest—was the attempt to turn Teresa into a model of "National Catholicism" and "Christian feminism." The Fascist objective was to "re-Christianize" Spanish women, that is, to turn them away from modern liberal models of womanhood, especially Marxist ones, and have them return to their "natural" role as mothers and housekeepers who were totally subservient to their husbands.[54]

No one embraced this campaign with more zeal than Pilar Primo de Rivera, younger sister of the fallen Falangist/ Fascist leader José Antonio Primo de Rivera, who had been one of Franco's closest associates.[55] The Falange was an anti-Communist movement eventually absorbed by the Fascists in Spain, which Franco ably used to suit his needs. In 1937, Pilar Primo de Rivera, leader of the Women's Section of the Falange (Sección Femenina [SF])—who had once been offered to Adolf Hitler as a fitting bride—proclaimed Teresa the patron of that group, emphasizing her virtues as a role model: a thoroughly Spanish woman who worked hard, kept quiet, did her household chores, and obeyed her male superiors.[56] The chief message of the SF was simple enough: the "natural" identity of women is religious and subservient, and these characteristics were best exemplified by Teresa. It is no mere coincidence, then, that the SF's "magazine for women" was given the title *Teresa*.

Members of the SF were loyal to the Falangist version of Fascism and to a very specific "eternal essence" of Spain embodied in two women: Queen Isabel I, "the Catholic queen," and Saint Teresa. Queen Isabel was the monarch who took charge of "cleansing" Spain by ridding it of Jews, Muslims, and heretics, and of bringing Catholicism to the Americas while being subservient to her husband, King Ferdinand. Teresa was the saint who combined faith ("a pure knowledge of God") with utilitarian action ("having her feet on the ground").[57] Pilar Primo de Rivera was fond of comparing SF members with *teresianas*, laywomen who had vowed to dedicate their lives to the education of children. As Pilar Primo de Rivera saw it, women did not need to develop creative talents, for they had none. According to her, women can never discover anything, for God had given that kind of intellectual ability to men only. The highest aim women could have was to be like Teresa, who, according to Pilar, constantly relied on her male superiors and confessors to tell her what to think.[58] Whether or not Pilar Primo de Rivera ever read the *Vida* is immaterial: she had an agenda to promote, and her version of Teresa's life served that agenda perfectly. Or so she thought.

The SF was no frothy lunch club for the wives and daughters of Falangist Fascists. After the war, its power—and that of Pilar Primo de Rivera—grew considerably. From the end of the war in 1939 to the death of Franco in 1975, Pilar ran the SF as a member of Franco's Council of State, and the SF was a branch of the Fascist state that wielded considerable power over the women of Spain. Any woman who aspired to land a government job or who needed official documentation, such as a passport or driver's license, had to serve the SF for six months. Consequently, the SF and its office of Social Service for Women provided quasi-mandatory training in a very peculiar kind of Teresian piety, much as mandatory military service provided training in Fascism for men.

This nationalistic Catholicism imposed on Spain during Franco's dictatorship might have been somewhat superficial, but it was nonetheless intense. Although many Spaniards were forced to dissemble, conforming to Catholicism was equated with being Spanish, and any offense against the Catholic faith could be punished by the civil authorities. Moreover, certificates of baptism were required for routine functions of life, religious instruction was required in all schools, and all print media were carefully censored, along with radio and television broadcasts and films.

Embedded in this forced re-Catholization effort, Teresa's *Vida* enjoyed a rebirth, with many new editions being published, and many students being required to read it. Consequently, it could be argued that more people were exposed to it or forced to read it during these thirty-six years than at any other time in history. It could also be argued that by promoting Teresa and her *Vida* in such a repressive way, Franco's Fascist regime might have also made more people despise Teresa and her autobiography than ever before, or since. The Fascist appropriation of Teresa, which included a propagandist use of the *Vida*, had little impact outside of Spain—save for making available more editions of the *Vida* in the Spanish-speaking world—but within Spain itself, turning Teresa into a Fascist icon did much to create hostility toward her rather than devotion or admiration, for there were many Spaniards who resented the Franco regime and loathed what its hijacked Teresa represented.

As the world was plunged into war in 1939, and far too many unimaginable horrors, the Fascist Teresa would become an odd curiosity, and would soon be eclipsed by other surprising Teresas, some as previously unimaginable as the Fascist one, and as shocking to the devout.

The Post-Mystical Intermillennial *Vida*

In 1926, before Teresa became the darling of Fascists, the Spanish cultural historian Américo Castro observed that the saint had three kinds of readers: "the devout, the erudite, and those who search for nervous disorders."[1] Little did he suspect how much this would change in the years that followed, especially in the second half of the twentieth century and the first two decades of the twenty-first—the intermillennial era—when the *Vida* began to attract various types of readers who would subject it to new interpretations and appropriations. Some of these interpretations would be as much of a departure from tradition as those of the psychoanalysts and Fascists, and perhaps as shocking or potentially offensive to Teresa's devotees. They would also be no less intent on revealing the "real" Teresa as all previous interpretations, even while admitting that their aim was to reveal a Teresa who was intensely relevant to immediate this-worldly concerns and scholarly trends.

These recent interpretations approach the *Vida* from various perspectives: as a literary gem, an icon of Hispanic culture, a feminist or queer manifesto, a mirror of sixteenth-century attitudes toward race, class, and gender, and various other issues of interest to scholars and activists. At the same time, some of these recent approaches have broadened the scope of the *Vida*'s context, including previously ignored perspectives that allow us to understand Teresa's spirituality as encompassing more than her ecstasies, visions, and levitations. In addition, the *Vida* has also continued to hold its significance as a religious otherworldly text among devotees with divergent beliefs and agenda: Protestants who wished to reclaim the mystical tradition, conservative Catholics who wished to do the same, liberal Catholics who favored a larger role for women in their church, and others who disagreed with these three camps and with one another on how best to interpret Saint Teresa and her autobiography.[2]

In brief, as the twentieth century ended and the twenty-first began, Saint Teresa's *Vida* became a Rorschach test of sorts, in secular as well as religious circles: something akin to the inkblots employed by psychologists to elicit interpretations from their patients, attracting variant readings, each of which mirrored issues of great concern for those doing the interpreting.[3] Consequently, the *Vida*'s significance—while contested—actually increased at the turn of the millennium.

One of the most salient features of Western culture during the intermillennial age was the proliferation of interpretive schools of thought that identified themselves as definitive breaks with the past and proudly employed the prefix "post" in naming themselves: such as postmodern, poststructural, postfeminist, postsecular, and postcolonial, to name but some of the most prominent. While there was no agreement on the exact meaning of these terms, or about their significance, one assumption did link those who identified with any or all of these "posts": the conviction that

Western culture had arrived at some sort of apogee (or nadir) that transcended history, and that such a turning point allowed Western intellectuals to discard the past and finally embrace some unassailable obvious truth that had eluded all their benighted ancestors. Consequently, these various "posts" shared in a common epistemological and historical conceit, as well as in a triumphalist claim to finality, each proclaiming itself an interpretive end point, a "post" after which there could be no more "posts." Ironically, although the denial of epistemological certainty marked the age, these various post-whatevers shared a cocky, self-assured certainty that resembled that of the eighteenth-century Enlightenment.

Given the intensity with which these interpretive approaches took hold, it stands to reason that some of the new secular approaches to Teresa and her *Vida* in the inter-millennial decades could be classified as post-mystical, that is, as interpretations that focused on dimensions of the *Vida* other than the one that was of the greatest interest to Teresa, her fellow nuns, confessors, superiors, contemporaries, and spiritual devotees. This is not to say that some of these interpretations refused to take the mystical dimension seriously—for some have most certainly done so—but rather that they deliberately chose to examine Teresa's text from a this-worldly rather than an otherworldly vantage point. And these new approaches can be placed on a spectrum, varying in the intensity of their interest in the transcendental dimension of the text, with great interest at one end and none whatsoever at the other, and a somewhat scrambled mix in between. At their most extreme, some of these interpretations have assumed that the *Vida*'s supernatural dimension is of secondary significance, or no significance whatsoever.

To a considerable extent, the psychoanalysts and Fascists had already taken a post-mystical approach, each with some this-worldly pragmatic end in mind, one medical-scientific, the other political. In contrast, most of Teresa's intermillennial interpreters—most of whom have been scholars—have taken a more abstract approach. Although some have had a specific ideological agenda in mind, such as feminism, their take on Teresa and the *Vida* has been more of a search for historical or interpretative truth than an attempt to reshape the mundane world. In this respect, then, ironically, the post-mystical interpreters share much with the spiritual seekers for whom the mysticism of the *Vida* is so important.

During the intermillennial age, much has been written about Saint Teresa, but not all of these publications have focused on the *Vida* per se, or on its legacy. Consequently, our focus here shall be limited strictly to those publications that have relied on the *Vida* or sought to interpret it and its author in a new light. Curiously, the vast majority of such studies come from North American scholars. And the reasons for this cultural shift remain unanalyzed.

Historical Approaches

In the Catholic world, all developments in the intermillennial period were linked in one way or another to the Second Vatican Council (1963–65). Every aspect of Catholic life, thought, and devotion was affected by the changes this council brought about, many of which were immense, and all of which were put into effect quickly in the second half of the 1960s.

It stands to reason, then, that the study of Teresa within the Catholic world was affected by the spirit of *aggiornamento*—or "updating"—breathed into all things Catholic by the council. The Discalced Carmelite order, in particular, embraced this process of *aggiornamento*, and as a result, some of the younger Discalced Carmelite friars in Spain took up the challenge of updating Teresian studies and placing Teresa and her writings in the context of the history and culture of her day and age, taking factors into account beyond theology and hagiography.

In the 1970s Discalced Carmelite scholars such as Teófanes Egido, Enrique Llamas, and Tomás Alvarez began to publish essays and books based on new approaches to Teresa's texts, and on new evidence that they and others began to unearth from Spanish archives. In addition, this generation of Discalced Carmelites began to establish closer relations with secular scholars, and to collaborate with them. Certain subjects previously ignored came to the fore as a result, such as Teresa's Jewish background, her role as a woman in a misogynist church and society, her relations with the Inquisition, and her connections to other reformers. Links established between Carmelites and secular scholars such as Franciso Márquez Villanueva and Rosa Rossi cleared a path for a new generation of scholars in the 1980s and 1990s, many of whom were Americans, a national cohort that had previously shied away from Teresian studies.

One of the most significant developments in the years after 1980 has been the interest taken in Teresa and her *Vida* by English-speaking historians whose studies have combined social and intellectual history. One of the most significant examples of this post-mystical historical turn is Jodi Bilinkoff's *The Avila of Saint Teresa*, which draws heavily on the *Vida* in order to analyze the social context of Teresa's life and of her reform of the Carmelite order.[4] Focusing on the political, social, and economic structures of the city of Ávila, as well as on the issues of class differences and of Teresa's Jewish lineage—which made Teresa something of an outsider—Bilinkoff analyzes how the radical novelty of Teresa's reform caused considerable friction and how that dissonance shaped Teresa's life and work, and even her mysticism. The issue of the prayer of quiet, for instance, is set in a socioeconomic context. Silent prayer was viewed as threatening, she argues convincingly, not only for theological reasons but practical ones as well, because vocal prayer was the lynchpin of the patronage system that funded convents. By insisting on silent prayer and on radical poverty, Teresa rejected the symbiotic relationship between Ávila's elites and her nuns. Since patrons relied on the vocal prayer of the nuns they funded, and since the city of Ávila relied on that funding to sustain its convents, the city's elites felt threatened by Teresa and her silent prayer. And since Teresa also rejected dowries as absolutely necessary for entrance into her convent, the economic threat posed by her was viewed as doubly threatening. Bilinkoff's perspective has helped to set the *Vida* in its social context, and to make its readers aware that Teresa's mysticism was not confined to the supernatural realm.

Another significant post-mystical historical study is Gillian Ahlgren's *Teresa of Avila and the Politics of Sanctity*, which analyzes Teresa and her *Vida* from a sociopolitical perspective, with a touch of feminist theorizing.[5] According to Ahlgren, Teresa's life and work—and her mysticism too—can be best understood as a woman's constant struggle for recognition as saintly in a male-dominated church that was always suspicious of female ecstatics and visionaries. Ahlgren's Teresa is not so much a mystic as a master strategist who could unerringly disarm her male superiors by carefully constructing an image of herself as obedient and subservient to them. Viewing sanctity as a political construction, that is, as a status that is always contested and is never achieved without controversy or negotiation—especially in the case of women who claim intimacy with God in a repressive patriarchal society—Ahlgren approaches the *Vida* as self-fashioning, that is, as a conscious strategy for the achievement of that rare status. Like Bilinkoff, Ahlgren relies heavily on the *Vida* and turns it into something that is more than a mystical text. In the process, she recovers certain important aspects of the historical Teresa while constructing a post-mystical Teresa: a feisty woman who is no more immune to the politics of sanctity in the twenty-first century than she was in her own day.

Ahlgren's take on Teresa is not entirely post-mystical, however, as evidenced in her negative review of Rowan Williams's *Teresa of Avila* (1991), in which she excoriates the former archbishop of Canterbury for saying, "On the place of women in the twentieth-century Church, Teresa has no conclusions to offer us." Her criticism of Williams's statement is a succinct summation of her feminist take on Teresa, which does not exclude the mystical dimension at all:

Williams does not recognize Teresa's categorization of mystical experience as representative of her desire for women to achieve spiritual autonomy. Teresa was in fact empowering religious women to validate their experiences of God and to take control of their own spiritual direction by providing them with the theological vocabulary, categories, and concepts that would enable them to recognize the operation of Christ in their own lives. This is no less true for women today than in Teresa's own time.[6]

Literary Approaches

Analyzing women authors as *writers*—rather than as representative of other roles they might have played—is a perspective that became increasingly favored at the end of the twentieth century, especially in the case of mystics. Consequently, Teresa and her *Vida* have become subjects for literary scholars and other experts in critical theory and interpretative methodologies. In the case of Teresa, much of the theorizing has been shaped by feminism, in one way or another, as well as by various other intermillennial concerns.

Three pioneers who blazed a trail in the study of Teresa as an author and of her writings as literature—as texts with contexts other than mysticism—were Victor García Concha, Francisco Márquez Villanueva, and Rosa Rossi.[7] Inspired by their work, a new generation of scholars began to take a new approach to Teresa, and to the social, cultural, and political context in which she wrote. The most significant pioneering study of this kind is Alison Weber's *Teresa of Avila and the Rhetoric of Femininity*, which analyzes the *Vida* and other Teresian texts as strategically crafted to ensure acceptance by the male clerics who had the power to brand Teresa as a heretic, a fraud, or a demoniac. In Weber's post-mystical reading, the *Vida* is not so much an attempt by a mystic to elucidate her ecstasies, trances, and visions as it is a work of careful self-fashioning by a woman monastic who was skating on thin ice, so to speak, ever in peril of being condemned. Weber's book—which predates Ahlgren's—introduces readers to a Teresa who is a master at crafting "covert strategies of empowerment,"[8] and a genius at employing a disarming rhetoric of feminine self-deprecation that convinced her male readers to not just approve of her but to exalt her as an extraordinary saint. Weber's Teresa perfects several strategic moves in the *Vida* that she will continue to employ for the remainder of her life. These strategies involve paradoxical inversions of expectations: a posture of modesty and humility that disarms any male critic potentially threatened by her claims; a constant harping on her sinfulness and unworthiness that frames all claims to intimacy with God yet fails to reveal any specifics of her misbehavior; and a deference to authority that couches all outrageous claims—such as that of understanding the Trinity—in a rhetoric of imprecision, that is, in a unique mix of apophatic dumbness and abject weakness of intellect that her male readers could appreciate as properly feminine. As Weber sees it, then, the writing of the *Vida* allows Teresa to devise a template for subsequent texts, principally because she was placed in a perilous bind by the superiors who ordered her to prove that she was at once extraordinary and humble, obedient, deferent, and meek.

Weber's Teresa is most definitely no "patron saint of hysterics" but rather of bright, assertive, self-assured women: she is no Jamesian shrew or sexually repressed Lacanian basket case but rather an immensely talented wordsmith and self-promoter who was so perceptive and so well grounded in the realities of her world that she could turn the misogyny of those who could damn her into the chief instrument of her elevation to sainthood. Whether her mystical experiences were genuine or merely another clever device of her rhetorical strategy is beside the point. This is the post-mystical Teresa, after all, a brilliant author who is fully in command of her text and deliberately employs male prejudices to outwit the men who have the power to condemn her. As Dominique de Courcelles has also argued, by writing the *Vida* as she did, Teresa crafted a remarkable instrument of legitimation and authority, and also managed to uphold the integrity of female religious experience in a world dominated by men.[9]

All in all, this clever protofeminist Teresa is thoroughly intermillennial, yet enmeshed in the complexities of her own era. Some traditionalists and devotees find this post-mystical Teresa inauthentic and unattractive, as one might expect, and argue that she is incompatible with Teresa the sublime mystic. But there are also many others in that circle who appreciate this new light that has been shed on Teresa's unique genius. To them, interpreters such as Weber and De Courcelles make the mystic Teresa seem even more sublime, and her descriptions of mystical experiences more realistic and comprehensible.

Another post-mystical feminist interpretation of Teresa is Carol Slade's *Teresa of Avila: Author of a Heroic Life*, which appeared five years after Alison Weber's study and builds on it. As the subtitle suggests, Slade focuses extensively on the *Vida*. Much like Weber, Slade interprets Teresa as a master strategist and a very adroit manipulator of gender stereotypes, as well as of texts and literary genres.

As she sees it, Teresa's *Vida* and her other texts were "an elaborate project of self-representation and self-interpretation" through which she sought to win favor from potentially hostile male superiors.[10] Slade's Teresa skates on thinner ice than Weber's, so to speak, and much more attention is paid to the Spanish Inquisition and the sinister inquisitorial context within which the *Vida* was written. That context shaped the *Vida*, argues Slade, for the text is in essence a judicial confession in which she had to simultaneously abase, excuse, and exalt herself in order to prove the divine origin of her mystical experiences. According to Slade, Teresa succeeded by interweaving narrative strands that mirrored various genres, including scriptural exegesis, first-person hagiography, and confession narratives (especially those of Saint Augustine)—a clever strategy that allowed her to craft an undetectable subversive subtext within her outwardly submissive narrative.

To anyone unfamiliar with literary studies, Slade's analysis will be less accessible than Weber's, not only because of her reliance on esoteric concepts such as Mikhail Bakhtin's "hidden polemic" and "dialogized heteroglossia," but also because of the intense attention paid to an assortment of critical theories in several fields, including hermeneutics, semiotics, feminist and gender studies, new historicist literary analysis, genre studies, and psychoanalysis.[11] In sum, Slade interprets Teresa in a highly specialized academic way, and in her Rorschach inkblot test, Teresa turns out to be an intermillennial feminist heroine who penned a masterpiece of covert subversion.

Issues of sex and gender being such a consuming interest among intellectuals and academics of the intermillennial period, it is no surprise that the *Vida* has also attracted post-mystical queer readings that would have left Teresa in apoplectic shock or prompted her to greater austerities and ascetic extremes than the ones she inflicted on herself to atone for the apostasy of all Lutherans. As Paola Marín points out—by means of highly specialized terminology—queering Teresa makes perfect sense due to what she sees as the sexually charged challenge that mystical experiences pose to the hegemonic patriarchal-misogynist hierarchical authority structure of the Catholic Church. "The ecstatic union is transgressive because it does not depend on *logos* or an external authority," argues Marín. "It overcomes the restrictions of the phallogocentric theological discourse, since the mystic develops an erotic and violent language that points toward the rupture of the incest interdiction." In other words, mystical ecstasy blurs boundaries between binary opposites such as male/female, straight/gay, or familial/extrafamilial. Teresa is queer, beyond a shadow of a doubt, and her mysticism is highly sexed.

> Queer is a quality related to any expression that may be considered "contra-, non-, or anti-straight." In Teresa's writings, it is possible to find an explicit "anti-straight" attitude in the sense that she puts at stake the paradigms of a social organization based on heterosexuality—that is, a phallocentric regime.[12]

Marín is far from alone in seeing Teresa as a sexually charged transgressor of boundaries. As David William Foster explains, while "patriarchy" controls discourse by insisting on fixed gender (masculinity/femininity) and defining identity on the basis of genitals, mystical discourse is inherently "queer" due to its highly unstable and fluid parsing of gender differences. In a similar vein, relying on Julia Kristeva's theories, Paul Julian Smith interprets Teresa's visions—especially the transverberation—as "acts of disavowal," and as a negation of the "phallic order." As Smith sees it, the transverberation is not a "penetration" by a spiritual otherworldly phallus, as Freud and Lacan saw it, but rather a bold denial of sexual difference.[13]

Marín, Foster, and Smith are just the tip of the iceberg when it comes to queering Teresa and the *Vida*. Many other intermillennial post-mystical interpreters have turned Teresa into a "queer icon"; so many, in fact, that we cannot devote equal attention to them in a brief survey such as this. Suffice it to say that there are a variety of interpretations of the queerness of the *Vida*. While some argue that the text was written in the "epistemological space of the closet," others consider it a defense of her "unruly pleasures" or of the "homosocial milieu" in which she lived. Some see the *Vida* as an expression of Teresa's "female homoeroticism," "homoerotic passion," or "experiential homoeroticism"; some even praise her "protolesbian *butchness*" (my italics).[14] In sum, a surprisingly high number of scholars see her as a closeted lesbian and interpret her mysticism as an alternative to "penetration and the presence of the penis," while bemoaning the fact that the world has for far too long ignored the fact that Teresa is "the symbol of the queers of all nations, sexes, and colors, who have resisted obliteration even as they continue to endure social isolation, dispersion, and silencing."[15] Needless to say, most traditionalists and devotees find these interpretations wrong and offensive.

Not all post-mystical literary analyses of the *Vida* in the intermillennial period have taken a feminist approach or focused on gender or queerness. Ten years after the publication of Slade's study, Elena Carrera challenged Weber, De Courcelles, and Slade, arguing that the feminist Teresa was inauthentic and that gender issues are not the key to interpreting the *Vida*. Teresa, she proposes, should not be read through the "prejudiced" lens of "the gender studies perspective" but instead approached as a "Christian subject, subjected both to language and to the authority of the Church and Tradition."[16] Carrera's Teresa is no crafty subversive or activist: she is merely a product of the religiosity of her day, and her *Vida* but a means of self-discovery. In her conclusion, Carrera says:

> I hope to have demonstrated that Teresa's sense of self and the mode of writing she chose for her autobiography were shaped by ideas promoted by sermons and devotional books, as well as by cultural practices such as examination of conscience, confession, spiritual direction and mental prayer. The *Vida*, therefore, cannot be seen simply as the expression of a coherent self which pre-existed the writing or as the product of an objective transmission of infused or borrowed ideas, but as evidence for its author's process of self-interpretation through writing.[17]

While it may seem that Carrera departs from the theory-driven interpretations so common in the intermillennial age, constant references and challenges to French theorist Michel Foucault place Carrera within the fold of the theorist-quoting interpreters from whom she tries to distance herself. Much like Slade, Carrera identifies Saint Augustine's *Confessions* as an essential textual model for the *Vida*, but Carrera's conclusions differ greatly from Slade's. According to Carrera, it is Teresa's reading of Augustine that ultimately determines the narrative structure and rhetorical strategies of the *Vida*, rather than the fact that she was a woman facing prosecution by male inquisitors. As one might expect, Carrera's rejection of gender as a determining factor in the structure and content of the *Vida* has been challenged by those with whom she disagrees.[18]

Alternative Vidas

Pitching a book as peculiar as the *Vida* to devotees and seekers is one thing, and pitching it to a narrow scholarly audience is quite another. The devotees and seekers are always out there, it seems, eager to encounter Teresa and venerate her, and they are numerous. The scholars, in contrast, are a select and demanding audience—fussy and cantankerous, ever on the lookout for errors of fact or opinion—and they number in the mere hundreds, at best. Pitching the *Vida* to a broad audience is a challenge entirely different from the other two just mentioned. Can a book about a sixteenth-century nun's mystical experiences ever be made appealing or accessible to the great masses, or even to some peculiar segment of the entertainment-consuming market? Surprisingly, a few brave individuals have taken on this challenge in the intermillennial period, with varying degrees of success.

Most recently, as mentioned in chapter 6, linguist, psychologist, and novelist Julia Kristeva published a lengthy novel, *Teresa My love*, which is set in two time periods: Teresa's own lifetime and the author's present.[19] Writing historical fiction that is at once accurate and engaging is enormously difficult, and the more the author cares about little details, the more difficult the task becomes. As a scholar and novelist, Kristeva is well suited to handle the historical details, large and small. Nonetheless, intermingling fictive characters from the present with historical ones from the distant past requires unique talents. A fussy and cantankerous skeptical scholar might ask: Can Kristeva pull off this trick? Can anyone do it, really? Kristeva's publisher wants potential readers to think she can do just about anything. The pitch from Columbia University Press reads: "*Teresa, My Love* interchanges biography, autobiography, analysis, dramatic dialogue, musical scores, and images of paintings and sculpture." As if this were not already stunning or disconcerting enough, the publisher adds that Kristeva mixes "fiction, history, psychoanalysis, and personal fantasy," and "turns a past world into a modern marvel" while sharing "unprecedented insights into her own character" and providing "a fascinating dual diagnosis of contemporary society and the individual psyche."[20]

Kristeva does indeed insert herself into the novel, as the publisher promises. She does so principally through her alter-ego present-day character, Sylvia Leclercq, a multi-talented psychologist-academic-writer. She also enters into the novel through her Lacanian psychoanalytic take on Teresa, which gives shape to that character and to the narrative. All of the "Freudian-Lacanian mumbo-jumbo" inserted into the novel—described in those exact terms by one of the protagonist Sylvia's friends—forms a thick, foggy lens through which the reader is forced to see the historical Teresa. Needless to say, that lens can easily annoy some readers, especially of the devout or academic sort, or even of a secularist bent. Her *New York Times* reviewer summed up the value of the novel by asking, "Does Ms. Kristeva really need nearly six hundred pages to expound on the reading she has given the saint elsewhere?"[21]

Fifteen years before Kristeva's "imagined life" was published, a very different nonscholarly approach to Teresa's *Vida* had been taken by Cathleen Medwick in *Teresa of Avila: The Progress of a Soul*. Although she has earned two master's degrees in literature from Columbia University, Medwick has not pursued an academic career. A former features editor for *Vogue, Vanity Fair, Mirabella*, and *House and Garden*, and a freelance writer for other mass media, Medwick makes her scholarly training evident in *Progress of a Soul*, which is duly graced with proper academic bells and whistles, including endnotes. Medwick is no Catholic or Anglican seeker—she describes herself as having a Jewish "background"—but rather a writer who first encountered Teresa by chance in Richard Crashaw's seventeenth-century poems. Medwick's aim is somewhat emotional and novelistic: to engage readers in Teresa's search for God, which, as she puts it, is a journey as "full of wonder and terror as any ocean voyage through uncharted seas."[22] As one might expect from a features editor for fashion and design magazines, Medwick's reframing of the *Vida* pays close attention to small details in the scenery, and those details claim a substantial amount of space in many pages. Medwick's Teresa is a heroine, for sure: the polar opposite of a patron saint for hysterics, a busy woman who gets things done. Although her post-mystical Teresa is not constantly psychoanalyzed, as is Kristeva's, or nearly as needy, she does resemble that Teresa in one way, by thinking and acting more like a self-assured intermillennial entrepreneur than as a mystic who had frequent intimate encounters with the divine. When all is said and done, Medwick's Teresa ends up being a part-time mystic who had to shoehorn her spiritual life in between the few tight gaps left open between her personal goal-seeking and her business transactions.

In the area of theatrical and visual arts, the *Vida* has barely attracted any attention in the intermillennial age. Paintings and sculptures have been limited to parishes here and there, such as the church of Santa Teresa de Jesús in Tres Cantos, a thoroughly postmodern suburb of Madrid, where an image of a levitating Teresa seems awkwardly out of place. Stage plays have been scarce too. Perhaps no playwright felt confident enough to top Gertrude Stein's lesbian-themed 1927 play *Four Saints in Three Acts*, in which the characters of the younger and older Teresa "interact" intimately within sight of two female angelic lovers.[23]

Nonetheless, a few years after the death of Generalissimo Franco and the demise of Fascism in Spain, an eight-episode miniseries produced by Televisión Española aired in the spring of 1984, when all of Teresa's troublesome associations with Fascism were still vividly etched in the memories of many Spaniards. Directed by Josefina Molina—one of the first women directors to gain prominence in Spain[24]—*Teresa de Jesús* traces the life of the saint from the age of twenty-three to her death at sixty-seven. Molina's non-Fascist Teresa, portrayed by actress Concha Velasco, is not exactly post-mystical, since some of Teresa's ecstasies and visions were recreated for viewers on the small screens of that era, along with her struggles against her confessors and the Inquisition, but the main thrust of the narrative, which closely follows that of the *Vida*—where applicable—is her active life as a nun and reformer, not her mysticism. Molina's miniseries won several awards, and in the 1990s a video-cassette version with subtitles became available to English-speaking audiences, followed in 2008 by a digital video disk set. In 2018, all eight episodes are still available on the Internet. Ironically, it is highly likely that this miniseries has already acquainted more human beings with Teresa than the text of her *Vida* ever did. Such is the power of film and the nature of post-everything intermillennial culture.

Nonetheless, the definitive status of Molina's interpretation has not gone unchallenged. Unintimidated by the popularity of Molina's work, perhaps irked by its reverent approach or inspired by Freudian and Lacanian perspectives, Spanish filmmaker Ray Loriga wrote and directed a highly erotic film, *Teresa: The Body of Christ* (2007), in which actress Paz Vega portrays Saint Teresa's mystical ecstasies as sexual encounters with a very handsome and very physical Jesus. Needless to say, the film scandalized devotees and traditionalists. And, as if two conflicting cinematic versions of Teresa's life were not enough, director Jorge Dorado and scriptwriter Juanma Romero Gárriz teamed up to offer Spanish television audiences a third film on Saint Teresa in 2015, to mark the five-hundredth anniversary of her birth. Their production, titled *Teresa*, was inextricably tied to the *Vida* and marketed as a retelling of the life of the saint "through the eyes of a young woman of our own day who reads one of Saint Teresa's principal works, *El Libro de su Vida*."[25] Despite their self-conscious attempt to appeal to divergent contemporary sensibilities, neither of these films has attracted as wide an audience as Molina's 1984 miniseries.

Evaluating Rorschach Teresa

Some intermillennial post-mystical interpretations of Teresa and her *Vida* would have baffled, shocked, and offended Teresa and her contemporaries, and even some of the skeptics who came along in the centuries after her death in 1582. Simply put, it is highly likely that some interpretations of the post-mystical Teresa would have been unrecognizable and unintelligible to just about everyone born before 1900 or thereabouts, due to the colossal shifts in weltanschauung, or worldview, that emerged in the twentieth century. What is one to make of this interpretative dissonance between past and present? Does it nullify all post-mystical interpretations or does it nullify Teresa's own view of things, as expressed in the *Vida*? Or are all interpretations immune to invalidation, always, regardless of how outrageous they seem to anyone in the past or present?

One might as well ask whether any interpretation of a Rorschach inkblot is "invalid" or open to nullification by some other interpreter. An interpretation is what it is, and that interpretation itself is open to interpretation, and to challenges. That is the basic premise of the Rorschach inkblot test, and also a largely uncontested premise of early twenty-first-century secular Western culture. This is the epistemological impasse that we intermillennial Westerners find ourselves in, where the chasm separating the seekers who venerate the mystic Teresa and the interpreters who prefer the post-mystical Teresa can sometimes seem as unbridgeable as the void between galaxies.

When all is said and done, however, the very fact that Teresa's *Vida* continues to elicit so many discordant or incompatible interpretations four and a half centuries after it was written—and that some devout seekers can appreciate the post-mystical Teresa *more* than some intermillennial interpreters can appreciate Teresa the mystic—validates the text's inherent value as a truly *great* religious book.

Religion is never some isolated dimension of human existence immune to the world in which humans live and breathe, eat and drink, buy and sell, toil and rest, or shout and whisper. Mystics have to engage in innumerable tasks other than praying and fasting, and the world is as much a part of their mysticism as their asceticism, no matter how thick the walls are that enclose them. This is what Teresa the mystic knew all too well, and affirmed when she told her nuns that "God walks among the pots and pans." And this is what the post-mystical intermillennial *Vida* reveals to us, too, even when its Teresa offends some of the devout.

Religion is a highly charged interpretative sphere of human experience, as likely to elicit discord and disagreement as sweet harmony and mutual understanding. Consequently, the interplay of discordant voices found in the *Vida*'s intermillennial trajectory is not too surprising. In fact, the apparent cacophony may very well be some inevitable paradoxical hum, and the surest indication we can have of the book's enduring significance.

DOCTOR OF THE CHURCH,
SIGN OF CONTRADICTION

On 27 September 1970, three and a half centuries after her canonization, Teresa's Rorschach inkblot received a very special interpretation by Pope Paul VI, a reading that seemed out of sync with the secularist spirit of the times, especially for those in the avant-garde who embodied that spirit. That Sunday, at the Vatican, Pope Paul proclaimed Saint Teresa a doctor of the church, along with Catherine of Siena, singling out both of them as the first women ever to be honored with this rare title. Their road to the doctorate had been long indeed. Unlike many of the previous figures raised to this exalted rank—such as Saint Augustine, Saint Ambrose, Saint Anselm, Saint Bonaventure, and Saint Thomas Aquinas—neither one of these women had studied theology or held a position of authority in the hierarchy of the Catholic Church. Even more surprising, one of them, Teresa, had been sorely tested by the Inquisition during her lifetime.

Teresa the doctor was quite different from Fascist Teresa or the hysterical or nymphomaniac Teresa of the psycho-analysts, or the feminist or queer Teresa that had yet to emerge in the not-too-distant future.[1] But there she was, at the Vatican, this apparent anachronism, this first woman doctor of the autocratic, male-dominated Catholic Church, this weird sign of contradiction to the zeitgeist of the age of post-everything, who in her own day was a sign of contradiction to that same church.

To be proclaimed a doctor in the Catholic Church, three conditions need to be met: *eminens doctrina*, *insignis vitae sanctitas*, and *Ecclesiae declaratio* (eminent learning, a high degree of sanctity, and proclamation by the church through the pope). The practice of naming stellar saints as doctors began in the Middle Ages. By 1568, in Teresa's lifetime, only ten saints had been elevated to this special rank. Since then, only twenty-six more have joined the elite list: four in the eighteenth century, nine in the nineteenth, ten in the twentieth, and three thus far in the first two decades of the twenty-first. Of these thirty-six, only four are women: Catherine of Siena (fourteenth century) and Teresa of Avila (sixteenth century), jointly proclaimed in 1970; Thérèse of Lisieux (nineteenth), proclaimed in 1997; and Hildegard of Bingen (twelfth century), proclaimed in 2012.

A custom dating back to medieval times also assigns specific titles to some doctors, creating a first- and second-class ranking among them by reserving this distinction for only fifteen out of the thirty-six on the list. For instance, Augustine is the *doctor gratiae* (doctor of grace), Anselm of Canterbury the *doctor magnificus* (magnificent doctor), Bernard of Clairvaux the *doctor mellifluous* (doctor as sweet as honey), and Thomas Aquinas the *doctor angelicus* (the angelic doctor).

Out of the four women doctors, Teresa is the only one thus far to be assigned one of these honorific titles, and in her case it is that of *doctor orationis* (doctor of prayer). That title is immensely significant and indicative of her unique spiritual talents, but the irony with which this title is laced cannot be missed by anyone who knows that prayer was the main source of Teresa's troubles with the Inquisition, especially her prayer of quiet. Tellingly, John of the Cross, Teresa's friend and fellow Carmelite reformer, earned his rank as doctor before Teresa, in 1926—although it took him a century longer than Teresa to be canonized—and was given the title *doctor mysticus*, or mystical doctor. So John became *the* expert on mysticism and Teresa *the* expert on prayer, although both of them would have protested that the two things are one and the same. The fact that they prayed and levitated together in ecstasy seems to have been overlooked by those who assigned such titles.

Pope Paul VI began his sermon that Sunday by saying, "We have just conferred the title of Doctor of the Church—or, rather—*recognized* that she is such," implying, of course, that she had truly earned the title long ago but was finally getting the honor she deserved, a bit late.[2] Much of Pope Paul's sermon is descriptive rather than analytical, and replete with laudatory hyperbole, but no mention of the ordeals Teresa's male superiors made her endure. Teresa, he said, was "an exceptional woman" whose doctrine "shone brightly with the gifts of truth, fidelity to the Catholic Church, and usefulness for the shaping of souls." Her most attractive gift, continued Pope Paul, was also the biggest mystery of all: the divine inspiration that made her such a prodigious mystical writer. What was the source of the "treasure of her doctrine?" asked Pope Paul. His answer to that rhetorical question is quite revealing of his desire to interweave intellectual and spiritual elements. In brief, every aspect of her life played a part.

> Without any doubt, the source was her intelligence and her cultural and spiritual formation, her reading, her acquaintance with the great teachers of theology and spirituality, her unique sensibilities, her constant and intense ascetic discipline, her contemplative meditation, in sum, her response to the grace that flowed into her soul, which was extraordinarily fertile and prepared by the practice and experience of prayer.

This was the human side of the story, and it was very Catholic, basically a "response to grace" that required effort and the proper training. But could that have been all? Pope Paul asked: Was Teresa herself the ultimate source of her "eminent doctrine"? The answer to that rhetorical question was no surprise. Of course not: She was not the active agent, he said, but only a passive one, a conduit for the "extraordinary action of the Holy Spirit." Teresa experienced intimate union with God, said Pope Paul, and that mystical embrace was turned into "light and wisdom" in her. Teresa's teaching is full of wisdom about divine and human things, he continued, because these are "secrets of prayer" that she was privileged to plumb and pass on to the Catholic Church. Teresa, then, is not only the *doctor orationis* but the *mater spiritualium*, the mother and teacher of all spiritual people. In other words, the first woman doctor is assigned the ultimate traditional woman's role, that of mother.

Making an overt reference to modern psychiatry, Pope Paul stressed that Teresa, as mother, is in charge of teaching her children to pray and to rely on prayer as a means of prevailing over the "confused murmuring of our animal subconscious and the screams of the unconquered passions and of our desperate anxiety." To underscore this point, Pope Paul then quoted Teresa's *Vida*, saying that her simple and sublime message as doctor and mother is that "mental prayer is nothing more than friendship and frequent solitary conversation with Him Who we know loves us" (8:5.61). Finally, with no apparent awareness of alternative interpretations to Teresa's last words on her deathbed—"At the end, I am a daughter of the Church"—which postmystical interpreters attribute to her constant fear of the Inquisition, Pope Paul exhorted all the faithful to join Teresa in proclaiming that they, too, are children of the church. Forty years later, Pope Benedict XVI, the well-trained German theologian, would reiterate Pope Paul VI's assessment of Teresa as an expert on prayer rather than on theology, saying at a General Audience, "Rather than a pedagogy Teresa's is a true 'mystagogy' of prayer: she teaches those who read her works how to pray by praying with them."[3]

The papal Teresa, then, seems at odds with that of many modern and postmodern interpreters. In the early twenty-first century, there seem to be as many different Teresas as the hundreds of pages in her *Vida*, or perhaps as many as all the words in that text. Yet, Teresa the mystic survives amid all the other Teresas that seek to crowd her out, and her *Vida* continues to serve as the most direct doorway for those who seek to gain access to that unique mystic. Her doctorate does not in any way erase or excuse the harsh treatment she received in her own day, so different from that of intermillennial Western folk. Some might even see it as more of an insult to

Teresa than an honor, something akin to a posthumous prize awarded by some dictator to a victim of his own torturers. As some see it, papal recognition came way too late, without proper contrition—no *mea culpa, mea maxima culpa*—and no apologies for the church's opposition to the ordination of women as priests. Despite Pope John Paul II's many profuse apologies for many of the Catholic Church's past sins, including all the injustices committed against women, that doctorate rings hollow.[4] Such is the tenor of the times. Fortunately, for Teresa the mystic, tough times—*tiempos recios*—are familiar territory.

Papal recognition of Teresa's contribution to Catholicism, tardy as it may seem to some, is nonetheless significant, for it is itself a sign of contradiction, much like Teresa herself, so hounded in her own day, and much like her *Vida*, locked up by the Inquisition, nearly consigned to the flames. Signs of contradiction are at the very heart of the Christian religion, and they speak most eloquently of redemption and of what Dante dared to call the Divine Comedy.[5]

In the fourteenth century, Meister Eckhart, a German mystic who influenced Teresa indirectly, once said, "Whether you like it or not, whether you know it or not, secretly all nature seeks God and works toward him."[6] Teresa could not have read Meister Eckhart's German sermons, but she was nonetheless his heir, through translations of the texts of his disciples. Paraphrasing Eckhart seems appropriate now, as intermillennial interpreters hover over Teresa's Rorschach inkblot, all eager to find the true meaning of her *Vida*. Whether you know it or not, whether you like it or not, when all is said and done, Teresa was a mystic, and her *Vida* was—and continues to be—a religious book, regardless of what anyone wants to see in it or do with it, or of what any-one has seen in it or done with it.

In fact, it could be argued that few other texts propose as optimistic an evaluation of human existence and human potential, or as eloquent a defense of the power of love over evil and our own worst shortcomings.

And this makes it a great religious book.

So it goes. *Plega al Señor.*[7]

PREFACE: THE CHARACTER OF THE *VIDA*

1. Archivo Historico Nacional, Inquisición, file 2.072n43. See Enrique Llamas Martínez, *Santa Teresa de Jesús y la Inquisición Española* (Madrid: CSIC, 1972), 311–12.

2. *Vida*, 38:7.209, in Efrén de la Madre de Dios, OCD, and Otger Steggink, O. Carm., eds., *Obras Completas de Santa Teresa* (Madrid: Biblioteca de Autores Cristianos, 1997). Subsequent citations from the *Vida* are from this edition and are given parenthetically in the main text by chapter, section, and page number, respectively. All translations from this text are my own.

3. Francisco de Ribera, *La vida de la madre Teresa de Jesús* (Barcelona: Gili, 1908), xvi.

4. *Oxford English Dictionary* online, http://www.oed.com /view/Entry/124654?redirectedFrom=mysticism#eid.

5. Saint Teresa shared this honor with Catherine of Siena. Paul VI said of Teresa: "St. Teresa of Avila's doctrine shines with charisms of truth, of conformity to the Catholic faith and of usefulness for the instruction of souls." Homily of the Holy Father Paul VI, 27 September 1970, http://w2.vatican .va/content/paul-vi/it/homilies/1970/documents/hf_p-vi _hom_19700927.html.

CHAPTER 1: TERESA'S LIFE STORY

1. Conversos—also known by the pejorative name *marranos* (swine)—have attracted a considerable amount of scholarly interest. See Yirmiyahu Yovel, *The Other Within: The Marranos* (Princeton: Princeton University Press, 2009);

Rene Levine Melammed, *A Question of Identity: Iberian Conversos in Historical Perspective* (Cambridge: Cambridge University Press, 2004); Michael Alpert, *Crypto-Judaism and the Spanish Inquisition* (New York: Palgrave, 2001); and Benzion Netanyahu, *The Marranos of Spain* (Ithaca: Cornell University Press, 1999).

2. See Narciso Alonso Cortés, "Pleitos de los Cepeda," *Boletín de la Real Academia Española* 25 (1946): 85–110.

3. Quoted in *Tiempo y Vida de Santa Teresa*, ed. Efrén de la Madre de Dios and Otger Steggink (Madrid: Biblioteca de Autores Cristianos, 1968), 6n31.

4. Ibid., 63.

5. See Hans-Jürgen Prien, *Francisco de Osuna: Mystik und Rechtfertigung* (Hamburg: Verlag Dr. Kovac, 2014); Efrén de la Madre de Dios and Otger Steggink, *Santa Teresa y su tiempo* (Salamanca: Universidad Pontificia, 1982), 1:239–50; Fidèle de Ros, *Un maître de Sainte Thérèse: Le père François d'Osuna* (Paris: Gabriel Beauchesne, 1936).

6. See Carlos Eire, "Early Modern Catholic Piety in Translation," in *Cultural Translation in Early Modern Europe*, ed. Peter Burke and Ronnie Po-chia Hsia (Cambridge: Cambridge University Press, 2007), 83–100.

7. See Elena Carrera, *Teresa of Avila's Autobiography: Authority, Power and the Self in Mid-Sixteenth-Century Spain* (London: Legenda, 2005), 47–49; Gillian Ahlgren, *Teresa of Avila and the Politics of Sanctity* (Ithaca: Cornell University Press, 1996), 10–20, 38, 87–92.

8. See Arcángel Barrado Manzano, *San Pedro de Alcántara* (Cáceres: San Antonio, 1995).

9. Immortalized by Bernini's sculpture (see chapter 5). To "transverberate" is "to strike through" or "to pierce through." The term is derived from the Latin "transverberare" (prefix, trans/through) plus (verb, verberare/to strike).

10. See Jodi Bilinkoff, *The Avila of Saint Teresa: Religious Reform in a Sixteenth-Century City* (Ithaca: Cornell University Press, 1983), 123–33.

11. Ana de San Bartolomé, "Ultimos años de la Madre Teresa de Jesús," in *Obras Completas de Ana de San Bartolomé* (Rome: Edizioni Teresanium, 1981), 1:26; my translation. For a published translation, see Darcy Donahue, ed. and trans., *Ana de San Bartolomé: Autobiography and Other Writings* (Chicago: University of Chicago Press, 2008).

12. Diego de Yepes, *Vida, virtudes y milagros de la Bienaventurada Virgen Teresa de Jesús*, chap. 39 (Buenos Aires: Emecé Editores, 1946), 414; originally published in Madrid, 1599.

13. *Procesos de Beatificación y Canonización de Santa Teresa de Jesús*, ed. Silverio de Santa Teresa (Burgos: Editorial Monte Carmelo, 1934–35), 1:172, 197.

14. Sermon by Tomás de San Vicente, *Relación sencilla y fiel de las fiestas que el Rey Don Felipe IV nuestro Señor hizo al Patronato de sus Reinos* (Madrid, 1627), 13.

15. Yepes, *Vida, virtudes y milagros*, 17–18.

CHAPTER 2: HOW, WHEN, AND WHY THE BOOK WAS WRITTEN

1. On judicial confession, see Carole Slade, *St. Teresa of Avila: Author of a Heroic Life* (Berkeley: University of California Press, 1995), xii, 13–14, 22, 25, 159n1.

2. See Andrew Keitt, *Inventing the Sacred: Imposture, Inquisition, and the Boundaries of the Supernatural in Golden Age Spain* (Leiden: Brill, 2005).

3. See Carole Slade, *St. Teresa of Avila*, esp. 65–78.

4. See José Ignacio Tellechea Idígoras, *El arzobispo Carranza: "Tiempos recios"* (Salamanca: Universidad Pontificia de Salamanca, 2003).

5. See Doris Moreno, "Los Jesuitas, la Inquisición y la frontera espiritual de 1559," *Bulletin of Spanish Studies* 92.5 (2015): 655–75; Melquíades Andrés Martín, "Common Denominator of Alumbrados, Erasmians, 'Lutherans' and Mystics," in *The Spanish Inquisition and the Inquisitorial Mind*, ed. Angel Alcalá (Boulder, CO: East European Monographs, 1987), 457.

6. Luis de Granada, *Historia de Sor María de la Visitación y Sermón de las caídas públicas*, ed. Alvaro Huelga (Barcelona: Juan Flors, 1962).

7. See Geraldine McKendrick and Angus McKay, "Visionaries and Affective Spirituality during the First Half of the Sixteenth Century," in *Cultural Encounters: The Impact of the Inquisition in Spain and the New World*, ed. by Mary Elizabeth Perry and Anne J. Cruz (Berkeley: University of California Press, 1991), 93–104.

8. In the words of Saint Paul the Apostle, "Satan himself masquerades as an angel of light" (2 Corinthians 11:14).

9. "Bula de canonización de Santa Teresa de Jesús," in *Biblioteca mística carmelitana*, ed. Silverio de Santa Teresa (Burgos: El Monte Carmelo, 1934–49), 2:219–21.

10. See Alison Weber, *Teresa of Avila and the Rhetoric of Femininity* (Princeton: Princeton University Press, 1996).

11. See Alastair Hamilton, *Heresy and Mysticism in Sixteenth-Century Spain: The Alumbrados* (Cambridge: J. Clark, 1992); and Pedro Santoja, *La herejía de los alumbrados y la espiritualidad en la España del siglo 16* (Valencia: Generalitat Valenciana, 2001).

12. Enrique García Hernán emphasizes the saint's links to alumbradismo. See his *Ignacio de Loyola* (Madrid: Taurus, 2013).

13. Elizabeth Rhodes has called attention to the perils of interpreting the *Vida* as an autobiography in "What's in a Name: Teresa of Avila's Book," in *The Mystical Gesture*, ed. Robert Boenig (Farnham, UK: Ashgate, 2000), 79–106.

14. See Alison Weber, "The Three Lives of the Vida: The Uses of Convent Autobiography," in *Women, Texts and Authority in the Early Modern Spanish World*, ed. Marta Vicente and Luis Corteguera (Farnham, UK: Ashgate, 2003), 109.

15. See facsimile edition: Santa Teresa de Jesús, *Libro de la Vida, Autógrafo de la Biblioteca del Real Monasterio de San Lorenzo de El Escorial*, ed. Tomás Alvarez (Burgos: Patrimonio Nacional, 1999).

16. Testimony of Isabel de Vivero, in *Procesos de Beatificación y Canonización de Santa Teresa de Jesús*, ed. Silverio de Santa Teresa (Burgos: El Monte Carmelo, 1934–35), 2:336.

17. Ibid., 2:220.

18. Ibid., 1:273.

19. Ibid., 1:398.

20. Ibid., 1:407.

21. Ibid., 1:53.

22. Enrique Llamas Martínez, *Santa Teresa de Jesús y la Inquisición Española* (Madrid: Consejo Superior de Investigaciones Científicas, 1972), 34.

23. Domingo Báñez, "Censura en el autógrafo de la Vida," in *Obras de Santa Teresa* (Madrid: Biblioteca de Autores Cristianos, 1997), 230–32.

24. Jéronimo Gracián, in Pierre Sérouet, *Glanes: Quelques brèves additions de la main du Père Jérôme Gratien à la premiére biographie de Thérèse d'Avila par le Père Francisco de Ribera* (Laval: Carmel de Laval, 1988), 57.

25. Ibid., 59–61.

26. *Obras Completas* (Madrid: Biblioteca de Autores Cristianos, 1997), Letter 183, 1089.

27. Joseph Pérez, *Teresa de Ávila y la España de su tiempo* (Madrid: Algaba, 2007), 269n2. Julián de Ávila's *Vida de Santa Teresa de Jesús* was eventually edited by Vicente de la Fuente and published in 1881 (Madrid: Antonio Pérez Dubrull, 1881).

28. *Compendium Vitae B.V. Teresiae a Iesu Fundatricis Fratrum Discalceatorz et Monialium Bmae. Virg. M. de Monte Carmelo* (Rome, 1609).

29. *Declamacion en qve se trata de la perfecta vida y virtudes heroycas de la B. Madre Theresa de Iesus, y de las fundaciones de sus Monasterios* (Brussels, 1611).

30. *Procesos de Beatificación y Canonización*, ed. Silverio de Santa Teresa, 2:276.

1. See Jure Kristo, "The Interpretation of Religious Experience: What Do Mystics Intend when They Talk about Their Experiences?," *Journal of Religion* 62.1 (Jan. 1982): 21–38.
2. *Camino de la Perfección*, Valladolid manuscript, chap. 25.2.
3. *The Interior Castle* (*El Castillo Interior*) or *Las Moradas* (*The Mansions*), third morada, chap. 1.8.
4. "Imaginaria," the term employed by Teresa for these visions, is commonly translated as "imaginary" in English, but the connotations of unreality conveyed by that word make it inappropriate. "Imaginative" is a more accurate translation.
5. Teresa was aware of these dangers posed by corporeal visions. See *Vida*, 28:4.149–50.
6. The most thorough survey of Christian levitation is Olivier Leroy, *Levitation: An Examination of the Evidence and Explanations* (London: Oates & Washbourne, 1928). See Carlos Eire, "The Good, the Bad, and the Airborne: Levitation and the History of the Impossible in Early Modern Europe," in *Ideas and Cultural Margins in Early Modern Germany: Essays in Honor of H. C. Erik Midelfort*, ed. Marjorie E. Plummer, Robin B. Barnes, et al. (Farnham, UK: Ashgate, 2009), 307–24.
7. For instance, *Procesos de beatificación y canonización de Santa Teresa de Jesús*, 2:297.
8. *Vida*, 20:4; 20:7.109–10. Thirteen years later, in the *Moradas* (*Mansions*, 6.5.9), Teresa said the following about the speed and force with which the soul is drawn upward in rapture: "I am not really sure how to say this, but what happens is that the soul rises interiorly in flight, and goes far outside of itself, as fast as a bullet is shot out from a gun, only without making any noise."
9. Cited by Leroy, *Levitation*, 71.

1. Luis de León, ed., *Obras de la gloriosa Madre Santa Teresa de Jesús* (Brussels: Francisco Foppens, 1674), 6.

2. Ibid.

3. See the introduction in *Procesos de beatificación y canonización*, ed. Silverio de Santa Teresa, 1:vii–xxviii. For details on "Informative" and "Remissory" inquests, see Andre Vauchez, *Sainthood in the Later Middle Ages* (Cambridge: Cambridge University Press, 2005), 42–43.

4. Miguel de Cervantes, *Poesías completas*, ed. Vicente Gaos (Madrid: Castalia, 1981), 2:385.

5. Lope de Vega, *Vida y muerte de Santa Teresa de Jesús*, ed. Elisa Aragone Terni (Messina/Florence: Casa Editrice D'Anna, 1970), 100. For information on other plays, see Nicolás Martín, "Teresa de Jesús en el teatro barroco," *Actas del Congreso Internacional Teresiano, II, Salamanca, 4–7 Octubre 1982* (Salamanca: Universidad Pontificia de Salamanca, 1984), 699–719.

6. For more information on these sermons, see Carlos Eire, *From Madrid to Purgatory: The Art and Craft of Dying in Sixteenth-Century Spain* (Cambridge: Cambridge University Press, 1995), 392–94.

7. *The Life of the Holy Mother S. Teresa: Foundress of the Reformation of the Discalced Carmelites, according to the Primitive Rule*, trans. Abraham Woodhead (London, 1671), 25–26.

8. Archivo Historico Nacional, *Inquisición*, file 2.072n43. See Enrique Llamas Martínez, *Santa Teresa de Jesús y la Inquisición Española* (Madrid: CSIC, 1972), 311–12.

9. Quoted by Llamas Martínez, *Santa Teresa y la Inquisición*, 380.

10. Ibid., 382–88.

11. Sermon by Fray Tomás de San Vicente, *Relación sencilla y fiel de las fiestas que el Rey Don Felipe IIII, nuestro Señor hizo al Patronato de sus Reinos de España* (Madrid, 1627), 13.

12. See Erin Rowe, *Saint and Nation: Santiago, Teresa of Avila, and Plural Identities in Early Modern Spain* (University Park: Pennsylvania State Press, 2011).

13. Woodhead, *The Life of the Holy Mother S. Teresa* (1671), 39.

14. Ibid., 37–38.

15. See Raymond Deville, *The French School of Spirituality: An Introduction and Reader* (Pittsburgh: Duquesne University Press, 1994).

16. Jean de Brétigny (1556–1634), who had a Spanish father and a French mother, is also known as Jean de Quintana Dueñas, Jean de Quintanadueñas, and Jean de Quintanadoine.

17. Joseph Pérez, *Teresa de Ávila y la España de su tiempo* (Madrid: Algaba, 2007), 285.

18. *The Complete Works of Richard Crashaw* (Perfect Library, 2015), 1:128–29. Crashaw is explicitly referencing Teresa's poem "Vivo sin vivir en mi" and especially the refrain "que muero porque no muero."

19. Ibid.

CHAPTER 5: THE LIFE OF THE *VIDA* IN ART

1. E. Allison Peers, a translator of Teresa's texts, coined the term and tallied up the number of "pictorial" descriptions in the *Vida*. See his *St. Teresa of Jesus and Other Essays and Addresses* (London: Faber & Faber, 1951), 87–88.

2. Margarete Salinger was one of the first to do so in "Some Representations of St. Teresa," *Metropolitan Museum of Art Bulletin* 8, 3 (1949): 97–108, especially 106–8. Victor Stoichita has linked some of Teresa's visions to specific works of sacred art that she could have seen. See his *Visionary Experience in the Golden Age of Spanish Art* (London: Reaktion Books, 1995), 58–59.

3. See *Visioni ed Estasi: Capolavori dell'arte europea tra Seicento e Settecento*, ed. by Giovanni Morello (Milan: Skira, 2003).

4. John B. Knipping, *Iconography of the Counter Reformation in the Netherlands* (Nieuwkoop: B. de Graaf, 1974), 7, 258.

5. See María José Pinilla Martín, "La ilustración de los escritos Teresianos: Grabados de la primeras ediciones," *Boletín del Seminario de Estudios de Arte y Arqueología, arte* 74 (2008): 185–202.

6. Quoted by Joseph Pérez, *Teresa de Ávila y la España de su tiempo* (Madrid: Algaba, 2007), 169n155.

7. Psalm 88:2 in the Vulgate Latin Bible; Psalm 89:2 in Protestant Bibles.

8. See León Carbonero y Sol, ed., *Homenaje a Santa Teresa de Jesús gloria del carmelo* (Madrid, 1882), 60–61.

9. See Maria Berbara, "'Esta pena tan sabrosa': Teresa of Avila and the Figurative Arts in Early Modern Europe," in *The Sense of Suffering: Constructions of Physical Pain in Early Modern Culture*, ed. Jan Frans van Dijkhuizen and Karl A. E. Enenkel (Leiden: Brill, 2009), 285n48.

10. See introduction by María José Pinilla Martín to the facsimile edition: *Iconografía Teresiana: Colección de 25 grabados sobre la vida de Santa Teresa* (Madrid: Editorial de Espiritualidad, 2012).

11. *Vita Beati Patris Ignatii Loyolae Religionis Societatis Iesu Fundatoris* (Antwerp, 1610). See Walter S. Melion, "The Jesuit Engagement with the Status and Function of the Visual Image," in *Jesuit Image Theory*, ed. W. de Boer, K.A.E. Enerkel, and W. Melion (Leiden: Brill, 2016), 1.

12. See Luis Mebold, SDB, *Catálogo de Pintura Colonial en Chile: Obras en Monasterios de Religiosas de Antigua Fundación* (Santiago: Ediciones Universidad Católica de Chile, 1987).

13. *Vita effigiata di S. Teresa Vergine: Reparatrice dell'antico Ordine Carmelitano e Fondatrice de' Padri, e Monache Scalze del medesimo Istituto Originario dal Gran Profeta, e Patriarca S. Elia* (Rome, 1655).

14. *La vie de la séraphique Mère Sainte Térèse de Iésus, fondatrice des Carmes Déchaussez et des Carmélites Déchaussées* (Lyons, 1670).

15. See María José Pinilla Martín, "Dos 'vidas gráficas' de Santa Teresa de Jesús: Amberes 1613 y Roma 1655," *Boletín del Seminario de Estudios de Arte y Arqueología, arte* 79 (2013): 183–202.

16. The event is depicted in an engraving by Matthäus Greuter. See Irving Lavin, "Bernini and the Crossing of Saint Peter's," plate 5, in his *Visible Spirit: The Art of Gianlorenzo Bernini* (London: Pindar Press, 2007), 1:62–185.

17. A simple Internet search for images of the transverberation yields more than a hundred as of early 2018. Five decades ago, Robert Peterson listed more than forty in his *The Art of Ecstasy: Teresa, Bernini, and Crashaw* (New York: Atheneum, 1970), and Andor Pigler listed fifty-four in *Barockthemen: Eine Auswahl von den Verzeichnissen zur Ikonographie des 17 und 18 Jahrhunderte* (Budapest: Akademiai Kiado, 1970).

18. Giovanni Giacomo de Rossi, *Sanctissimae Matris Dei Marie de Monte Carmelo Beatae Teresiae humilis filiae* (Rome, 1622).

19. He may not have been the first painter to depict the transverberation. In 1615, the Venetian artist Jacopo Negretti, better known as Giacomo Palma il Giovane, painted a depiction of the transverberation full of angels in which a bright ray of light links the wound in Christ's side directly to Teresa.

20. Some later versions of this engraving employ the Vulgate text.

21. See Walter Melion, Ralph Dekoninck, and Agnes Guiderdoni-Bruslè, eds., *Ut pictura meditatio: The Meditative Image in Northern Art, 1500–1700*, Proteus: Studies in Early Modern Identity Formation 4 (Turnhout: Brepols, 2011).

22. For example, see *Descripción del túmulo y relación de las exequias que hizo la ciudad de Sevilla en la muerte del Rey don Felipe II* (1599), ed. Francisco Gerónimo Collado (Seville: J. M. Geofrin, 1869).

23. See Peter M. Daly, *Literature in the Light of the Emblem* (Toronto: University of Toronto Press, 1998).

24. See James Clifton, "Secret Wisdom: Anton Wierix's Engravings of a Carmelite Mystic," in *The Authority of the Word:*

Reflecting on Image and Text in Northern Europe, 1400–1700,
ed. Celeste Brusati and Karl Enenkel (Leiden: Brill, 2012),
639–66.

25. Quoted by Franco Mormando in *Bernini: His Life and His Rome* (Chicago: University of Chicago Press, 2011), 162.

26. *The Seminar of Jacques Lacan XX, Encore, 1972–1973,* trans. J. Miller (London: W. W. Norton, 1998), 76; Irving Lavin, *Bernini and the Unity of the Visual Arts* (Oxford: Oxford University Press, 1980), 2:121.

27. Mormando, *Bernini*, 161.

28. Session 25, 1563, *The Canons and Decrees of the Council of Trent,* trans. H. J. Schroeder (Charlotte, NC: TAN Books, 2009), 215–16.

CHAPTER 6: FROM ENLIGHTENMENT TO MODERNITY

1. *Principles of Philosophy,* in *Descartes: Selected Philosophical Writings,* trans. John Cottingham, Robert Stoothoff, and Dugald Murdoch (Cambridge: Cambridge University Press, 1988), 160.

2. See Carlos Eire, *Reformations: The Early Modern World* (New Haven, CT: Yale University Press, 2016), chaps. 23 and 24.

3. Francis de Sales, *Oeuvres de Saint François de Sales,* ed. Benedict Mackey et al. (Annecy: Niérat, 1892–1932), 15:377.

4. Cited in D. J. Enright, *The Oxford Book of Death* (Oxford: Oxford University Press, 1987), 330.

5. Stephen Greenblatt, *The Swerve: How the World Became Modern* (W. W. Norton, 2011), 182–202.

6. Pierre Viret, *Instruction Chrestienne en la doctrine de la loy et de l'Evangile* (1564), vol. 2, fols. iii–iii verso.

7. Paul Heinrich Dietrich, Baron d'Holbach, *The System of Nature* (London: G. Kearsley, 1797), 1:25.

8. Thomas Paine, *The Writings of Thomas Paine,* ed. M. C. Conway (New York: G. P. Putnam and Sons, 1908), 4:22.

9. The martyrs of Compiègne attracted considerable artistic attention in the twentieth century. In 1931 Gertrud von

Le Fort published a novel about them, *The Last One at the Scaffold*, which inspired Georges Bernanos to write a poetic play, *Dialogues of the Carmelites*, and that play, in turn, led composer Francis Poulenc to produce an opera in 1957 with the same title, and Père Brückberger and Philippe Agostini to create a film in 1959, also with the same title. See Eithne O'Sharkey, "Fact into Poetic Fiction: Bernanos's 'Dialogues des Carmelites,'" *Studies: An Irish Quarterly Review* 57, no. 225 (1968): 67–77.

10. See Emmanuel Renault, *L'influence de sainte Thérèse d'Avila sur Thérèse de Lisieux* (Toulouse: Carmel, 2009).

11. Sister Geneviève of the Holy Face, *A Memoir of My Sister, St. Thérèse* (New York: P. J. Kenedy, 1959), 74.

12. See *Fundaciones* (*Foundations*), 5:8, in *Obras*, 690.

13. See Thomas R. Nevin, *Thérèse of Lisieux: God's Gentle Warrior* (Oxford: Oxford University Press, 2006).

14. Evelyn Underhill, *Mysticism: A Study in the Nature and Development of Man's Spiritual Consciousness* (London: Methuen, 1911).

15. The road for Underhill's philo-Catholicism had been paved earlier in the nineteenth century by the Anglo-Catholics of the Oxford Movement. See *The Oxford Handbook of the Oxford Movement*, ed. Stewart J. Brown, Peter Nockles, and James Pereiro (Oxford: Oxford University Press, 2017).

16. Quoted in Teresia Posselt, *Edith Stein: The Life of a Philosopher and Carmelite*, ed. Susanne M. Batzdorff, Josephine Koeppel, and John Sullivan (Washington, DC: ICA Publications, 2005), 63. See Joyce Avrech Berkman, "Edith Stein and Theatrical Truth," in *Edith Stein: Women, Social-Political Philosophy, Theology, Metaphysics and Public History*, ed. Antonio Calcagno (New York: Springer International, 2016), 228n3.

17. See "Love for Love: The Life and Works of St. Teresa of Jesus," in *Hidden Life: Essays, Meditations, Spiritual Texts* (*The Collected Works of Edith Stein, Vol. 4*) (Washington, DC: ICS Publications, 1992), 29–66.

18. *Edith Stein Gesamtausgabe* (Freiburg: Herder, 2001–); *The Collected Works of Edith Stein: Sister Teresa Benedicta of the Cross* (Washington, DC: ICS Publications, 1986–).

19. See Mary Catharine Baseheart, "Edith Stein's Philosophy of Woman and of Women's Education," *Hypatia* 4.1 (Spring 1989): 120–31; K. M. Haney and J. Valiquette, "Edith Stein: Woman as Ethical Type," in *Phenomenological Approaches to Moral Philosophy: A Handbook*, ed. J. J. Drummond and L. Embree (Dordrecht: Kluwer Academic, 2002), 451–73; and Antonio Calcagno, *Lived Experience from the Inside Out: Social and Political Philosophy in Edith Stein* (Pittsburgh: Duquesne University Press, 2014).

20. Dorothy Day, *The Long Loneliness* (New York: Harper & Row, 1952), 115.

21. Ibid., 140–41.

22. Quoted by Kathleen Fischer, *Women at the Well: Feminist Perspectives on Spiritual Direction* (Mahwah, NJ: Paulist Press, 1988), 144.

23. For a brief survey of early psychological dismissals of Teresa as a hysteric, see Cristina Mazzoni, *Saint Hysteria: Neurosis, Mysticism, and Gender in European Culture* (Ithaca: Cornell University Press, 1996), 37–41.

24. "No amount of genuine, solid mental endowment is excluded by hysteria . . . After all, the patron saint of hysteria, St. Theresa, was a woman of genius with great practical capacity." Josef Breuer and Sigmund Freud, *Studies in Hysteria* (Boston: Beacon Press, 1950), 232.

25. See Doriano Fasoli and Rosa Rossi, *Le "estasi laiche" di Teresa d'Avila: Psicoanalisi, misticismo e altre esperienze culturali a confronto* (Rome: Edizioni Associate, 1998).

26. William James, *Varieties of Religious Experience* (New York: Longmans, Green, 1902), 379.

27. James, *Varieties*, 428.

28. Ibid., 346–47.

29. Ibid., 347–48.

30. Underhill, *Mysticism*, 28.

31. Bertrand Russell, *Religion and Science* (Oxford: Oxford University Press, 1997), 188.

32. See Marcella Biro Barton, "Saint Teresa of Avila: Did She Have Epilepsy?," *Catholic Historical Review* 68.4 (Oct. 1982): 581–98, esp. 583.

33. See Niall McCrae and S. Elliott, "Spiritual Experiences in Temporal Lobe Epilepsy: A Literature Review," *British Journal of Neuroscience Nursing* 8.6 (Dec. 2012/Jan. 2013): 346–51; and Niall McCrae and R. Whitley, "Exaltation in Temporal Lobe Epilepsy: Neuropsychiatric Symptom or Portal to the Divine?," *Journal of Medical Humanities* 35.3 (Sept. 2014): 241–55.

34. L. A. Ruttan, M. A. Persinger, and S. Koren, "Enhancement of Temporal Lobe-Related Experiences during Brief Exposures to MilliGauss Intensity Extremely Low Frequency Magnetic Fields," *Journal of Bioelectricity* 9.1 (1990): 33–54; and M. A. Persinger et al., "The Electromagnetic Induction of Mystical and Altered States within the Laboratory," *Journal of Consciousness Exploration & Research* 1.7 (2010): 808–30.

35. Some experts argue that attempts to link religiosity and temporal lobe epilepsy are based on "flawed and outdated" assumptions. See Craig Aaen-Stockdale (2012), "Neuroscience for the Soul," *Psychologist* 25.7 (2012): 520–23.

36. See Christopher Bache, "A Reappraisal of Teresa of Avila's Supposed Hysteria," *Journal of Religion and Health* 24.4 (1985).

37. *The Seminar of Jacques Lacan XX, Encore 1972–1973*, trans. J. Miller (New York: W. W. Norton, 1998), 76.

38. Luce Irigaray, *Speculum of the Other Woman* (Ithaca: Cornell University Press, 1985), 91. For an analytical synopsis of Irigaray's argument, see Carole Slade, *St. Teresa of Avila: Author of a Heroic Life* (Berkeley: University of California Press, 1995), 133–38.

39. Julia Kristeva, *Teresa, My Love* (New York: Columbia University Press, 2014).

40. Julia Kristeva, *Black Sun: Depression and Melancholia* (New York: Columbia University Press, 1989), 14, 54, 61, 78. See Slade, *St. Teresa*, 138–44.

41. For a superb summary of Spanish interpretations of Teresa in the late nineteenth and early twentieth century, see Denise DuPont, *Writing Teresa: The Saint from Ávila at the fin-de-siglo* (Lewisburg, PA: Bucknell University Press, 2012).

42. Marcelino Menéndez Pelayo, *La ciencia española* (Madrid: Pérez Dubrull, 1887), 1:124.

43. José Dueso, "Leyendo a Santa Teresa," in *Homenaje literario a la gloriosa doctora Santa Teresa de Jesús en el tercer centenario de su beatificación* (Madrid: Alrededor del Mundo, 1914), 104.

44. Américo Castro, *The Structure of Spanish History* (Princeton: Princeton University Press, 1954), 10–11, 54–55, 555–71.

45. Emilio Sánchez, *Santa Teresa de Jesús, patrona del Cuerpo de Intendencia Militar* (Avila: Senén Martín, 1922), 95.

46. Gabriel de Jesús, *La Santa de la Raza: Vida gráfica de Santa Teresa de Jesús*, 3 vols. (Madrid: Voluntad, 1930).

47. Silverio de Santa Teresa, *Santa Teresa: Modelo de feminismo cristiano* (Burgos: El Monte Carmelo, 1931).

48. See Carlos Eire, *From Madrid to Purgatory* (Cambridge: Cambridge University Press, 1995), 425–71.

49. *Boletín Oficial del Obispado de Salamanca*, 27 February 1937, 55–56. "Caudillo" is a Spanish term for a military or political leader.

50. Silverio de Santa Teresa, "La mano de la Santa redimida de la esclavitud bolchevique," *El Monte Carmelo*, 1 April 1937, 148. General Villalba commanded the Republican troops in Málaga.

51. "La mano incorrupta y el dictador obsesionado," *El País*, 19 December 2014.

52. *Boletín Oficial de la Diócesis de Málaga*, 1939, 625–28.

53. "La mano incorrupta," *El País*, 19 December 2014.

54. See Mary Nash, "Towards a New Moral Order: National Catholicism, Culture, and Gender," in *Spanish History Since 1808*, ed. José Alvarez Junco and Adrian Shubert (Oxford: Oxford University Press, 2000), esp. 291–92; and also Nash's "Pronatalism and Motherhood in Franco's Spain," in *Maternity and Gender Policies*, ed. Gisela Bock and Pat Thane (London: Routledge, 1991).

55. See Stanley G. Payne, *A History of Fascism, 1914–1945* (Madison: University of Wisconsin Press, 1995); and Kathleen Richmond, *Women and Spanish Fascism: The Women's Section of the Falange, 1934–1959* (London: Routledge, 2003).

56. See Inbal Ofer, *Señoritas in Blue: The Making of a Female Political Elite in Franco's Spain* (London: Sussex Press, 2009); and Jessica Davidson, "Women, Fascism and Work in Francoist Spain: The Law for Political, Professional and Labour Rights," *Gender and History* 23.2 (2011): 401–14.

57. "Lecciones de Santa Teresa, conferencia pronunciada por Pilar Primo de Rivera en el Casón del Buen Retiro" (pamphlet) (Madrid: Ruan, 1971), 11.

58. Stanley G. Payne, *Fascism in Spain, 1923–1977* (Madison: University of Wisconsin Press, 1999), 324.

CHAPTER 7: THE POST-MYSTICAL INTERMILLENNIAL *VIDA*

1. Américo Castro, *Teresa la santa, Gracián y los separatismos, con otros Ensayos* (Madrid: Alfaguara, 1972), 41.

2. For various Catholic interpretations, see *La recepción de los místicos Teresa de Jesús y Juan de la Cruz*, ed. Salvador Ros García (Salamanca: Universidad Pontificia de Salamanca, 1997), 43–229; 769–86.

3. The Rorschach inkblot test—developed in the 1920s—is a diagnostic tool that was widely used in the twentieth century. See Katherine Hubbard and Peter Hegarty, "Blots and All: A History of the Rorschach Inkblot Test in Britain," *Journal of the History of the Behavioral Sciences* 52.2 (2016): 146–66.

4. Bilinkoff, *Avila of Saint Teresa*. Some reviewers faulted Bilinkoff for relying too much on the *Vida*. See review by Gillian Ahlgren, *Journal of Religion* 72.1 (1992): 106–7.

5. Gillian Ahlgren, *Teresa of Avila and the Politics of Sanctity* (Ithaca: Cornell University Press, 1996).

6. Rowan Williams, *Teresa of Avila* (Harrisburg, PA: Morehouse, 1991), 165. Gillian Ahlgren review in the *Journal of Religion* 73.1 (Jan. 1993): 89–90.

7. Victor García de la Concha, *El arte literario de Santa Teresa* (Barcelona: Ariel, 1978); Francisco Márquez Villanueva, "La vocación literaria de Santa Teresa," *Nueva Revista de Filología Hispánica* 32.2 (1983): 355–79; Rosa Rossi, *Teresa d'Avila: Biografia di una scrittrice* (Rome: Riuniti, 1983); Rosa Rossi, *Esperienza interiore e storia nell'autobiografia di Teresa d'Avila* (Bari: Adriatica, 1977).

8. Weber, *Rhetoric of Femininity*, 15.

9. Dominique de Courcelles, *Thérèse d'Avila: Femme d'écriture et de pouvoir dans l'Espagne du Siècle d'Or* (Grenoble: Jérôme Millon, 1993).

10. Slade, *Teresa*, 1.

11. Ibid., 4, 12, 14, 17.

12. Paola Marín, "Teresa de Ávila," *Spanish Writers on Gay and Lesbian Themes: A Bio-Critical Sourcebook*, ed. David William Foster (Westport, CT: Greenwood Press, 1999), 160–61.

13. David W. Foster, *Producción cultural e identidades homoeróticas* (Editorial de la Universidad de Costa Rica, 1999); Paul Julian Smith, "Visions of Teresa," in *Representing the Other* (Oxford: Clarendon Press, 1992), 97–127. See Marín, "Teresa," 160–61.

14. For these and many other queer interpretations of Teresa, see Corinne Blackmer, "The Ecstasies of Saint Teresa: The Saint as Queer Diva," *En Travesti: Women, Gender Subversion, Opera*, ed. C. Blackmer and P. J. Smith (New York: Columbia University Press, 1995), 306–47.

15. Blackmer and Smith, eds., "The Saint as Queer Diva," in *En Travesti*, 339.

16. Elena Carrera, *Teresa of Avila's Autobiography: Authority, Power and the Self in Mid-Sixteenth-Century Spain* (London: Legenda, 2005), 8, 108. For a briefer critique of the approach of the "American" feminist approach, see Mercedes Blanco, "Les raisons de la jouissance chez Thérèse d'Avila," *Savoirs et Clinique: Revue de Psychanalise; L'écriture et l'extase* 1.8 (2007), 13–25.

17. Carrera, *Teresa of Avila's Autobiography*, 191.

18. See Alison Weber's review of Carrera's book in *Iberoamericana* 6.24 (December 2006): 213–15.

19. Julia Kristeva, *Thérèse mon amour* (Paris: Fayard, 2008). English translation: *Teresa, My Love: An Imagined Life of the Saint of Avila* (New York: Columbia University Press, 2014). Another historical novel about Teresa's life appeared about the same time, written by Barbara Mujica, a scholar of Spanish literature at Georgetown University. Her novel *Sister Teresa* (Overlook, 2007) is much less ideologically charged but does stress Teresa's efforts to overcome the misogyny of her age.

20. Columbia University Press online, https://cup.columbia.edu/book/teresa-my-love/9780231149600.

21. Carlene Bauer, "Imagining a Saintly Life, Some of It Not So Holy: Julia Kristeva's Latest Novel," *New York Times*, 14 December 2014.

22. Cathleen Medwick, *Teresa of Avila: The Progress of a Soul* (New York: Knopf, 1999), xvii.

23. See Corinne Blackmer, "The Saint as Queer Diva," in *En Travesti*, 335.

24. Molina collaborated on the screenplay with highly acclaimed novelist Carmen Martín Gaite and Teresian scholar Victor García de la Concha.

25. "Nuestro profesor Jorge Dorado, estrena la TV Movie Teresa en TVE," https://www.escueladecinedemalaga.com/nuestro-profesor-jorge-dorado-estrena-tv-movie-teresa-tve/.

EPILOGUE: DOCTOR OF THE CHURCH, SIGN OF CONTRADICTION

1. For an assessment of the impact of Teresa's new status on Catholic theology at the end of the twentieth century, see Jesús Castellano Cervera, "El doctorado de Teresa y su nueva presencia teológica," in *La recepción de los místicos Teresa de Jesús y Juan de la Cruz*, ed. Salvador Ros García (Salamanca: Ediciones Universidad Pontificia, 1997), 205–28.

2. "Proclamación de Santa Teresa de Jesús como doctora de la Iglesia, Homilia del Santo Padre Pablo VI," 27 September 1970, http://w2.vatican.va/content/paul-vi/es/homilies /1970/documents/hf_p-vi_hom_19700927.html.

3. Benedict XVI, General Audience, 2 February 2011, https:// w2.vatican.va/content/benedict-xvi/en/audiences/2011 /documents/hf_ben-xvi_aud_20110202.html.

4. "Letter of Pope John Paul II to Women," 29 June 1995, http://w2.vatican.va/content/john-paul-ii/en/letters/1995 /documents/hf_jp-ii_let_29061995_women.html.

5. Pope John Paul II, *Sign of Contradiction* (New York: Seabury Press, 1979).

6. *Meister Eckhart: A Modern Translation*, trans. Raymond Blakney (New York: Harper Perennial, 1941), 168.

7. *Vida*, 40:25.229.

SELECTED BIBLIOGRAPHY

PRIMARY SOURCES

The Collected Works of St. Teresa of Avila. Translated by Otilio Rodriguez and Kieran Kavanaugh. 2 vols. Washington, DC: ICS Publications, 1987, 2012.

Madre de Dios, Efrén de la, OCD, and Otger Steggink, O. Carm, eds. *Obras Completas de Santa Teresa*. Madrid: Biblioteca de Autores Cristianos, 1997.

Ribera, Francisco de. *La vida de la madre Teresa de Jesús* (1590). Barcelona: Gili, 1908.

Santa Teresa, Silverio de, ed. *Procesos de Beatificación y Canonización de Santa Teresa de Jesús*. 3 vols. Burgos: Editorial Monte Carmelo, 1934–35.

Sermones predicados en la Beatificación de la B.M. Teresa de Jesús. Madrid: A. Martin, 1615.

Urkiza, Julián, ed. *Obras Completas de Ana de San Bartolomé*. 2 vols. Monumenta Historica Carmeli Teresiani, 5. Rome: Teresianum, 1981.

Yepes, Diego de. *Vida, virtudes y milagros de la Bienaventurada Virgen Teresa de Jesús*. Buenos Aires: Emecé Editores, 1946 (originally published in Madrid, 1599).

SECONDARY SOURCES

Chapter 1: Teresa's Life Story

The most thorough and scholarly modern biography of Teresa is *Tiempo y Vida de Santa Teresa*, ed. Efrén de la Madre de Dios and Otger Steggink (Madrid: Biblioteca de Autores Cristianos, 1968).

The most concise introduction to Teresa's life and work written
for a wide audience is that of onetime archbishop of Canterbury Rowan Williams, *Teresa of Avila* (Harrisburg, PA:
Morehouse, 1991).

An essential introduction to the social, political, and economic set-
ting of Teresa's life and her monastic reforms is Jodi Bilinkoff's
The Avila of Saint Teresa: *Religious Reform in a Sixteenth-
Century City* (Ithaca: Cornell University Press, 1989).

For an overview of the plight of Jewish converts and their descendants in the Spain of Teresa's day, see Benzion Netanyahu, *The
Marranos of Spain* (Ithaca: Cornell University Press, 1999).

For an indispensable introduction to the cultural context of
Teresa's life and work, see LuAnn Homza, *Religious Author-
ity in the Spanish Renaissance* (Baltimore, MD: Johns
Hopkins University Press, 2004).

Chapter 2: How, When, and Why the Book Was Written

For two concise and definitive introductions to the monastic context of Teresa's *Vida*, see Alison Weber, "The Three Lives of
the Vida: The Uses of Convent Autobiography," in *Women,
Texts and Authority in the Early Modern Spanish World*,
ed. Marta Vicente and Luis Corteguera (Farnham, UK:
Ashgate, 2003); and "Saint Teresa, Demonologist," in *Culture and Control in Counter-Reformation Spain*, ed. Anne J.
Cruz and Mary Elizabeth Perry (Minneapolis: University of
Minnesota Press, 1991).

For an account of the suspicions surrounding all Spanish mystics
in Teresa's day, which gave shape to the writing of her *Vida*,
see Andrew Keitt, *Inventing the Sacred: Imposture, Inquisition, and the Boundaries of the Supernatural in Golden Age
Spain* (Leiden: Brill, 2005).

Gillian Ahlgren analyzes the expectations placed on Teresa by
her superiors, as well as those she willingly embraced on her
own, in *Teresa of Avila and the Politics of Sanctity* (Ithaca:
Cornell University Press, 1996).

An excellent analysis of Teresa's *Vida* as a confessional document can be found in Elena Carrera's *Teresa of Avila's Autobiography: Authority, Power and the Self in Mid-Sixteenth-Century Spain* (London: Legenda, 2005).

Chapter 3: The Mysticism of the Vida

Bernard McGinn's *Mysticism in the Golden Age of Spain, 1500–1650* (New York: Crossroad, 2017) offers a new magisterial survey of the spiritual and cultural context of Teresa's ecstatic life.

Mónica Balltondre analyzes Teresa's mysticism in *Éxtasis y visiones: La experiencia contemplativa de Teresa de Ávila* (Barcelona: Erasmus Ediciones, 2012).

For an overview of the mystical trends suspected of heresy in Teresa's day, see Alastair Hamilton, *Heresy and Mysticism in Sixteenth-Century Spain: The Alumbrados* (Cambridge: J. Clark, 1992).

For a concise introduction to the institution that enforced orthodoxy in Teresa's day, see Helen Rawlings, *The Spanish Inquisition* (Oxford: Blackwell, 2006).

Cathleen Medwick's *Teresa of Avila: The Progress of a Soul* (New York: Knopf, 1999) interprets the links between the active and the contemplative dimensions of Teresa with a popular audience in mind.

Chapter 4: The Life of the Vida, 1600–1800

For an overview of religious attitudes toward Teresa's mysticism, see Salvador Ros García, ed., *La recepción de los místicos Teresa de Jesús y Juan de la Cruz* (Salamanca: Universidad Pontificia, 1997).

For a brief survey of the intellectual climate of the baroque age, see Carlos Eire, *Reformations: The Early Modern World, 1450–1650* (New Haven, CT: Yale University Press, 2016), chapters 20–26.

For a detailed survey and analysis of the growth of rational skepticism, see Jonathan Israel, *Radical Enlightenment: Philosophy and the Making of Modernity, 1650–1750* (Oxford: Oxford University Press, 2001).

José Luis Sánchez Lora's *Mujeres, conventos y formas de la religiosidad barroca* (Madrid: Fundación Universitaria Española, 1988) provides a thorough analysis of Spanish convent culture in the baroque age.

Erin Rowe, in *Saint and Nation: Santiago, Teresa of Avila, and Plural Identities in Early Modern Spain* (University Park: Pennsylvania State Press, 2011), analyzes the postmortem popularity of Teresa in Spain.

Chapter 5: The Life of the Vida in Art

Victor Stoichita's *Visonary Experience in the Golden Age of Spanish Art* (London: Reaktion Books, 1995) is the most thorough and perceptive English-language survey of the genre in which depictions of Teresa's ecstasies belong.

The Italian-language complement to Stoichita's survey is Giovanni Morello's richly illustrated *Visioni ed Estasi: Capolavori dell'arte europea tra Seicento e Settecento* (Milan: Skira, 2003).

For an incisive analysis of representations of Teresa's ecstasies, see Maria Berbara, "'Esta pena tan sabrosa': Teresa of Avila and the Figurative Arts in Early Modern Europe," in *The Sense of Suffering: Constructions of Physical Pain in Early Modern Culture*, ed. J. F. van Dijkhuizen and K.A.E. Enenkel (Leiden: Brill, 2009).

Irving Lavin's *Bernini and the Unity of the Visual Arts*, 2 vols. (Oxford University Press, 1980), provides a brilliant analysis of the best-known depiction of Teresa's transverberation.

María José Pinilla Martín provides an introduction to early depictions of scenes from Teresa's *Vida* in "La ilustración de los escritos Teresianos: Grabados de la primeras ediciones," *Boletín del Seminario de Estudios de Arte y Arqueología, arte* 74 (2008): 185–202.

Chapter 6: From Enlightenment to Modernity

Edith Stein's fascination with Teresa is summed up in "Love for Love: The Life and Works of St. Teresa of Jesus," in *Hidden Life: Essays, Meditations, Spiritual Texts (The Collected Works of Edith Stein, Vol. 4)* (Washington, DC: ICS Publications, 1992), 29–66.

Christopher Bache examines psychoanalytic perspectives on Teresa in "A Reappraisal of Teresa of Avila's Supposed Hysteria," *Journal of Religion and Health* 24.4 (1985).

Marcella Biro Barton proposes a neurological etiology for Teresa's ecstasies in "Saint Teresa of Avila: Did She Have Epilepsy?," *Catholic Historical Review* 68.4 (Oct. 1982).

For a survey of the Spanish fascist fixation on Teresa, see Giuliana de Febo, *La Santa de la Raza, Teresa de Ávila: Un culto barroco en la España Franquista* (Barcelona: Icaria, 1987).

Denise DuPont surveys the impact of Teresa on Spanish writing of the late nineteenth and early twentieth centuries in *Writing Teresa: The Saint from Ávila at the fin-de-siglo* (Lewisburg, PA: Bucknell University Press, 2012).

Chapter 7: The Post-Mystical Intermillennial *Vida*

For a lucid and immensely influential feminist interpretation of Teresa's writing, see Alison Weber, *Teresa of Avila and the Rhetoric of Femininity* (Princeton: Princeton University Press, 1996).

Although a work of fiction, Julia Kristeva's *Teresa, My Love* (New York: Columbia University Press, 2014) sums up significant feminist and psychological perspectives on Teresa.

For an introduction to queer interpretations of Teresa, see Paola Marín, "Teresa de Ávila," in *Spanish Writers on Gay and Lesbian Themes: A Bio-Critical Sourcebook*, ed. David William Foster (Westport, CT: Greenwood Press, 1999); and Corinne Blackmer, "The Ecstasies of Saint Teresa: The Saint as Queer Diva," in *En Travesti: Women, Gender Subversion,*

Opera, ed. C. Blackmer and P. J. Smith (New York: Columbia University Press, 1995), 306–47.

A significant collection of intermillennial interpretations of Teresa can be found in *Teresa of Avila: Mystical Theology and Spirituality in the Carmelite Tradition*, edited by Peter Tyler and Edward Howells (London: Routledge, 2017).